D1474431

JUNIPER WATERWAY

A History of the Albemarle and Chesapeake Canal

JUNIPER WATERWAY

A HISTORY OF THE

ALBEMARLE AND CHESAPEAKE CANAL

BY ALEXANDER CROSBY BROWN

Published for the MARINERS' MUSEUM, Newport News, Virginia,
and the NORFOLK COUNTY HISTORICAL SOCIETY, Chesapeake, Virginia,
by the UNIVERSITY PRESS OF VIRGINIA, Charlottesville

NC
386.48
B

FOR *Charles and Eleanor Cross and Johanna Brown*—
Shipmates on the good ship *Whim* during our spring cruise
through the Albemarle and Chesapeake Canal in April 1972

FRONTISPIECE: *The 600-foot guard lock at Great Bridge looking east to the Virginia Cut of the Albemarle and Chesapeake Canal. U.S. Army Corps of Engineers compound shows on the right and the drawbridge of Battlefield Boulevard at the top. (1973 photo courtesy U.S. Army Corps of Engineers)*

THE UNIVERSITY PRESS OF VIRGINIA
Copyright © 1981 by The Mariners' Museum, Newport News,
Virginia

First published 1981
Mariners' Museum publication no. 39

Printed in the United States of America
Library of Congress Cataloging in Publication Data

Brown, Alexander Crosby, 1905–
   Juniper Waterway, a history of the Albemarle and
Chesapeake Canal.

   (Mariners' Museum publication; no. 39)
   Bibliography:
   Includes index.
   1. Albemarle and Chesapeake Canal, Va. and N.C.—
History.
   I. Title. II. Series: Mariners' Museum, Newport
News, Va.   Museum publication; no. 39.
HE396.A4B76   386'.48'0975551   80-14093
ISBN 0-917376-35-8

NORTH CAROLINA ROOM
NEW HANOVER CO   IC LIBRARY

c.1
NCR

22.50

CONTENTS

LIST OF ILLUSTRATIONS

LIST OF TABLES

FOREWORD

Alec Brown's love affairs with the many components of the Chesapeake Bay began with the first book published by the Mariners Museum. This is the thirty-ninth such book, but, of course, not even Brown's prodigious production accounted for every one of the Museum's rapidly expanding contributions to maritime history, economics, and science. The agility of his mind continues unabated despite his 1973 retirement as literary editor of the *Newport News Daily Press*. Years earlier, Brown had served as an assistant to the dean of United States naval historians, Samuel Eliot Morison, during preparation for publication of the definitive *History of United States Naval Operations in World War II*. He was also associate editor of the *American Neptune: A Quarterly Journal of Maritime History* from 1941 to 1979. In the years since Brown took his typewriter home from the *Daily Press* office, he has turned out a number of specialized histories of maritime subjects, many of them reflecting his consummate skill as a sensitive photographer of top rank.

Several of these authoritative research works, done with a great dollop of understated humor and a thick slice of wry, resulted in such appropriate recognition as the United Daughters of the Confederacy's Jefferson Davis Medal, the Certificate of Commendation of the American Association of State and Local History, and the Distinguished Service Medal of Christopher Newport College. Residents of Virginia's Lower Peninsula are indebted to him for research into the locations of historical events and places and the establishment of a veritable forest of highway markers identifying these spots.

This latest publication authorized by the Mariners' Museum, *Juniper Waterway: A History of the Albemarle and Chesapeake Canal*, is the first full account of the seventy-five mile link of the Intracoastal Waterway that runs along the rim of the Dismal Swamp—that primeval eruption of amber-colored, medically antiseptic water that bubbles out of the Dismal Swamp aquifer, getting its rich color from the juniper trees that saturate this unique geological formation.

First proposed in 1728 by Col. William Byrd II of Westover on the River James, the canal was not completed until 1858, after steam shovels had made it possible to clear away the petrified logs that had languished for millennia. At that, Virginia's General Assembly had moved with all deliberate speed to procrastinate almost another half century before authorizing the project in 1772.

Author Brown's incredible scope of technical knowledge, catalyzed from the classrooms of Yale '28 to the deck of a schooner circumnavigating the globe, results in this elegant little gem, which takes its place proudly with the other significant maritime contributions to literature sponsored by the Mariners Museum. We are pleased to be associated in this venture with the prestigious Norfolk County Historical Society of Chesapeake.

GEORGE W. PASSAGE
President, The Mariners' Museum

FOREWORD

The enthusiastic reception by the public of Alexander Crosby Brown's the *Dismal Swamp Canal* (republished by the Norfolk County Historical Society of Chesapeake, Virginia, in 1970) was endorsed by the American Society of State and Local History when it awarded their Certificate of Commendation to the *Dismal Swamp Canal* and its author.

Meanwhile, the Historical Society was making plans to prepare and publish a history of the Albemarle and Chesapeake canal as a companion volume. It was only natural for them to commission Alexander Crosby Brown as the author of the projected book. On this new project, Brown focused his considerable knowledge, experience, background, and enthusiasm. He has more than fulfilled the expectations of the society. The product of Mr. Brown's labors is published herewith under the title *Juniper Waterway*.

In order to give *Juniper Waterway* the highest quality production and the widest possible public exposure, the society entered into an agreement with the Mariners' Museum of Newport News, Virginia, for *Juniper Waterway* to become a joint publication of the two institutions.

The Norfolk County Historical Society of Chesapeake, Virginia, is proud to be associated with Alec Brown and the Mariners' Museum in this joint venture.

CHARLES B. CROSS, JR.
Publications Chairman
Norfolk County Historical Society of Chesapeake, Virginia

ACKNOWLEDGMENTS

One pleasant duty in connection with gathering the material and writing an historical work consists in attempting to pay at least partial tribute to the many well-disposed persons who have helped along the way—indeed, those who in many instances went beyond the call of duty to steer the bemused writer around historical potholes and to aid him in presenting his text in reasonably readable English prose.

The encouragement of Charles B. Cross, Jr., former City of Chesapeake Clerk of Courts and a founder and moving spirit of the Norfolk County Historical Society of Chesapeake, now elevated to Judge, General District Court, Chesapeake, Virginia, was in large part responsible for the successful reception of a previous book I wrote, *The Dismal Swamp Canal,* which was published by his society. The present endeavor covering the alternate canal through Dismal Swamp, the Albemarle and Chesapeake, was suggested by him and is a logical successor, made possible by his continued help and gentle prodding.

While I was doing the research for *Juniper Waterway,* Charles Cross contrived to arrange for microfilming, on one continuous reel, two separate but incomplete holdings of considerable rarity of the annual reports of the Albemarle and Chesapeake Canal Company. This produced a virtually continuous set of these invaluable documents from 1855 to 1885. This work was performed under his direction by the Virginia State Library (of which he was then Chairman of the Library Board), so combining copies of the reports housed in the Sergeant Room of the Norfolk Public Library and in the archives of the U.S. Army Corps of Engineers at District Headquarters, Fort Norfolk. The latter collection, acquired when the federal government took over the canal in 1913, had been the personal possession of canal-company founder and long-serving president Marshall Parks.

Mrs. William S. Portlock, who graciously presides over the Norfolk Public Library's rare books, not only made her copies of the reports available for microfilming, but also has been kind enough to handle a variety of research chores on my behalf. They ranged from tracking down obituary notices of the Parks family to forwarding useful historical items about the canal itself.

J. Thomas Lawless III, veteran chief of the operation and maintenance branch of the Corps of Engineers—following the courtesy of former Corps Executive Assistant John H. Pruhs—has been of tremendous help, not only in locating all sorts of necessary engineering detail but in arranging visits and tours of the canal locks and other facilities. He made it possible for me to consult both Canal Company and Army Chief of Engineers reports and maps at Fort Norfolk, and he also read and corrected several parts of my manuscript and suggested and made available a considerable quantity of official Corps of Engineers photographs for use as illustrations.

The photography department of the Newport News *Daily Press* has, over the years when I worked there, given me the benefit of its expertise in processing my films, which provide the greater part of the following illustrations. Particularly I want to thank Bea Kopp and Jim Livengood.

I cannot praise too highly the invaluable assistance and courtesies extended over the years by various people on the staff of the Mariners' Museum of Newport News, and I am profoundly grateful that the museum elected to join forces with the Norfolk County Historical Society of Chesapeake in the publication of this volume. The museum has also helped out in countless ways by assisting in various research tasks and in granting permission to reproduce many valuable old photographs from their extensive collections.

Former museum librarian John L. Lochhead, now retired, passed me along to the courteous ministrations of his successors, library assistant Linda Kelsey and the present librarian, Ardie L. Kelly, who very graciously assumed the task of assisting in preparing the book for publication by the University Press of Virginia, at the end taken over by his colleague, Museum archivist Dr. Paul B. Hensley. Museum docent Mary W. Phillips assisted with the indexing.

A happy event was when Col. C. W. Tazewell, former president of the Norfolk Historical Society, introduced me to his sprightly octogenarian godmother, Mrs. Charles Turnstall. This daughter of Marshall Parks graciously received me in 1976 and allowed me to photograph and to reproduce here the family portrait of her illustrious ancestor.

Countless other individuals and institutions from Richmond to Raleigh replied to requests for information. It would be impossible to cite them all, but certainly mention should be made of the indefatigable Portsmouth historian John C. Emmerson, Jr., whose compilations of data gleaned from old Norfolk newspaper files have been invaluable. I mention, too, Thomas J. Wood, the amiable retired railroad man from Munden Point, Virginia, on the Norfolk Southern's Currituck Branch, and F. Roy Johnson, steamboat historian of Murfreesboro, North Carolina.

The well-known railway authority Richard E. Prince of Omaha, Nebraska, straightened out several points for me about the canal's railroad affiliations and competition. He kindly reviewed in manuscript the chapter on this involved topic and made useful suggestions. Likewise, Bill Wright, editor of *The State* (Raleigh, North Carolina), included a portion of chapter 6, covering the Civil War years, as an article for his magazine and assisted in searching for pictures.

My debt to my good friend and long-suffering colleague in the field of maritime history, Dr. James M. Morris, professor of history at Christopher Newport College, is incalculable. He read and corrected the entire manuscript, both as an historian and as a grammarian, so saving me many blushes. I shudder to think what the book might have been like without his ministrations, but the boo-boos he failed to exorcise are all mine.

My friend and former newspaper associate *Times-Herald* editor George W. Passage* has, in a dual capacity as President of the Mariners' Museum, contributed a graceful and gracious foreword to this volume for which I am profoundly grateful.

Finally, I express especial gratitude to my daughter, Johanna Hewlett Brown, my pleasant companion of several trips—not only on our first canal cruise, when she was thirteen, but also on subsequent expeditions while she was working for the *Daily Press* photography department. Her skill with the camera has been reflected in several of the illustrations we reproduced here.

To one and all, most profoundly, many thanks.

Alexander Crosby Brown

———

*Mr. Passage died suddenly, September 30, 1980, less than a week after the above lines were written.

1

An Introduction to the Albemarle and Chesapeake Canal and the Atlantic Intracoastal Waterway

riginally planned and even surveyed in colonial times, the Atlantic seaboard's Albemarle and Chesapeake Canal, connecting the sound and bay for which it is jointly named, is one of the nation's most beautiful as well as most useful artificial waterways. Acquired by the federal government in 1913, when it had already been in operation for fifty some years, the modern Albemarle and Chesapeake Canal is a comparative newcomer in the family of Virginia and North Carolina man-made channels. Its construction had to be postponed until technical advances of the machine age became available. Considering the terrain that had to be traversed, it would have been virtually impossible in the pioneer days of canal building to dig it without the aid of steam power, by mere pick, shovel, and grub hook.

First opened in 1859, the Albemarle and Chesapeake Canal today provides an important link in that engineering marvel, the Atlantic Intracoastal Waterway—a system of canals, dredged channels, and protected natural bays, rivers, and sounds which extends from New England to the tip of the Florida Keys, affording small craft a safe and protected "inside route" up and down the coast.[1]

The Albemarle and Chesapeake Canal is not a continuous ditch like the famous Erie Canal, however. In

---

[1] The Atlantic Intracoastal Waterway is well described and illustrated in Allan C. Fisher, Jr., and James L. Amos, *America's Inland Waterway.* See also U.S. Army Corps of Engineers, *The Intracoastal Waterway Atlantic Section.*

its seventy-mile length, extending from Hampton Roads and the Elizabeth River in Virginia to the North River and Albemarle Sound in North Carolina, there are only two major land cuts through widely separated stretches of solid ground. The rest consists of the dredged channels of two curving rivers, in addition to the upper part of landlocked Currituck Sound.

The almost-nine-mile-long Virginia Cut through what was once the eastern part of Dismal Swamp runs eastward from the town of Great Bridge—the principal settlement of the city of Chesapeake, famed for the early Revolutionary War battle fought there[2]—to the head of the North Landing River, which drains the southern portion of former Princess Anne County, now the city of Virginia Beach.

The twisting North Landing River flows generally southward into the northern end of shallow Currituck Sound. Having entered the Tarheel State, the route then follows a straight, dredged channel cut through the middle of the sound to the entrance of the North Carolina Cut at Coinjock Bay. This north-south North Carolina Cut bisecting Currituck County is about 5½ miles long. It emerges near the upper end of the gently curving North River which flows southward into Albemarle Sound. Here, off Camden Point, the Albemarle and Chesapeake Canal officially terminates with the total "line of navigation" of natural channels, dredged rivers, and fully excavated land cuts slightly more than seventy-three miles in length.

Though chartered in 1772 by the colonial Virginia Assembly, the Albemarle and Chesapeake Canal was not the first artificial waterway to connect Chesapeake Bay and Albemarle Sound. The Dismal Swamp Canal—today also a part of the Intracoastal Waterway, which provides an alternate route—was first envisaged in 1728 and was authorized by the Virginia and North Carolina state legislatures in 1787 and 1790. It was opened for limited through navigation in 1805, then was enlarged as a shoal-draft ship canal in 1826. Its fortunes became inextricably entwined with those of the Albemarle and Chesapeake Canal from the moment the newer waterway emerged as a rival in 1859.[3]

Passage of an act by the Virginia House of Burgesses in February 1772 provided for opening a canal from the headwaters of either the Southern or the Eastern branches of the Elizabeth River to the head of the North Landing River—which, as stated, drains into Currituck Sound, thence to the Albemarle. Although surveyors were engaged and plans drawn, no further action was taken in the colonial era. However, only fifteen years later, with the Revolutionary War successfully terminated, the then-constituted Assembly of the Commonwealth of Virginia, encouraged by Governor Patrick Henry, authorized the newly formed Dismal Swamp Canal Company to build a north-south canal on a more westerly course running through the middle

---

[2] For an interesting account of this important 1775 battle, called "The Bunker Hill of the South," see Elizabeth B. Wingo, *The Battle of Great Bridge*.

[3] The history of the Dismal Swamp Canal is covered in detail in Alexander Crosby Brown, *The Dismal Swamp Canal*. This 1970 edition updates previous editions of 1946 and 1967.

of the swamp. This plan was endorsed by the North Carolina General Assembly in 1790.

Starting in the Southern Branch of the Elizabeth River below Norfolk, the route of the Dismal Swamp Canal initially followed the circuitous course of Deep Creek, a tributary stream. Thence, via an elevated lock canal of several different levels starting at the village of Deep Creek, Virginia, and running south to the village of South Mills, North Carolina, it at length joined the headwaters of the Pasquotank River, a northern tributary of Albemarle Sound.

The Dismal Swamp Canal was first planned as a means of floating lumber out of the swamp. Actual work on it began in 1793, and it was opened for the limited navigation of log rafts and flatboats in 1805, but for some time to come the canal would be of only local significance.

The Dismal Swamp Canal's subsequent enlargement as a shoal-draft ship canal did not materialize until the 1820s. But those improvements rendered superfluous at the time the original need for what was to eventuate in the more easterly sea-level Albemarle and Chesapeake Canal, for the Dismal Swamp Canal had by then already effectively united the bay and the sound, so providing a long-sought back-door route inside Cape Hatteras.

The Dismal Swamp Canal's twenty-one mile elevated channel was maintained by a series of locks—originally seven—fed by a lateral feeder ditch bringing fresh water drawn from Lake Drummond, in the center of the swamp. A tow-path, or tracking path, paralleled the canal for the entire distance between the terminal vil-lages of Deep Creek and South Mills. At length this was superseded by a stagecoach road and eventually by today's modern highway—Route 17, currently slated for upgrading to four lanes, with a dividing median strip.

As the size of vessels wishing to make the canal transit steadily increased during the second quarter of the nineteenth century, the Dismal Swamp Canal with its many locks and narrow, twisting river approaches increasingly demonstrated its inconveniences. This justified the construction of the wider and deeper sea-level Albemarle and Chesapeake Canal, encumbered by only a single lock, to make its appearance in the 1850s.

It was only within the decade preceding the outbreak of the Civil War that the eighteenth-century concept of canal building in southeastern Virginia and northeastern North Carolina was revived. Then, at long last—after fourscore years of debate—actual work on the Albemarle and Chesapeake Canal began in 1855. While the Dismal Swamp Canal had been dug by hand, nine steam dredges (then styled "Iron Titans") were now assembled at various points along the Albemarle and Chesapeake's "line of navigation." Some of these powerful machines grubbed out a sea-level swath through a seemingly impenetrable morass for the Virginia Cut. Colossal stumps as hard as rock from a primeval forest were uprooted in the process, and a mucky channel below sea level was cleared out, which immediately filled with water. Other dredges attacked the more easily cut sandy soil of the North Carolina Cut and removed shoal spots in the rivers and Currituck Sound.

While all this was taking place, a steam pile driver positioned at the west end of the Virginia Cut at Great Bridge was laying the foundations for what was to be a national engineering wonder—a large, double-gated, reversible-head guard lock built of masonry, the first such device constructed in the nation. This lock was necessary to prevent tidal flow in the Elizabeth River from ranging through the canal cut. It also kept salt water from getting into the freshwater sounds beyond, insuring that they remain filled with the mahogany-colored, sweet juniper water of the adjacent swamps, rich in tannic acid and renowned for its purity for drinking. Other work consisted of converting the two narrow low-level bridges across the streams at Great Bridge and North Landing into drawbridges—providing unlimited height for masted vessels using the canal—and of building a brand-new drawbridge across the Carolina Cut at Coinjock, then effectively severed by the canal into the upper and lower Currituck peninsula.

As private companies operating parallel routes connecting Chesapeake Bay with the North Carolina sounds, the two canals immediately became bitter rivals, each in its turn experiencing financial troubles as first one and then the other sought to improve its facilities in a bid to capture the available trade. As stated above, following a long period of study, the federal government in 1912, formally acquired all assets of the Albemarle and Chesapeake Canal Company and forthwith began a thorough process of upgrading the waterway. Neglected and now badly silted up, the Dis-

mal Swamp Canal barely remained open until 1925, when it too was purchased by the United States. It was then likewise improved, and today both canals exist side by side in amity as wards of the U.S. Army Corps of Engineers.

The Atlantic Intracoastal Waterway, of which both the Albemarle and Chesapeake and the Dismal Swamp canals are major segments, has been dubbed America's Grand Canal by affectionate partisans. A boon to yachtsmen and small commercial craft owners—not to mention the government itself—the waterway is jointly maintained and efficiently operated at no extra cost to civilian users—except through the federal taxes they pay—by the Corps of Engineers and the U.S. Coast Guard.

The waterway has had a gradual evolution, however, tying together various dredged channels of rivers, bays, and sounds with a number of independently owned canal schemes spotted along the Atlantic coast. The present continuous channel was envisaged as a unit as early as the beginning of the nineteenth century, and a survey by the national government was made in 1837. It was then suggested that owners of the various privately operated canals strive to maintain the same depth and use similar-sized locks where required.

Though the Intracoastal Waterway was not essentially completed for government operation until well into the first half of the twentieth century, its northernmost segment is claimed as its most venerable. In 1643, Massachusetts Bay colonists actually dug a half-mile-long tidal canal from Ipswich Bay to Gloucester Harbor, so making an island out of rocky Cape Ann and providing a safe, sheltered channel inside it between the Gulf of Maine and Massachusetts Bay. This was probably the earliest canal built in the Western Hemisphere.

Farther south along the Atlantic coast, a few years later the Plymouth settlers planned an eight-mile canal across the neck of Cape Cod, following the route of an ancient Indian canoe portage. This was in the year 1676, but the present sea-level Cape Cod Canal—a waterway of great importance, materially shortening the distance by water between Boston and New York—actually was not built until 1914. South of Cape Cod Bay and this canal, reasonably well protected natural water was afforded boatmen by Buzzards Bay, Vineyard Sound, Narragansett Bay, and Block Island and Long Island sounds all the way to the East River and New York Harbor.

Other coastal canals also envisaged in the colonial era as part of the southbound chain did not come into being until well into the nineteenth century. Had it not subsequently fallen into disuse and abandonment by reason of railroad competition as late as 1932, the then century-old, forty-four mile long Delaware and Raritan Canal spanning the state of New Jersey from New York Bay to the Delaware River near Trenton, might well have afforded a useful link in the modern waterway. All but vessels of extremely shoal draft now have to go "outside" for more than a hundred miles along the exposed Jersey coast between Sandy Hook and Cape May. Only the smallest can avail themselves of today's Garden State shoal-draft Manasquan Inlet–Cape May coastal canal, 106 miles long and authorized as a federal project in 1945.

Proceeding southward below New Jersey, the Chesapeake and Delaware—one of the nation's most logical ship canals—cuts off the neck of the Delmarva Peninsula, consisting of most of Delaware and the eastern shores of Maryland and Virginia, which make an inland sea out of Chesapeake Bay. The Chesapeake and Delaware Canal was initially surveyed in 1764, but was not actually started on its 13½ mile course between Back Creek and Elk River until 1802. Work soon came to a halt, however, and it was not revived until 1822. The canal was finally completed in 1829 as a narrow, elevated lock canal. But since there were no adjacent streams to provide water to feed the locks by natural drainage, the canal had to be replenished with water provided by enormous steam pumps located at Chesapeake City. They worked to keep the summit level full by replacing water lost through each lockage. Acquired by the federal government in 1919 and progressively widened and deepened over the years, the Chesapeake and Delaware Canal is today a modern, sea-level ship canal capable of handling the large, deep-draft vessels of many types which ply between the vital bays for which the canal is named—so serving the major bay ports of Philadelphia and Baltimore.

Though a considerable amount of protection is afforded boatmen by all these interconnecting rivers, bays, and sounds, the Intracoastal Waterway proper is held to begin its southbound course at the lower end of Chesapeake Bay inside Hampton Roads, with the zero-mile marker located in the Elizabeth River off downtown Norfolk. Though considerable open water lies ahead in shallow and potentially turbulent Albemarle and Pamlico sounds, during the remainder of its more than one-thousand-mile journey south the waterway lies for the most part behind snug, protecting banks paralleling the coastline. A project depth of twelve feet now prevails from Norfolk to Fort Pierce, Florida, 965½ miles; then a depth of ten feet to Miami, 123½ miles; and finally seven feet to Key West: a grand total of 1,244 miles for the complete waterway.

Vertical clearances, originally unlimited because of the drawbridges, are now governed by the sixty-five-foot elevation of several fixed interstate highway bridges which began to appear in the late 1960s. The dredged channels are a minimum of sixty feet wide.

Only a few miles south of where the Intracoastal Waterway officially commences at Norfolk, the south-bound navigator is afforded a choice of routes: the older and narrower Dismal Swamp Canal—the so-called alternate route, with lift locks at either end—or the newer and wider Albemarle and Chesapeake Canal, with its single guard lock. A sign on the west side of the channel set up on piles points out the routes. (See fig. 1.) The distance of seventy-odd miles is the same, and both routes effectively unite the waters of bay and sound by taking parallel courses. Pleasure boaters more frequently elect the Dismal Swamp Canal—which affords them an interesting overnight port of call at Elizabeth City, North Carolina—leaving the more commodious Albemarle and Chesapeake to non-stop commercial traffic. Hampton Roads yachtsmen often find it enjoyable to make a kind of circumnavigation of southeastern Virginia and northeastern North Carolina by way of both canals—going down to the Albemarle Sound region by one and returning to Tidewater Virginia by the other.

The southbound navigator of the Intracoastal Waterway, having gained the so-called common point where the lines of both these canals join, now has twenty miles of open water ahead while crossing Albemarle Sound on the next leg of his journey. He then enters the mouth of the Alligator River, a wide, sluggish stream hemmed in by forests. The river separates North Carolina's Tyrell and Dare counties and by way of the twenty-five mile long Alligator-Pungo Canal, completed in 1928, gives sheltered access into Pamlico Sound.

Exit from wide and open Pamlico is by way of a canal cut between the Neuse River and the Newport River. The route now leads past Beaufort Inlet and enters Bogue Sound. From this point onward, the Intracoastal Waterway stays close to the Atlantic coastline, taking advantage of a large number of salt marshes, rivers, bays, and inlets as it continues its southbound journey. It crosses the Cape Fear River near Wilmington, then Winyah Bay below Georgetown, Charleston Harbor, Port Royal Sound, the Savannah River mouth, Georgia's famed sea-island passages, the St. John's River, St. Augustine Harbor, and Indian River inside

FIG. 1. *Junction in the Southern Branch of the Elizabeth River. At this point Deep Creek branches off to the right, leading to the Dismal Swamp Canal, while the entrance to the Albemarle and Chesapeake Canal lies ahead to the left. When this August 9, 1977, photo was taken by Alexander C. Brown, the Dismal Swamp Canal was closed because of insufficient water to operate the locks, a not infrequent event.*

Cape Canaveral, and thence on to Stuart and a junction with the cross-Florida Okeechobee Waterway. Or, continuing on down past Palm Beach, Port Everglades, Miami, and Biscayne Bay, it finally terminates in the Florida Keys, with milepost 1,244 at Key West.

The Intracoastal Waterway is presently a necessity to a host of seafaring interests. It makes it possible for them to transfer up and down the coast in safety such unwieldly nautical creations as pipeline dredge rigs, ore and lumber barges with their accompanying tugs or pushers, and other craft like floating cranes, which it would be dangerous to attempt piloting out in the open ocean, particularly in the exposed stretch around Capes Hatteras and Lookout. Myriads of fishing boats, trawlers, small tankers, freighters, and other commercial vessels, together with pleasure craft of all types and sizes, contribute to the many million tons of shipping which annually use all or a part of this protected route. Some 4,470,292 net tons alone were recorded for 1976 via the stretch between Norfolk and the St. John River, Florida.[4] Fuel oil, fertilizers, liquid sulphur, and pulpwood logs make up the lion's share of commodities transported. Logs used to be rafted through the canals, but most all pulpwood is presently transported by barge.

A large proportion of this movement is seasonal, for, as with migratory birds, there is an annual passage of yachts going south in the autumn and north in the spring. The Atlantic Intracoastal Waterway makes this great movement of people, vessels, and goods convenient, efficient, and safe. The Albemarle and Chesapeake Canal is a vital link in this chain, and its long and interesting history will be traced in the succeeding chapters of this book.

---

[4] U.S. Army Corps of Engineers, *Waterborne Commerce of the United States, Calendar Year 1976*, pt. 1: "Waterways and Harbors, Atlantic Coast," p. 146.

Canal Schemes of
the Colonial Era,
1728–75

It was in 1772, toward the end of the colonial era, that (as we have seen) the first definite plans were proposed for the creation of the canal which turned out to be the Albemarle and Chesapeake. The Great Dismal Swamp, through which part of the canal was to run, then encompassed a far greater area than today's approximately 210,000 acres. At present, no more than a third of the Great Dismal's size—variously estimated to have been from seven hundred to two thousand square miles—survives to be classified as swampland.[1]

This vast tract of spongy forested terrain is the northernmost of a succession of large coastal-plain swamps which extend along the country's eastern seaboard all the way down to the Florida Everglades. The Dismal Swamp lies eastward of a ridge of elevated ground running from Suffolk, Virginia, to Edenton, North Carolina. Aeons ago, this ridge, termed the Nansemond Escarpment, was the original Atlantic coastline. But gradual emersion of the shallow ocean floor of the continental shelf widened the shore and resulted in the formation of flat, heavily forested swampland and the eventual deposit of layers of peat above what had once been the sandy sea bottom twenty feet below.

As a result of this rising of the land, the present ocean beach is now some forty miles farther east. Large parts of dry land in Virginia's former Princess Anne, Norfolk, and Nansemond counties—now the cities of Virginia Beach, Chesapeake, and Suffolk—together with those in Currituck, Camden, and Pasquotank counties in North Carolina, were originally included in the Dis-

---

[1] Paul W. Kirk, Jr., *The Great Dismal Swamp*, pp. 1–4, 167.

mal Swamp. Curiously, some of this swampy terrain is at a higher elevation than the dry land surrounding it, though much of it follows the course of meandering streams flowing eastward into now landlocked Currituck and Albemarle sounds.

When European discoverers first began to penetrate this newfound North American continent, they studiously skirted the swamps, considering them fearful, malevolent places.[2] Consequently, early cartographers did not have the means of delineating these areas accurately and so left them blank. Perhaps the earliest reference to Dismal Swamp, though not so named, occurs merely as a note appearing in a corner of the well-known map published in 1673 by Augustin Herrman. A Bohemian by birth, Herrman came to New Amsterdam around 1647 as a member of the Dutch West India Company. Later, he was commissioned by Lord Baltimore to survey the Chesapeake Bay area in return for an extensive grant of land in Maryland. His map, entitled "Virginia and Maryland—As it is planned and inhabited this present year 1670," shows merely a blank space where Dismal Swamp should appear. A number of places around the swamp's perimeter are properly identified, however: "Nantemond," "Lower Norfolk," "Corotuck" [Currituck], the "Nantemond River," "Chowann," and "Passpatank" [Pasquotank].[3]

It is unlikely that Herrman ever explored the area, and it was undoubtedly on the basis of local hearsay that he inserted the following descriptive note in the upper left-hand corner (the southwest region, as the map is oriented) of his chart. Incidentally, it was so drawn that the west is at the top, rather than the north, as is usually the case. It reads: "The land between the James River and Roanoke River is for the most parts [*sic.*] Low Suncken Swampy Land not well passable but with great difficulty. And therein harbours Tygers Bears and other Devouringe Creatures."[4]

Undoubtedly Herrman's "Tygers" would have to be downgraded to bobcats, but black bears up to five hundred pounds in weight were common in Dismal Swamp until even the recent past.With a large part of the swamp now under the control of the U.S. Department of the Interior, conservationists hope that much of the original fauna will be restored and that bears and all sorts of other wildlife will again thrive.

As the land surrounding the Great Dismal became settled, sporadic forays were made into it by hunters and woodsmen. As early as 1728, Virginia's famous resident Col. William Byrd II of Westover, describing the growing seaport city of Norfolk and its surroundings, reported: "This place is a mart for most of the Commodities produced in the Adjacent Parts of North Carolina. They have a pretty deal of Lumber from the Borderers on the Dismal, who make bold with the

[2] Bill Thomas, *The Swamp*, p. 11. See also chap. 3, "The Great Dismal Swamp," pp. 31–39.
[3] Coolie Verner, "The First Maps of Virginia 1590–1673," in *Virginia Magazine of History and Biography*, 58, no. 1 (January 1950): 14–15.

[4] Earl G. Swem, "Maps Relating to Virginia in the Virginia State Library," in *Library Bulletin*, vol. 7, nos. 2–3 (April–July 1914): 51–52.

King's Land there abouts, without the least Ceremony. They not only maintain their Stock's upon it, but get Boards, Shingles and other Lumber out of it in great Abundance."[5]

William Byrd probably furnished the first comprehensive description of Dismal Swamp when he wrote up his experiences in surveying, at the request of the Crown, the disputed Virginia-North Carolina boundary line. In the spring of 1728, Byrd's party of twenty men, including commissioners from both colonies, proceeded due west, starting from the Atlantic coast at Currituck Inlet, and passed directly through the center of Dismal Swamp while they were running the line. Byrd considered the place "a vast body of Mire and Nastiness," and he is responsible for assigning it the name *dismal*.[6] Curiously, though it had reputedly been discovered earlier by North Carolina's Governor William Drummond, oval-shaped Lake Drummond, the swamp's most significant feature, was not mentioned by Byrd, though the dividing-line surveyors passed less than half-a-dozen miles south of it.

In addition to the unsavory reputation Dismal Swamp had for being the cause of ill-health and distempers among those who lived nearby, one important reason for the unpopularity of the region with eighteenth-century settlers was that, as a virtually impenetrable barrier, it lay athwart the logical direct trade-routes running from the northeastern part of the Carolinas to Norfolk, which provided those regions' only available deepwater harbor. Carolina's ports located at the outlets of her rivers serving the vast hinterland were effectively denied access to the sea—and hence to coastwise or overseas markets. Only small, shoal-draft vessels could negotiate the treacherous bar-bound inlets that pierce the long Atlantic coastal-barrier beach islands and skirt the entire Currituck, Albemarle, and Pamlico sounds region, culminating eastward in Cape Hatteras.[7] For this reason, products for export and import were forced to take overland routes—slower and more costly—to gain a logical shipping port.

Throughout the eighteenth century, two dirt roads starting northward at Edenton, North Carolina, made long, circuitous routes around each side of Dismal Swamp, both necessitating frequent river crossings. Professor Thomas Jefferson Wertenbaker, a well known Virginia historian, states that these roads finally came together again at Great Bridge (fig. 2), a dozen miles south of Norfolk. From Great Bridge, freight was transported either by road or (preferably) by boat for the final leg of the journey to deep water via the Southern Branch of the Elizabeth River.[8]

---

[5] William Byrd, *Histories of the Dividing Line Betwixt Virginia and North Carolina*, p. 36. (Hereafter cited as Byrd, *Dividing Line*.)
[6] Byrd, *Dividing Line*, p. 70.

[7] Gary S. Dunbar, *Historical Geography of the North Carolina Outer Banks*. The various beach inlets and their migrations are well detailed in this scholarly work.
[8] Thomas Jefferson Wertenbaker, *Norfolk: Historic Southern Port*, p. 33.

Fɪɢ. 2. *An early view of Great Bridge, Va., as shown in a woodcut by Edward C. Bruce from* Harper's New Monthly Magazine, *May 1860.*

This nuisance was, of course, well understood by William Byrd, and in his account of the dividing line expedition, he voiced the prevailing sentiment of the area when he suggested that, even though: "It wou'd require a great Sum of Money to drain it [Dismal Swamp] . . . the Publick Treasure cou'd not be better

bestow'd than to preserve the Lives of His Majesty's Liege People and at the same time render so great a Tract of Swamp very Profitable." Byrd concluded prophetically by calling attention to "the advantage of making a Channel to transport by water-carriage goods from Albemarle Sound into Nansimond and Elizabeth Rivers, in Virginia." Logically this would entitle Byrd to the honor of being the spiritual parent of Dismal Swamp's various canals.[9]

Meanwhile, products obtained from the Dismal Swamp itself, particularly high-grade lumber, were enjoying increasing popularity, and, thirty-five years after Byrd's observations concerning the casual inroads made by neighboring citizens, in the 1760s George Washington and five business associates banded together in a speculative venture, styling their proposed activities as "Adventurers for Draining the Great Dismal Swamp." The company acquired some 40,000 acres of rich timberland which, Washington observed, contained "the finest cypress, juniper and other lofty wood."[10] Slaves owned by the group cut timber, built roads, and finally dug canals.

Unlike William Byrd, however, who considered the Dismal Swamp "dreadful," Washington recorded that the swamp was "a glorious paradise," and the half-dozen separate trips he made into it between May 1763 and October 1768 to examine his property and to talk

---

[9] Byrd, *Dividing Line*, pp. 84, 86.
[10] John C. Fitzpatrick, ed., *The Writings of George Washington.* 32: 350.

to his neighbors were described in glowing detail in his diaries.[11] As far as Dismal Swamp was concerned, the first mention of the word *canal* in connection with the area appears in the January 1764 charter granted to Washington's company by the Virginia assembly. This prestigious body passed "An Act to enable certain adventurers to drain a large tract of marshy grounds in the Counties of Nansemond and Norfolk" and allowed them "to enter upon and have such a free passage and make such canals or causeways" as they felt were necessary.[12]

One of the first acts of the company was to make a "corduroy causeway" of transverse-laid saplings starting at high ground east of the Suffolk-Edenton Road and leading into the northwest shore of Lake Drummond. This is shown on a plat of the company's property dated November 20, 1763, which was prepared for the "Adventurers" by Norfolk County surveyor Gersham Nimmo.[13] Apparently the Nimmo map was the first to chart accurately the position and extent of the lake.

A modest beginning toward that goal—fortunately never fully achieved—of draining Dismal Swamp occurred in the early 1760s, when the bumpy road to Lake Drummond was replaced by a five-mile-long,

twelve-foot-wide canal, subsequently carrying Washington's name. This modest waterway, first used to transport timber, is still employed for drainage and might well qualify as the nation's first "monument" to the man who later became known as the Father of his Country.[14] Apparently no records survive to pinpoint the date of digging the ditch, but a casual mention of its existence appears in an advertisement in the *Virginia Gazette* of November 19, 1772, offering for sale a tract of land "joining the great ditch in the Dismal Swamp." Also for sale was a "large gondola," presumably used in navigating it.[15]

The prime function of Washington Ditch was merely to afford a better way of getting wood products out of the swamp than by using carts to haul them over the original rough, timber-laid road. But the date of the advertisement is significant, for "canal talk" was then in the air. The year 1772 witnessed a surge of interest in all Virginia waterways, including the first positive record of the plan previously mentioned for a ship canal to run through Dismal Swamp and connect Albemarle Sound and the Chesapeake Bay. Charles B. Cross Jr., Chesapeake Clerk of Courts and a moving spirit in the Norfolk County Historical Society of Chesapeake, has covered this matter thoroughly, and we are pleased to be able to follow his scholarly account in detail.[16]

---

[11] John C. Fitzpatrick, ed., *George Washington Diaries*, 1:189–94.

[12] William Waller Hening, ed., *The Statutes at Large: Being a Collection of All the Laws of Virginia*, 8:18–19.

[13] This map is reproduced in Brown, *Dismal Swamp Canal*, p. 18. Biographical information concerning Nimmo is given on pp. 25–26 n. 16.

[14] Brown, *Dismal Swamp Canal*, p. 29.

[15] Williamsburg *Virginia Gazette* (Purdie and Dixon), November 19, 1772, p. 2, col. 3.

[16] Cross, "The Canal," episode I, pp. 11–19.

In many respects Virginia's 1772 colonial assembly, presided over by Royal Governor Dunmore, was remarkable for the number of acts it passed for the promotion of internal improvements.[17] In his foreword to the *Journal of the House of Burgesses, 1770–1772*, historian John Pendleton Kennedy cited: "such important matters as improving the navigation of the Potomac; the opening of a road from Warm Springs to Jenning's Gap; the determination to clear the Mattapony River, and of circumventing the falls of the James River by a canal from Westham to a point below Richmond; and a canal from Archer's Hope Creek to Queen's Creek, through Williamsburg, to connect James River with the York River." And, Kennedy continued in his introduction to the *Journals of the House of Burgesses*, "At no time in the history of the colony had such stupendous undertakings been suggested, much less received serious consideration."[18]

When the "Act for opening the Falls of James River" was introduced, Norfolk County burgesses James Holt and Thomas Newton, Jr., as well as Joseph Hutchings, representing the borough of Norfolk—assisted by neighbors from Princess Anne County—tacked on the end of this James River act the further "provision for opening a canal from the head of the southern or eastern branch of Elizabeth River, to the head of the north [Landing] river." The full text of this act reads:

VII.   And whereas the opening of a canal from the head of the southern or eastern branch of Elizabeth River, to the head of the north [Landing] river, will greatly increase the commerce of this colony: Be it therefore enacted, by the authority aforesaid, That Joseph Hutchings, Thomas Newton, junior, James Webb, John Wilson, Abraham Wormington, Edward Hack Mosely, junior, Christopher Wright, Anthony Walke, David McClenahan, George Logan, Peter Singleton, Lemuel Riddick, Severn Eyre, and James Holt, gentlemen, or any seven of them be, and they are hereby authorized and required to view the lands, between the heads of the said rivers, and to make, or cause to be made, an exact survey, of such parts thereof, through which the said canal may be the most conveniently cut, and shall moreover make as exact an estimate as may be of the expense of opening and rendering such canal navigable for the passage of boats, or other vessels, which estimate, together with a plan of the survey, the said trustees, or a major part of them, shall return to the next session of assembly, and it shall be lawful for the said trustees, or the major part of them, or the persons employed by them in the execution of this act, to pass through the lands of any person, or persons, whatsoever, for the purpose aforesaid.[19]

Charles Cross points out[20] that James Holt was undoubtedly the father of the plan that, more than four-

---

[17] Hening, *Statutes*, 8:556–81.
[18] John Pendleton Kennedy, ed., *Journals of the House of Burgesses, 1770–1772*, p. XXXV, and *1773–1776*, p. 246.

[19] Hening, *Statutes*, 8:564–70.
[20] Cross, "The Canal," episode I, p. 14.

score years later, was to become today's Albemarle and Chesapeake Canal. He, along with Peter Singleton of Princess Anne County, went ahead to engage surveyors, and Holt put up the funds to hire chain carriers in order to measure the projected routes. One route proceeded eastward from the head of the Elizabeth River's Southern Branch at Great Bridge—the eventual canal route—and the other ran southward from the high point of navigation on the Eastern Branch at Kemps Landing. Both aimed directly toward the headwaters of Virginia's North Landing River, which leads down into Currituck Sound.[21]

Thomas Reynolds Walker, Princess Anne County surveyor and one of Washington's Dismal Swamp "Adventurers," undertook the Eastern Branch survey, determining the distance to North Landing by that line to be "seven Miles and one hundred forty Perches." Meanwhile, Josiah Ives, deputy surveyor of Norfolk County, examined the Southern Branch route (fig. 3), finding that distance to be "Six Miles and a quarter."[22]

In 1774, "when the need for engineering advice be-

came apparent," Cross states that James Holt retained the services of Isaac Hildrith. Backed by practical experience in building canals in Wales, Hildrith examined both suggested routes. He toured Kemps Landing on March 28, 1774, and explored the Southern Branch by canoe on March 29. Inclement weather cut short his physical survey at North Landing, however. Nevertheless, he got out an engineering report the next month, in which he compared both feasibility and cost of the two separate lines. (See table 1.) Each was designed to handle vessels sixty feet long by fifteen feet wide and drawing up to four feet. These cost estimates were merely for cutting the canal, however. Not included

Table 1—Hildreth's comparison of two proposed canal routes

Kemp's Landing to North River		The Great Bridge to North River
7¼ miles	Length	6¾ miles
7 feet	Mean depth	6 feet
30 feet	Width at top	28 feet
16 feet	Width at bottom	16 feet
	Cost in pounds	
7057 . . 6 . . 4	sterling	6666 . . 19 . . 3

Source: Charles Cross, "The Canal," episode 1 in *An Historical Review* (Chesapeake, Va.: Norfolk County Historical Society of Chesapeake, 1966), p. 14, quoting Hildreth's report from folder 50, item 23, pts. 1–3, Colonial Papers, 1753–78, Virginia State Library, Richmond.

---

[21] Although generally referred to merely as Virginia's North River in the early records, wherever pertinent in this account we have added the word "Landing" in brackets lest the identities of the Virginia and North Carolina streams became confused. In Virginia it is the North Landing River and in North Carolina, the North River, both parts of the Albemarle and Chesapeake Canal route.

[22] Quoted in Cross, "The Canal," p. 14.

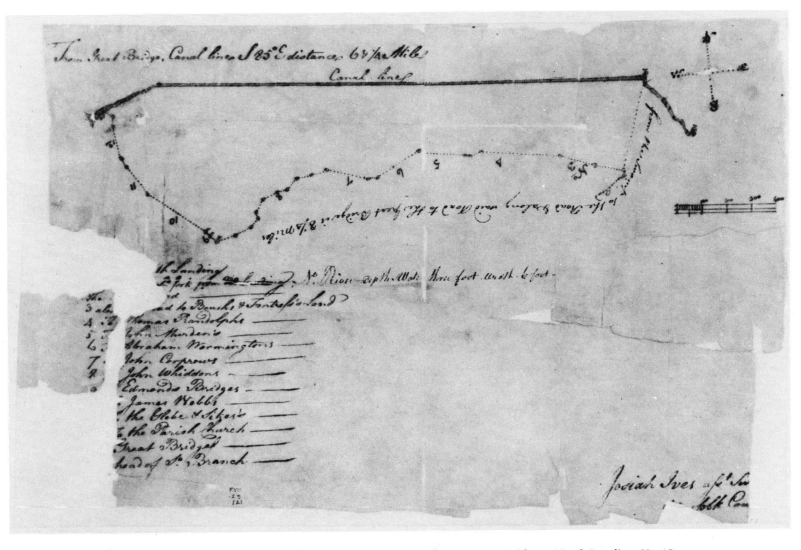

FIG. 3. *Josiah Ives's survey of the proposed canal route, 1772, covering Great Bridge to North Landing, Va. (Courtesy Virginia State Library, Richmond.)*

was the purchase price of the land the lines would have to traverse, about which Hildrith commented:

> It will likewise be necessary to have the most advantageous Course for the Canal, Planned from a careful Survey, that the value of such grounds as are private property, through which the canal must pass be exactly known, and whether there may be any Necessity of laying Bridges over it to unite Estates as may be severed thereby.
>
> It is observed that from the Southern Branch of Elizabeth River, it will pass chiefly through waste Lands or such as are of small value, but from the Eastern Branch through such as are or may be cultivated, the value of which I have not attempted to ascertain as I am not a competent Judge.[23]

It is significant to note that, although none were then in existence in colonial America, Hildrith also designed a canal lock suited to either one of the routes which might be chosen. This lock could raise the Elizabeth River water level to match that of the North Landing River. However, no mention was made of the necessity of having the lock operate in the other direction when, for example, the heights of water in the rivers were reversed. This would require a reversible head lock, as was subsequently installed at Great Bridge when the canal was actually constructed many years later. Cost of Hildrith's lock was estimated at £758, and he rec-

ommended that it have a floor of timber and sides of asher stone—of which he said 350 tons would be required. Labor costs were appraised at 12 to 14 shillings a week (about $1.80) for masons; 10 shillings, 6 pence, to 12 shillings for carpenters; and from 10 to 12 shillings for laborers.

Governor Dunmore, who had already demonstrated his enthusiasm for canals by subscribing £500 of his own funds for the projected canal through Williamsburg to unite the James and York Rivers,[24] also recommended that James Tait, a Scot then living on the Eastern Shore of Virginia, be employed to make an independent examination and compile estimates for both the proposed canal lines.

Tait's report, dated April 17, 1774, at Norfolk, included drawings showing comparable canal sections for both routes (see fig. 4),[25] and his cost estimates turned out to be practically the same as those determined by Hildrith—approximately £7,000 for the Eastern Branch line and £6,500 for the Southern. Tait included the cost of drawbridges—one "over the canal for the Road leading from the Great Bridge to Kemp's Landing," and the other at Great Bridge itself. Like Hildrith, Tait made no estimate "for either the value of Ground or manager's wages."[26]

---

[23] Cross, "The Canal," pp. 14–15, cites Hildrith Report, in folder 50, item 23, pts. 1–3, Colonial Papers, 1753–78, Virginia State Library, Richmond.

[24] Brown, "Colonial Williamsburg's Canal Scheme," This article cites Williamsburg *Virginia Gazette* (Purdie and Dixon), January 16, 1772. Reprints were issued as pub. no. 1 of the 1977-formed Virginia Canals & Navigation Society, Williamsburg, Va., 1977.
[25] Cross, "The Canal." pp. 16–17.
[26] Ibid.

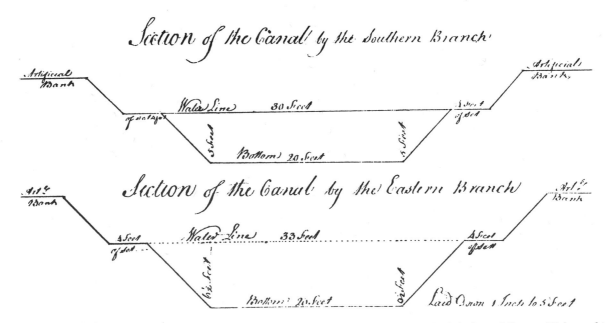

Section of the Canal by the Southern Branch

Section of the Canal by the Eastern Branch

FIG. 4. *Drawing filed with James Tait's report, dated April 17, 1774. (Courtesy Virginia State Library, Richmond.)*

Though more than three years had elapsed since the passage of the February 1772 act of the House of Burgesses, Joseph Hutchings, Thomas Newton, Jr., James Webb, John Wilson, Abraham Wormington, Peter Singleton, and James Holt made on June 16, 1775, their combined formal report certifying that Messrs. Hildrith and Tait, "persons skilful in such Works," had determined that it was "practicable to cut a Canal from the head of one of the said branches of *Elizabeth River,* to the Head of the *North [Landing] River.*"[27]

This report was duly referred to the Committee of Trade, of which Hutchings and Newton were members. However, this committee recommended on June 20, 1775, that further consideration be "deferred till the next session of the General Assembly."[28]

That next session was never held, however, for far more important things were taking place. The patriots' move for independence was just around the corner, and Lord Dunmore had slipped quietly out of the Governor's Palace in Williamsburg by June 8, 1775, hastened to Capitol Landing, and then sought safety on board H.M.S. *Fowey* in the York River—never to return to his colonial residence again. Meanwhile, canal-building schemes had to await a more propitious climate for their revival by the new nation.

[27] Kennedy, ed., *Journal of the House, 1773–1776*, p. 246.

[28] Ibid., pp. 269–70.

3

Plans to Connect
Chesapeake and Albemarle
Waters, 1783–1850

Although the Revolution called an effective halt to Virginia's extensive plans for internal improvements, these were to be revived soon after the war under the leadership of none other than George Washington. Now the country's revered hero, Washington was to be a leader in the movement he first envisaged as an important way to bind the newly formed states together as a nation. Two years after the great victory at Yorktown, the Virginia General Assembly, meeting now in Richmond, passed a new "Act for cutting a navigable canal" in October 1783. This started off with virtually the same preamble as its predecessor: "Whereas the opening of a communication of the waters of Elizabeth River with those of North [Landing] River will be of great benefit and advantage. . . ."[1]

With the sole exception of Peter Singleton, however, a whole new group of trustees were appointed. They included: "Thomas Brown, George Kelley, Peter Singleton, Josiah Parker, William White, James Hunter, John King, Daniel Sandford and Solomon Shepherd, gentlemen." These men were authorized to: "take and receive subscriptions . . . to go on the lands of any persons whatsoever, and to dig, cut out, and open such canals or aqueducts, for the passage of the waters of the said rivers, and to build and place such locks therein

---

[1] Hening, *Statutes*, 11:332–34.

as they shall think proper."[2] John Coleman, Joel Watkins, James Wall, James Mason, Samuel Goode, Isaac Coles, and Andrew Meade—also "gentlemen"—were appointed commissioners, and they were enjoined to select the route the canal would follow.

Presumably the prewar surveys of Hildrith and Tait were known to the new commissioners, but no mention of them occurs in the 1783 act, nor were the two separate routes originally under consideration described in any way in the act.

As before, apparently no one was then in any particular hurry to get the project started, and it was two full years following the passage of the act before Virginia's Governor Patrick Henry had chosen to appoint William Ronald "as one of the commissioners in the Canal Business." Henry had also named Robert Andrews "to fix on the most convenient course for a canal between the waters of Eliz [*sic*] River in this state and those passing through North Carolina." Ronald subsequently declined the appointment, and Andrews suggested John Cowper of Portsmouth as a substitute, advising Governor Henry that "Cowper has an intimate acquaintance with the principal characters of N. Carolina, and he is much interested in this measure."[3]

At length, Andrews and Cooper, representing Virginia, met with North Carolina commissioners William McKenzie, James Galloway, and John Stokes at Fayetteville, North Carolina, and on December 12, 1786, the five men hammered out an agreement. This declared that Virginia waters "should be free forever for vessels belonging to citizens of North Carolina" on the one hand, and that North Carolina waters should be similarly free for the passage of Virginia craft on the other.[4] The waters of Chesapeake Bay, Hampton Roads, the Elizabeth River, and Virginia's section of the upper Roanoke River were specified in both agreements. The lower part of the Roanoke—together with the Meherrin, Nottoway, and Chowan rivers—plus Albemarle Sound took care of North Carolina. These measures were to prevent either state legislature from subsequently deciding to levy tolls or otherwise penalize its neighbor once their inland waters were joined.

Despite this agreement, and the authorization to proceed granted by the October 1783 act, what was ultimately to become the Albemarle and Chesapeake Canal scheme went once more into a decline. It was

---

[2] Ibid.

[3] *Calendar of Virginia State Papers* (Richmond, Va., 1884) vol. 4: letter, William Ronald to Governor Henry, February 21, 1785, p. 12; letter, Robert Andrews to Governor Henry, March 9, 1785, p. 14; letter, Robert Andrews to Governor Henry, October 2, 1786, p. 176.

[4] Charles Clinton Weaver, *Internal Improvements in North Carolina Previous to 1880,* p. 70; John W. Moore, *History of North Carolina from the Earliest Discoveries to the Present Time* 1:401–2. Both Moore and Weaver presume that the appointment cited of Andrews, Cooper, et al. pertains to the subject of the Dismal Swamp Canal rather than to the then-proposed Albemarle and Chesapeake Canal.

about the same time, however, that the plan to dig the Dismal Swamp Canal on a line farther west through the greater part of the swamp was first broached. Although initially he felt that this would be "tedious and attended with an expense which might prove discouraging," Washington, as a former Dismal Swamp property owner, stated that he had "long been satisfied of the practicability of opening communication between the waters which empty into Albemarle Sound thro' Drummond's Pond and the Waters of Elizabeth or Nansemond Rivers."[5]

Three years after a preliminary survey had been made by Nicholas Forster, the Virginia assembly passed on December 1, 1787, its "Act for cutting a navigable canal from the waters of Elizabeth river, in this state, to the waters of Pasquotank river, in the state of North Carolina." The act was to come in force "after the passage of a like act by the General Assembly of North Carolina."[6] This eventuated during the November 1790 session, and actual work on building the canal began with slave labor in 1793.

The Dismal Swamp Canal was laid out as a continuous elevated cut some twenty-one miles in length, with Deep Creek (a narrow westward-flowing branch of the Elizabeth River six miles from Norfolk) as its northern entrance, and Joyce's Creek (a tributary of the upper Pasquotank River) its southern. Lake Drummond was bypassed but was subsequently tapped by a 3½-mile-long feeder canal designed to draw water for lockage in the main canal. Major lifts were required at both ends, and there were supplementary locks along the way, which, when first completed made the canal's summit level some 21½ feet above mean low water in tidal Deep Creek and only 3 feet lower than Lake Drummond. The Dismal Swamp Canal has remained an elevated waterway, though the summit level was lowered to 12 feet in 1899.[7]

Once Chesapeake waters were united with those of Albemarle Sound by the Dismal Swamp Canal, the need for building the originally conceived canal by way of Currituck Sound was effectively eliminated, though by no means was the plan entirely forgotten. It has already been noted that, at length, half a century later, the advent of larger vessels and greater communication requirements in the age of steam contrived to bring the new canal into being.

Due to unforeseen difficulties in digging the Dismal Swamp Canal—including lack of funds—the work proceeded with agonizing slowness. It was not until 1805 that canal-company president Richard Blow could report that an actual "junction has been effected betwixt the waters of Elizabeth River and Pasquotank." "It is navigable to admit shingle flats to pass the whole distance river to river," he continued, but reminded his

---

[5] George Washington to Dr. Hugh Williamson, Mount Vernon, March 31, 1784, in Fitzpatrick, ed. *Writings of George Washington*, 27:380.
[6] Hening, *Statutes*, 12:478–94.

[7] Brown, *Dismal Swamp Canal*, p. 140.

patrons that locks were still needed at both ends of the canal.[8]

As might have been expected, the passage of mere shingle flats and lumber rafts alone did not meet the promotors' lofty aims of an inland seas connection between bay and sound for the passage of ships. Yet it was actually not until June 1814 that the channel was deep enough to permit the arrival at Norfolk, from Scotland Neck on the Roanoke River, of a twenty-ton decked boat carrying a cargo of bacon and brandy.[9] Norfolk was jubilant, and presumably some of the cargo was immediately consumed. However, disappointment in the facilities of the Dismal Swamp Canal provided those partisans who still favored a route running via the branches of the Elizabeth River ample opportunity to continue their promotion of one or another of the original sea-level routes suggested in the 1772 act of the House of Burgesses and confirmed by the 1783 act of the Virginia legislature.

The Elizabeth River–North Landing routes soon received endorsement from a new, outside source. Albert Gallatin, Swiss-born secretary of the treasury under Thomas Jefferson and a financial wizard, took a special interest in the new nation's roads and canals. Planning to submit a comprehensive report to Congress on the matter, in 1807 he wrote to the steamboat inventor and civil engineer Robert Fulton to request that he secure information for the report, knowing that Fulton was keen on such matters.[10]

Fulton made a personal survey of Virginia's coastal canal areas and subsequently set forth his views at considerable length in a letter to Gallatin, which was made part of the official report. Fulton had gained much of his enthusiasm while visiting English canals, and he envisaged the time when in America, "canals should pass through every vale, wind around every hill, and bind the whole country together in the bonds of social intercourse." He prophesied grandiosely that "Cheap and rapid transport will draw forth the ponderous riches of the earth and circulate our minerals for the benefit of the whole community," concluding, "There is no country whose waters are so favorable to the application of this new art [canal building], as those of the United States."[11]

Fulton's personal examination showed "excellent water" in Currituck Sound past Knotts Island and on up to North Landing. And he remarked—erroneously, as it turned out—that a canal joining North Landing and the headwaters of the Elizabeth River could be "easily cut." He also praised the existing twenty-mile overland road from North Landing to Norfolk as "equal to any in the world."[12]

Gallatin's report, a year in the making, was presented

---

[8] *Calendar of Virginia State Papers*, 9:460–61.
[9] Norfolk, Va., *Gazette and Public Ledger*, June 11, 1814.

[10] Thomas W. Knox, *The Life of Robert Fulton and a History of Steam Navigation*, pp. 23–27.
[11] Robert Fulton, *Report on the Practicability of Navigating with Steam Boats*, pp. 11–12.
[12] Ibid.

to the U.S. Senate on April 4, 1808. It strongly urged further canal building and particularly stressed improvements in communication along the seaboard states, at an estimated cost of $3,000,000. Canals such as the projected Cape Cod Canal and those contemplated in New Jersey, Delaware, and North Carolina would provide continuous inland navigation south to the Cape Fear River.[13] Gallatin was impressed with the potential of the Dismal Swamp Canal and conceived it as becoming an important part of the system. Indeed, Charles Clinton Weaver observed, "to Gallatin, the Dismal Swamp Canal was of more importance than it has ever been considered since."[14]

In 1808, as established by the 1783 act of the Virginia legislature and encouraged by Gallatin's enthusiasm, the southern route from Kempsville—at the head of the Eastern Branch of the Elizabeth River—to North Landing was again before the assembly. Now it was supposed to provide an eight-foot channel and to have a capacity equal to that of the Delaware and Raritan and the Chesapeake and Delaware canals, then both in the planning stages, so forming a part of the north-south long-distance waterway in which the Federal government was showing interest. The act passed on February 4, 1809, incorporated a "Company to cut a canal from the Port of Norfolk through the Eastern Branch of Elizabeth River, to the Channel of Currituck Sound."[15]

This was styled grandly "The Great Coastwise Canal and River Navigation Company." Named as directors were Theodore Armstead, Luke Wheeler, and George Newton. But again war intervened—the War of 1812 began June 19—and nothing material was accomplished immediately. The unpopular war between Britain and her former colonies came to an end with the signing of the peace treaty at Ghent on December 24, 1814, although word did not reach New York until February of the next year. A reinstatement of canal-building intent was passed by the Virginia assembly on January 23, 1815, however, in "An Act concerning the Great Coastwise Canal and River Navigation." This put on record that the 1809 act was still in force for the construction of a canal at least six feet deep to run from the Eastern Branch to Currituck Sound.[16]

That autumn, the plans for what was to become the Albemarle and Chesapeake Canal were the subject of an official report made on November 5, 1815, by Maj. James Kearney of the U.S. Army Topographical En-

---

[13] U.S. Treasury Department, *Report of the Secretary of the Treasury on the Subject of Public Roads and Canals.* The report contains a letter by Robert Fulton dated December 8, 1807, p. 41. A French translation of the Hon. Albert Gallatin, *History of Interior Navigation (Histoire de la Navigation Intérieure,* 2 vols., Paris, 1820), cites the proposed Kempsville or Great Bridge routes to North Landing and also describes the Dismal Swamp Canal, (vol. 2, pp. 54–58).

[14] Weaver, *Internal Improvements,* pp. 69–73.

---

[15] *Acts Passed at the General Assembly of the Commonwealth of Virginia* (Richmond, Va., 1808), pp. 85–93. (Cited hereafter as *Acts of Virginia Assembly.*)

[16] *Acts of Virginia Assembly,* 1815, pp. 83–4.

gineers. Kearney cited anew the charters granted by both the Virginia and the North Carolina legislatures for the projected canal to start near Whitehouse Landing on the Elizabeth River's Eastern Branch and to run south to North Landing River, which he characterized as "rather a creek or arm of Currituck Sound." Kearney contrasted this route as being fifteen miles shorter from Norfolk to Roanoke Island than the faltering Dismal Swamp Canal.[17]

Major Kearney was apparently one of the first government engineers to recognize the major obstacles to building a canal in low ground, "below the level of the tides," where digging would have to be done under water.[18] And, no doubt, he realized that machinery powerful enough to cut through the virtually impenetrable barrier made by the petrified roots of a swamp forest had not yet been invented.

However—possibly on the strength of Major Kearney's endorsement, which Congress published February 20, 1817—the Virginia General Assembly at its session commencing December 7, 1818, considered an act with the convoluted and tongue-twisting title: "An act to revive and amend the act, entitled 'an act to revive and amend the act entitled "an act for cutting a canal from the waters of Elizabeth River, to the waters of the North [Landing] River."'" This was passed January 29, 1819, and the preamble stated that the spon-

sors of its predecessors "had been prevented by death, removal, or other causes" from being successful in their mission. Books of subscription were lawfully opened in Norfolk, Portsmouth, and elsewhere under the management of Miles King and John Capron in Norfolk; of Swepson Whitehead, William Wilson, and Arthur Emmerson in Portsmouth; of Nathaniel Paynter, Henry Sparrow, and James McAlpin in Kempsville; of John Cason, Samuel Bartie, Arthur Butt, Nehemian Freeman, and Samuel Miles at Great Bridge; and of William Davis and John Hodges in Washington. As soon as $10,000 should be subscribed, the company was to be organized at Great Bridge and incorporated under the name "The Great Bridge Canal Company."[19]

As before, apparently nothing tangible was accomplished, for an advertisement appearing in the Norfolk *American Beacon* on June 25, 1833, in behalf of the "Great Bridge and North Landing Canal" again solicited subscriptions to raise the expenses for building a canal "pursuant to an act of the General Assembly passed on the 26th of February last [1833]." Commissioners named were Thomas V. Webb, Jas C. Martin, Stephen B. Tatem, Agesilaus Foreman, Wilson B. Scott, Wm. Tatem, and Geo. T. Martin. Like their many predecessors, these men hoped that the money might soon be forthcoming "so the company may be organized immediately and the work be commenced and finished

[17] U.S. Congress, House, House doc. no. 93, February 20, 1817. Report of Major [James] Kearney, November 5, 1816.
[18] Ibid.

[19] *Acts of Virginia Assembly*, 1819, pp. 73–74 (chap. 29).

during the summer of the present year."[20] Alas, funds were apparently not readily available.

In his excellent review of pre–Civil War North Carolina canals, Clifford R. Hinshaw, Jr., mentions that the same course had been surveyed by Hamilton Fulton under the direction of the North Carolina Board of Internal Improvements. It was also examined by T. L. Patterson for the common council of Norfolk.[21]

Meanwhile the Dismal Swamp Canal was struggling along, trying to satisfy its customers with limited facilities. The canal had been deepened and substantially enlarged in 1826, and a good dirt road paralleled its elevated section, thus serving a stagecoach line between Norfolk and Elizabeth City. As vessels bringing cargo from ports on the Albemarle were prevalent in addition to continued traffic in log rafts and shingle flats, the Dismal Swamp Canal could, with some justification, now characterize itself as a ship canal. New and improved stone locks were built in several locations in 1840, and two years later considerable improvements were made at the north end by eliminating twisting and bar-bound Deep Creek from the system and substituting a direct overland cut from the outfall locks at Deep Creek Village that ran directly north to enter the Elizabeth River at the embryo village of Gilmerton. The new Gilmerton division of the Dismal Swamp Canal was 2½ miles long, and when it was opened in 1843, transit time for the entire canal had been materially reduced by eliminating the creek.[22]

Still another attempt to promote building the canal from North Landing to the Eastern Branch of the Elizabeth River, occurred in the latter part of the first half of the nineteenth century, almost seventy years after the initial proposal by the colonial House of Burgesses in 1772. This "new" canal was tied in with the suggestion that an additional canal be dug between North Landing and Lynnhaven Bay, which opens to the north directly into the lower Chesapeake. The canal was to run four miles across Princess Anne County to the same point at the headwaters of the Elizabeth River's Eastern Branch at Kempsville.[23]

Virginia's celebrated civil engineer Col. Claudius Crozet subsequently famed for the creation of the 1858 Blue Ridge railway tunnel at Rockfish Gap, carried out the necessary surveys for the Princess Anne and Kempsville Canal Company, incorporated in 1840. The completed line was to run southwestward from Lynnhaven to Kempsville, then join the seven-mile projected cut proceeding on to the North Landing River for the ship canal originally surveyed in

---

[20] Norfolk, Va., *American Beacon,* June 25, 1833.

[21] Clifford R. Hinshaw, Jr., "North Carolina Canals before 1860," p. 41 (pages 40–56 are devoted to the Albemarle and Chesapeake Canal).

[22] Brown, *Dismal Swamp Canal,* chap. 7, "The Canal is Improved," pp. 87–91; Dr. William E. Trout III, "The Gilmerton Lock," episode 2, pp. 20–33, in *An Historic Review* (Norfolk County Historical Society of Chesapeake, 1966).

[23] Dr. William E. Trout III, "The Kempsville Canal."

1774. Had this combined waterway, sixty feet wide and six feet deep, been constructed, it would have made it possible for vessels to sail a direct route from the lower Chesapeake to Albemarle Sound, bypassing Norfolk and the Elizabeth River entirely.

Colonel Crozet's estimate for the cut from Whitehouse Landing on the Eastern Branch to North Landing, including superintendence and the building of necessary bridges, amounted to $380,000, and he warned that "the appearance of the country is very deceiving." He had this to say about the tidal variations:

> The difference of the tide in North [Landing] River and Elizabeth River, the tide in the latter being that of the ocean, and the other regulated by the winds only, will be so small as to produce but an ordinary current in either direction, and, consequently, no locks will be required at the ends of the canal. But a bar may be expected to be formed at the opening into each river, by the oscillations of the waters lifting up sand into the canal; this is an unavoidable evil in all such canals, and occasional dredging must be expected.[24]

Crozet concluded his report by endorsing the potential usefulness of this canal, but this recommendation would have applied equally as well to the Southern

Branch line at Great Bridge as to the Eastern Branch line at Kempsville, which he surveyed:

> As regards the object of the canal, it would take a great deal of timber to market to Norfolk, from the extensive swamps of Currituck, Back Bay, and in North Carolina, as well as the common produce of the country, the cultivation of which it would promote and secure. Steamboats, and other crafts, would pass this short route to Currituck, Albemarle, and Pamlico Sound; and this would greatly benefit the commerce of the lower part of North Carolina, bordering on the Sound, and produce to that section of country, a short, safe, and easier way to market than by any other route, and particularly that by Ocracoke Inlet, the only opening now remaining between Pamlico Sound and the Atlantic.[25]

Although the Eastern Branch route was soon to be discarded for good in the face of a concerted and eventually successful attempt to use the Great Bridge–North Landing route, Virginia's dedicated canal historian Dr. William E. Trout III has traced the fate of the proposed Lynnhaven Bay–Kempsville canal in one of his monographs.[26] This canal amended its charter several times, and in 1861 it was reincorporated as the Kempsville Canal Company. Work began shortly thereafter on the four-mile-long proposed excavation. Despite the observation by Colonel Crozet that locks would be un-

---

[24] Quoted in William S. Forrest, ed., *Historical and Descriptive Sketches of Norfolk and Vicinity,* pp. 262–63.

[25] Ibid.
[26] Trout, "The Kempsville Canal."

necessary, wooden locks, presumably tidal ones, were in fact being considered.

By 1861 more than $17,000 had been spent, and two of four canal sections were practically finished. With the advent of the Civil War, however, the project faded into obscurity and was never successfully revived thereafter. Though some vestiges of canal construction are still visible today to those sufficiently knowledgable in canal archaeology to recognize them, Kempsville—once envisaged as a crossroads canal town—now exists as merely a Virginia Beach suburb at the head of a sluggish creek.

At the end of the first half of the nineteenth century, the apparently interminable period during which plans for canals in eastern Virginia were discussed, authorized, surveyed, and then shelved came to an end at last. Early in the 1850s, however, a remarkable Norfolk citizen named Marshall Parks, Jr., appeared on the scene and became the actual founder of the Albemarle and Chesapeake Canal. Parks had previously worked for the Dismal Swamp Canal Company, of which his father had been manager for a quarter of a century. He knew better than most the limitations of the old waterway and why a new one was a necessity. He also knew what to do to bring it into being.

4

Marshall Parks Lays
the Groundwork, 1850–55

Tidewater Virginian Marshall Parks, Jr. (fig. 5), the son of Marshall Parks and Martha Boush Parks, was born at Old Point Comfort on the southeastern end of the Virginia peninsula November 8, 1820, but lived for the greater part of his long, productive life in Norfolk. Known admiringly throughout the area as "Commodore" Parks, he founded the Albemarle and Chesapeake Canal Company and remained its president for almost thirty years. In addition, he performed many other civic duties, including serving terms both on the Norfolk city council and in the Virginia state legislature. During President Grover Cleveland's administration, (1885–89), he was appointed supervising inspector of steam vessels for the government district extending from Baltimore to Florida.[1] Marshall

Parks's father had also participated in a wide variety of activities, principally maritime. At one time, however, he had also been owner and manager of the elegant new Hygeia Hotel at Old Point Comfort—built close to the massive walls of what was then called Fortress Monroe, the bastion whose construction had begun the year before young Parks was born.[2]

Perhaps the senior Parks's most significant work, however, and that which had the greatest influence on the career of his son, was being superintendent and chief engineer of the Dismal Swamp Canal Company. This came at the time of the major enlargements made to the canal during the 1820s in an attempt to convert

---

[1] *Parks Families of Massachusetts*, (n.p., n.d.) pp. 120–21. See also obituary notices appearing in the Norfolk, Va., *Dispatch* and the Norfolk, *Public Ledger*, June 11, 1900; and in the Norfolk,

Virginian-Pilot, June 12, 1900.
[2] John C. Emmerson, *Steam Navigation in Virginia and Northeastern North Carolina Waters, 1826–1836*. Various newspaper references to Parks and the Hygeia Hotel are copied from Norfolk journals from 1826 to 1830 and are given on pp. 32, 181, 262.

FIG. 5. *Marshall Parks (1820–1900). This 1884 portrait by Mary J. Galt is owned by Parks's granddaughter, Mrs. Charles Tunstall of Norfolk. (Photo by Alexander C. Brown.)*

it to a ship canal. For his services, Parks received an annual salary in 1823 of $1,200.[3]

Parks apparently sold out his interest in the Hygeia Hotel in 1834, for, in addition to his work on the Dismal Swamp Canal, he had begun taking an increasingly active part in the operation of Norfolk's expanding steamboat lines, being listed in 1835[4] as agent for, and in some cases owner of, a variety of vessels performing a variety of services. Among these craft were the *Hampton,* the *Thomas Jefferson,* the *Chesapeake,* the *Columbia,* and the new, 1834-built *Old Dominion.* Described by contemporaries as a "useful and enterprising fellow citizen," Parks continued to be active in the management of the Dismal Swamp Canal and his other affairs until the time of his death in 1840.[5]

According to the well-known Virginia historian Dr. Leon Gardner Tyler, Marshall Parks, Jr., left school at the age of fifteen in order to accompany his father to the gristmills and sawmills the older Parks owned in North Carolina.[6] Evidently these were located at the

---

[3] Brown, *Dismal Swamp Canal,* p. 54.

[4] Norfolk *American Beacon,* June 30, 1835, quoted in Emmerson, *Steam Navigation,* p. 310.

[5] John C. Emmerson, comp., "Steamboats, 1837–1860; 1868–1878." Also "Dismal Swamp Canal, 1796–1848." Both are bound volumes of unpublished transcripts of articles copied from various Norfolk newspapers, deposited in the library of the Mariners' Museum, Newport News, Virginia. The Norfolk, Va., *American Beacon,* March 19, 1840, gives an advertisement of the forthcoming sale at auction of the steamboat *Old Dominion* by J. C. Colly, administrator of "Marshall Parks, dec'd."

[6] Leon Gardiner Tyler, *Encyclopedia of Virginia Biography* (New York: Lewis Historical Publishing Company, 1915), 3:369.

southern end of the Dismal Swamp Canal at South Mills—formerly known as Old Lebanon—for on his death, "extensive" properties there were offered for sale by his executors.[7] Tyler states that before Marshall Parks, Jr., even attained his majority, be became a postmaster and a major of militia.

Evidently young Parks had inherited a keen interest in steam navigation from his father, for after the latter's death, he began to devote himself seriously to it. Though only twenty-one years of age, in 1841 he reputedly became associated with Lt. William W. Hunter, USN, in the design of steamers propelled by the latter's revolutionary—but never to prove really successful—horizontal paddle wheels.[8] The steamer *Germ*, a fifty-two foot, wooden-hull experimental vessel, was little more than a launch. It was built for Hunter at the Gosport Navy Yard as the first example of this new form of underwater propulsion, and apparently Parks accompanied Hunter on the *Germ's* remarkable demonstration voyage from Virginia up to New York State during the summer of 1841.[9]

Parks was also responsible for the construction of an unusual iron vessel, the canal steamer *Albemarle*, an eighty-eight footer of about a hundred tons, "propelled by Worthington's Improved Vertical Wheels (the buckets being placed obliquely)." This vessel was expressly built in 1844 at the Novelty Iron Works in New York for Messrs. Reid and Anderson to establish regular steamboat service on the Dismal Swamp Canal. Parks took command in New York and brought the ship down in 3½ days, arriving at Norfolk on November 17, 1844. Here she joined her 1844-built contempories on the canal (also iron steamers), the *Pioneer, Conestoga,* and *Margaret Kemble*—the latter also pro-

[7] An advertisement in the Norfolk *American Beacon*, May 30, 1840, offered "in consequence of the death of Marshall Parks" both sawmills and gristmills at South Mills, North Carolina, "to close the concern," "Mr. Parks, Jr. will give the needful information as to the capacity and business of the mills." (From Emmerson, "Dismal Swamp Canal" transcripts.)

[8] John C. Emmerson, Jr., comp., "Experimental Steam Vessels." Transcripts in the author's files received from Mr. Emmerson provide contemporary news accounts of the steamboat *Germ's* voyage: the Norfolk *American Beacon*, August 11 and 21, 1841, quoting from Bennett's *Herald* (New York) and the Albany, N.Y., *Argus.*

[9] The voyage of the little *Germ* was by way of various bays and rivers from Hampton Roads up to New York Harbor, thence via the Hudson River into the Erie Canal, branching off northward to Oswego, N.Y., on Lake Ontario. The *Germ* then steamed across the lake to Kingston on the Canadian side and finally, retracing its course, returned to the Chesapeake again and its home port at Norfolk. Parenthetically, it might be observed that Lieutenant Hunter then proceeded to build for the federal government several full-scale iron naval vessels and revenue cutters propelled by his patented system, including the U.S.S. *Allegheny*—the largest, at 1,020 tons—which was launched in February 1847. The Norfolk *Southern Argus* of July 23, 1852, records the *Allegheny* "hauled out and improved" at Portsmouth "having 'Hunter's' propellers removed and a screw propeller substituted in its place." His other vessels also subsequently had their horizontal wheels removed in favor of conventional side paddles. No mention occurs of Parks's further connection with Lieutenant Hunter. Clark G. Reynolds, "The Great Experiment: Hunter's Horizontal Wheel," in *The American Neptune*, 24, no. 1 (January 1964): 5–24.

pelled by Hunter horizontal wheels. The propeller steamer *Loper* joined them the following year.[10]

Somewhat later, as agent for the city of Norfolk, Parks brought still another novel craft to the Elizabeth River. This was the iron ferry steamer *Princess Anne*, a hundred-foot-long, double-ended vessel built in 1853 at Wilmington, Delaware, and equipped with iron rails laid along the deck so that it could transport loaded freight cars. A pony engine turning a winch snaked them on and off the ferry. Until sold in 1860, the *Princess Anne* was successfully employed shuttling the freights between Norfolk and Portsmouth at the Seaboard and Roanoke Railway terminus.[11] Of major importance to canal building, however, and the most noteworthy craft introduced by Parks were the powerful steam dredges he assembled in order to dig the Albemarle and Chesapeake Canal.

As a former Dismal Swamp Canal Company official, young Marshall Parks appreciated better than most the many limitations of the older waterway. Perhaps the greatest of these was the inordinate length of time it normally took for sailing vessels and barges to pass through it. Often more than a week was consumed in making the fifty-mile run between Elizabeth City and Norfolk. Capt. Henry Cotton, master of the schooner *Industry* and a veteran of twenty-five years trading on the canal, wrote to Parks that on one occasion this trip had taken him fifteen days.[12] Indeed, even a twenty-day passage was not unheard of.

As had been stated, improvements were carried out at the Dismal Swamp Canal's north end beginning in the late 1830s. Completed in 1843, these eliminated bends and shoals in tidal Deep Creek by substituting the straight overland cut from the new entrance to the canal farther down the Elizabeth River at Gilmerton (named for Governor Gilmer), thence leading directly to the twin step-locks at Deep Creek Village.[13]

While this new approach speeded up canal transit at the northern end, the southern entrance to the Dismal Swamp Canal via the Pasquotank River's meandering tributary Joyce's Creek—often termed disparagingly the Old Moccosin Track—also had long proved a bottleneck. At length, another straight cut, just over four miles long, paralleling Joyce's Creek and leading directly from the upper Pasquotank to the canal's outfall locks at South Mills, eliminated the original, tortuous seven-mile-long creek channel. Named after the contractor who did the work, Turner's Cut was opened in 1856 and forthwith became a part of the Dismal Swamp Canal system, thus extended to almost thirty miles in length exclusive of river approaches.[14]

---

[10] Norfolk *American Beacon*, November 10, 1844; April 25, 1845, quoted in Emmerson, comp., "Dismal Swamp Canal" transcripts. See also Brown, *Dismal Swamp Canal*, p. 75.

[11] H. W. Burton, *History of Norfolk, Virginia, 1736–1877*, p. 16; Norfolk *Herald*, June 22, 1860.

[12] Great Bridge Lumber and Canal Company, *Report* (Norfolk, Va., February 1855), p. 16.

[13] Brown, *Dismal Swamp Canal*, pp. 87–89.

[14] Ibid., p. 91.

But neither of these expensive improvements could rectify the delays occasioned by the canal's time-consuming locking process. Just at the half-century, with the Albemarle and Chesapeake Canal then about ready to open, the Dismal Swamp Canal's original small timber locks were replaced by seven stone ones, the largest being 96 feet in length by 17½ feet wide. These still maintained the canal's summit level at its original elevation of 21½ feet above mean low water.

From north to south, the order of these seven stone locks was as follows: (*1*) the tidal lock at Gilmerton (still extant, but long without gates), which raised the water 5 feet more than the original canal entrance level at Deep Creek; (*2* and *3*) the twin step-locks at Deep Creek Village, which raised the channel to its northern level—extending 9½ miles to (*4*) Northwest Lock, from which the canal's middle, or summit, level was attained 8½ miles long and 4½ feet higher. (The feeder ditch emptied into this level.) Descending, was, first, by (*5*) Culpepper Lock, a drop of 7½ feet to the canal's south level, which was 3½ miles long; thence at South Mills by (*6* and *7*) tandem locks, the canal dropped 13 feet to navigable water in the upper Pasquotank.[15]

Obviously these locks took considerable time to operate and were inoperable in seasons of drought, even as today. In fact, Parks stated that one of the canal's "numerous defects is want of water."[16] Also, there were often delays for vessels waiting their turns to get into the locks. Likewise, the canal itself was narrow, and further delays might occur when vessels were too wide to pass conveniently, so that one of them had to pull over into one of the recesses which were cut into the banks at regular intervals for that purpose and to wait there until the other got by.

A large part of the Dismal Swamp Canal's traffic consisted of slow-moving log rafts and timber floats being pushed along by crewmen walking the towpath, breasting long poles that fastened transversely across the rafts and extended over the banks ashore. This method of propulsion, called tracking, could only be employed for the twenty-one-mile elevated central parts of the canal, where the channel was flanked by its parallel road, created from the spoil dredged from the canal bed and deposited along the bank. For the river approaches, however, where the swamp forest extended right out to the water's edge and there were no discernable banks, the rafts had to be poled. Occasionally, small steamboats operating from Elizabeth City advertised towing services in the upper Pasquotank up to the locks,[17] but poling was a common—and backbreaking—means of propulsion in a canal that was characterized by Parks as "not originally intended as a channel for the trade of North Carolina, but

[15] Ibid., pp. 87–93; Edmund Ruffin, *Agricultural, Geological and Descriptive Sketches of North Carolina*, p. 139.
[16] Great Bridge Lumber and Canal Company, *Report*, p. 4.

[17] Emmerson, comp., "Steamboats, 1837 1860," p. 127, cites the Norfolk *American Beacon*, October 13, 1847, advertising towing services of the "steamboat 'A', Capt. Jas. Kerby," of ten horsepower. See also Brown, *Dismal Swamp Canal*, p. 202.

merely for the purpose of obtaining lumber out of the Dismal Swamp."[18]

Adequate uninterrupted steam towing with powerful tugs proceeding through a wide, unencumbered sea-level channel without lift locks was, in Parks's opinion, requisite to any successful canal operation in the area, and the Dismal Swamp Canal could never be made to serve. But Parks was also a realist. Clifford Hinshaw points out in his excellent study of early North Carolina canals that Parks was well aware of the difficulties he might encounter in securing a charter and then actually funding a Virginia corporation whose activities would soon be in direct competition with the existing canal.[19] For, despite its limitations, the Dismal Swamp Canal had long been highly praised as an engineering wonder, and by this time, the Commonwealth of Virginia already held a considerable amount of Dismal Swamp Canal Company stock and naturally would not want its investment endangered.

On March 15, 1850, the Virginia legislature had incorporated the Great Bridge Lumber and Canal Company, which, in planning its operations only for the neighborhood of Great Bridge and lower Princess Anne County, did not seem, on the face of it, to pose any particular threat to the existing Dismal Swamp through-canal.[20]

Similarly, a bill to incorporate the Albemarle and Currituck Canal Company had been passed on December 27, 1850, by the North Carolina legislature for the purpose of the "establishment of a communication between the waters of Currituck Sound and those of North River by means of suitable canal. . . ."[21] Considered together, however, these two bills would, in effect, provide for the entire course of the long-projected Albemarle and Chesapeake Canal, with the first comprising the Virginia Cut from Great Bridge to North Landing and the second, the shorter of the two dredged sections, cutting through the Currituck peninsula—so joining Coinjock Bay at the southern end of upper Currituck Sound with what was then termed Doctor's Creek, a tributary of the North River. This North River was the true North River of North Carolina and not a truncated version of the name of the North Landing River in Virginia—with which, as pointed out, it was sometimes confused in the records. It was the revival of both these 1850 bills—which Marshall Parks undertook to combine—that had already been strongly endorsed on May 24, 1850, as "an important undertaking" by a writer in Norfolk's *Southern Argus.*[22]

---

[18] Great Bridge Lumber and Canal Company, *Report*, p. 3.
[19] Hinshaw, "North Carolina Canals," p. 41. One of Hinshaw's principal sources for his account of the early Albemarle and Chesapeake Canal is North Carolina General Assembly, *Governor's Message and Busbee's Report on the Albemarle and Chesapeake Canal Company*, pp. 8–9. Hereafter cited as *Busbee's Report.*

[20] *Hinshaw, "North Carolina Canals,"* p. 41.
[21] North Carolina General Assembly, *A Bill to Incorporate the Albemarle and Currituck Canal Company, December 27, 1850.*
[22] Norfolk *Southern Argus,* May 24, 1850, p. 2.

Parks also had a staunch ally in the Hon. Henry A. Wise of Accomac County, Virginia. On the evening of September 25, 1850, Wise delivered in Norfolk's Mechanics Hall what was described at the time as "a very able and eloquent address on the subject of connecting Norfolk and Portsmouth with the interior by means of railroads and canals." And the legislator also "urged with great energy and clearness. . . . the propriety and necessity of the contemplated canal," citing the "line of communication" commencing "at the head of the east fork of the South Branch of the Elizabeth River, a few miles above Great Bridge," and extending on to Currituck and Albemarle sounds.[23] In this, of course, Wise was merely retracing the long-familiar route which had been originally proposed in colonial days.

The latest survey for the proposed canal had been made in 1850 by G. P. Worcester of New York. Worcester's off-the-cuff estimate for building it with the two land cuts, tide lock, and necessary bridges came, he said, to "the comparatively small sum of $131,386."[24] Closer to reality had been T. L. Patterson's estimated cost of half a million dollars. Patterson had had considerable experience as chief engineer of the Chesapeake and Ohio Canal Company on the Potomac.[25] Although both estimates were below what would actually have to be spent to complete the project, Worcester was correct in stating, "this canal, when completed, will not only sustain itself, but make a handsome return for the capital expended in its construction, beside enriching the counties through which it passes, by the reduced cost of transportation which it will effect, compared with any facilities [i.e., the Dismal Swamp Canal] now in existence."[26]

Worcester also estimated that, with "a line of steam tow-boats in readiness, . . . boats carrying the produce from the interior and the coast of North Carolina would daily traverse the entire distance from Albemarle Sound to the harbour of Norfolk."[27]

Canal enthusiasm by Parks and others came at a singularly appropriate time for other reasons. Certain factions were again moving to demand that the federal government undertake to reopen Nag's Head Inlet, cutting through the Outer Banks from Roanoke Sound into the Atlantic Ocean. Ocracoke Inlet, farther south, the sometime haunt of the infamous pirate Blackbeard, had by then shoaled to only permit the passage of vessels drawing no more than six feet,[28] and Ocracoke and nearby Hatteras Inlet provided by that time the only reasonable access for shallow vessels sailing out of Pamlico Sound for the open sea. Unreliable Currituck Inlet—whence William Byrd had begun his

[23] Forrest, *Sketches of Norfolk*, p. 260.
[24] Ibid., pp. 261–62.
[25] Great Bridge Lumber and Canal Company, *Report*, p. 4.

[26] Forrest, *Sketches of Norfolk*, p. 261.
[27] Ibid.
[28] Gary S. Dunbar, *Historical Geography of the North Carolina Outer Banks*, pp. 21–23.

dividing line survey more than a century earlier—had gradually shoaled and had ultimately closed off entirely. Norfolk historian William Forrest mentions that subsequent to the building of the Dismal Swamp Canal, some of the water which would have flowed down the North West River into Currituck Sound was diverted laterally out through the ends of the canal.[29] Originally the North West River brought a considerable flow of water, but the canal contrived to interrupt the natural eastward drainage flow of the Dismal Swamp, desiccating former swampland to the east and diverting the seepage into the canal. It was shortly after the enlarged Dismal Swamp Canal was completed in 1826 that Currituck Inlet shoaled and then closed up for good. Back Bay, Currituck Sound, and other large expanses of brackish open water lying behind the barrier reefs then turned completely fresh, thereby promoting the growth of marsh grasses upon which migratory waterfowl thrive and introducing an extensive and profitable industry to the local economy.

The more southerly located Nags Head Inlet leading out of Albemarle Sound was undoubtedly the one originally known as Roanoke Inlet in the days of Sir Walter Raleigh's sixteenth-century pioneer colonial scheme. Through this inlet the British ships sailed when the ill-fated colonies were being established on Roanoke Island. It is possible, but not likely, that today's Oregon Inlet—south of Roanoke Island, and well known to

sports fishermen—was the passage that required improvement, so prompting the publication of the pamphlet entitled *Report of the Select Committee on the Re-Opening of Nag's Head Inlet in North Carolina*. This was issued at Raleigh in 1850, and it mentioned that dredging the inlet would be a "work of vast importance . . . and should be pressed upon the attention of Congress with a pertinence and zeal that should command success."[30]

Even then, the Nags Head region—still a long way off from the fame it later received because of the Wright Brothers and its popularity as a resort in the present century—was becoming a favorite summer-vacation spot for inland Carolinians. It had a sound-side wharf and direct steamboat connection with Elizabeth City, and its pioneer hotel was built there in 1838. Undoubtedly Nags Head could look forward to an increasingly thriving summer business with the encouragement of a deep-sea passage at its door.

Although they had always been treacherous and shifting, North Carolina's peripatetic inlets had, of necessity, experienced a vast amount of fair-weather commerce passing in and out over the bars from the seventeenth century on. Though geography had conspired against the state's connection with the open sea ever being able to serve other than shoal-draft vessels plying the shallow sounds, Gary Dunbar points out that

[29] Forrest, *Sketches of Norfolk*, p. 467.

[30] North Carolina General Assembly, Senate, *Report of the Select Committee on the Re-opening of Nag's Head Inlet in North Carolina*.

as early as 1787, the North Carolina legislature had passed an act authorizing the construction of a "useful inlet" through the banks near Roanoke Island, in order to provide the state with a market near the head of Albemarle Sound, which, hopefully, might rival Norfolk. Dunbar states that many North Carolinians were "humiliated by being under the necessity of seeking ships at Norfolk, instead of having them in their own ports."[31] This they had been forced to do for some time, however. First, they had had to use the overland routes going around Dismal Swamp, then to go by the Dismal Swamp Canal, and now (which would prove even more onerous) by the projected Albemarle and Chesapeake Canal. This waterway, many felt, would contrive Virginia's further "enslavement" of Carolina by drawing away the Tarheel State's commerce.

Surveys and plans for the Nags Head inlet project, with the federal government assuming the cost, had been made in 1816, 1820, 1829, and 1840. Only the proposal of 1850 (cited above) was actually implemented. Digging began through the sandy, banks island in 1856, Congress having appropriated $50,000 to get the work started. By the following year, however, the project was recognized as hopeless, and it was abandoned because, according to the official report submitted on September 1, 1857, to Col. J. J. Abert, head of the army's topographical engineers, "the drifting sand filled in the trench as fast as it was excavated by the dredging machine. In fact the machine became nearly imbedded in the sand, it filled up so rapidly behind it."[32]

This failure was a source of some satisfaction to proponents of the ship canal. They pointed out that not only was their project entirely practical, but it had the added advantage of being accomplished by private enterprise and not by the public's tax money.

Apparently no further attempts were ever made to create a ship canal through the shifting sands of Carolina's Outer Banks islands, although Ocracoke, Hatteras, and Oregon inlets continue to be used by small craft even today. As late as 1890, Ocracoke had been placed under government supervision, and a thorough examination of the inlet channels was made between 1891 and 1894. Despite the perennial demand of some North Carolinians for the creation of their own deepwater ports, the army engineers strongly advised against any attempts to dredge deep channels across the banks owing to the impermanency of any such work, which would so soon and effectively be nullified by natural causes.[33]

---

[31] Dunbar, *Historical Geography,* p. 26.

[32] Ibid., p. 137; the Albemarle and Chesapeake Canal Company's *Third Annual Report* (1858) cites the dredging of the inlet as "a "wanton waste of public money" (p. 9), then gleefully reported the abandonment of the project, citing the September 1, 1857, report of Topographical Engineer Colonel Abert as printed in U.S. War Department. *Report of the Secretary of War* (Washington: Government Printing Office, 1871), 2:659.

[33] Dunbar, *Historical Geography,* p. 46.

As planned, on March 2, 1854, Parks successfully steered a revival of the March 14, 1850, act through the 1854 Virginia state legislature, thus reviving the Great Bridge Lumber and Canal Company.[34] The new charter provided for the opening of subscription books at Norfolk and other designated locations to receive applications for stock. Shares were to equal $100 each, and the act stipulated that no less than $50,000 or more than $500,000 must be subscribed. The company was then permitted to secure lumber and to cut a canal from the Elizabeth River to the North Landing River. Landholdings authorized were not to exceed 30,000 acres in Norfolk and Princess Anne counties, and ownership of strips of land a hundred yards wide was permitted on each side of the canal for the entire length.[35] Whatever might be required in the way of boats, equipment, and machinery was also authorized, and when the canal should become active, the company might impose tolls similar to those collected on the Dismal Swamp Canal.

At the company's organizational meeting in November 1854, Asa Worthington was named president;

Marshall Parks, vice-president; and James Gordon, Thomas V. Webb, B. T. Simmons, and Addison M. Burt were directors. Though impressed by the venture, the city of Norfolk initially abstained from purchasing stock, and many Norfolk merchants still considered the scheme visionary.[36]

Parks had now accomplished the first part of his plan, and in order to promote further interest throughout North Carolina in the attainment of the second part, he undertook to write a pamphlet about his projected canal—extolling its expected virtues and predicting its certain accomplishments. This work he had published in Raleigh that same year, 1854. Estimated costs, forseeable profits, and other factors were glowingly presented against a background of disparagement of both the rival Dismal Swamp Canal and Ocracoke Inlet as alternate communication lines. The speed of transit and the safety of the projected new canal route were also emphasized in comparison with the existing routes.[37]

Shortly after Parks's pamphlet went into circulation, North Carolina's Senator Jones of Currituck County sought to receive and expand the December 27, 1850, bill incorporating the Albemarle and Currituck Canal Company by introducing on December 7, 1854, a new *Bill to Construct a Ship Canal to Connect the Waters of Albemarle, Currituck and Pamlico Sounds with Chesapeake Bay*

---

[34] Hinshaw, "North Carolina Canals," pp. 41–42; *Bushbee's Report*, p. 9.

[35] The deed for a strip of land 100 feet in width near Great Bridge is recorded in Deed Book 83, pp. 402–3, filed in the Clerk's Office of the Circuit Court of the City of Chesapeake (formerly Norfolk County), Virginia. By this deed Iverson N. Hall granted the Albemarle and Chesapeake Canal Company, "for one dollar and other consideration," a parcel of marshland on each side of the centerline of the canal.

---

[36] *Busbee's Report*, p. 9.

[37] North Carolina General Assembly, *A Bill to Construct a Ship Canal*, cited in *Busbee's Report*, pp. 8–10.

and for Other Purposes.[38] This bill was promptly referred to the state senate committee on internal improvements, where it received a favorable hearing. In the opinion of the committee, "the difficulties and handicaps encountered in navigating the Dismal Swamp Canal and Ocracoke Inlet made it necessary to offer the citizens of eastern North Carolina a new and better water route."[39] The hearing also suggested that the state endorse the bonds of the company as soon as sufficient security was furnished.

To report at length on the desirability of the projected canal, the table below was presented. Table 2 gives estimated figures for the expected amount of traffic the new canal would attract contrasted with the actual figures for the existing route.

With the committee report in hand, the legislature then duly passed an act incorporating the company, the preamble of which confirmed the necessity for the new canal, since "the state possessed no adequate channel from the sound region to the ocean." Hinshaw's article succinctly reports:

> As Virginia had incorporated the Great Bridge Lumber and Canal Company and granted it the right to connect the Elizabeth River with the North

Table 2—Estimated and actual quantities of produce through the proposed canal and through the Dismal Swamp Canal

Ship Canal		Dismal Swamp Canal
7,500	Bales of cotton	4,921
40,000	Barrels of fish	30,821
80,000	Barrels of naval stores	53,332
2,000,000	Bushels of corn	1,176,069
250,000	Bushels of wheat	113,004
50,000	Bushels of peas	17,428
100,000	Bushels of potatoes	10,374
500,000	Cubic feet of timber	164,089
10,000,000	Feet of lumber	5,945,186
10,500,000	Oak staves	7,164,490
60,000,000	Cypress and juniper shingles	44,364,420
50,000	Cords of firewood	5,623
200	Vessels with fresh fish	50
300	Vessels with vegetables	none

Source: Hinshaw, "North Carolina Canals," quoting North Carolina General Assembly, *Report of the Senate Committee on Internal Improvements* (Raleigh, N.C., 1855), p. 6.

Landing River, so North Carolina empowered the company to construct a canal from Currituck Sound to the North River, thus completing the route from Chesapeake Bay to Albemarle Sound. The act provided that the capital stock of the Great Bridge Lumber and Canal Company should form a part of the stock of the new company. It also provided that, for the purpose of raising additional subscriptions, the company could, upon thirty days notice, open books at Currituck Court House, Shiloe in Camden

---

[38] Hinshaw, "North Carolina Canals," p. 43; *Busbee's Report,* p. 10; North Carolina General Assembly, Senate; *A Bill to construct a Ship Canal to Connect the Waters of Albemarle, Currituck and Pamlico Sounds with Chesapeake Bay and for Other Purposes,* pp. 67–74.

[39] Ibid., p. 43.

County, Elizabeth City, Hertford, Edenton, Gatesville, Winton, Windsor, Jackson, Halifax, Plymouth, Williamson, Columbia, Hyde County Court House, Tarboro, Washington, New Bern, and other such places as it might direct. Subscriptions were not to exceed $300,000 in shares of $100 each. For each share $5.00 was to be paid at the time of purchase and the remainder of the sum was subject to call by the company. If a majority of the directors were residents of North Carolina, the company was to have the same officers as the Great Bridge Lumber and Canal Company and also the same rights and duties as were provided in the Virginia act of incorporation. To secure the land through which the canal must pass, the law stipulated that such property could be condemned upon the payment to the owner of a price designated as fair by a jury of twelve. As a further aid to the corporation, any county was allowed to subscribe to stock not exceeding $50,000, provided the matter had been first submitted to the voters. In addition, the state of North Carolina endorsed the bonds of the company for $250,000—for which the canal company mortgaged its entire works. The company was continued as the Great Bridge Lumber and Canal Company, but its name might be changed to the Chesapeake and Albemarle Canal Company—or any other—upon authorization of the Virginia Legislature.[40]

Then came a further act by the Virginia legislature, passed February 28, 1856, assenting to all the provisions of the North Carolina law and changing the corporation's name to its present one—the Albemarle and Chesapeake Canal. A combined total stock of $800,000 was authorized.[41]

---

[40] Hinshaw, "North Carolina Canals," pp. 44–45.
[41] Ibid., p. 45, cites North Carolina General Assembly, *Canal to Connect Albemarle, Currituck and Pamlico Sounds with Chesapeake Bay*, pp. 25–26.

5

Work Starts at
Last, 1855–60

hirty-five year old Marshall Parks had not waited for the 1856 canal enabling act of the Virginia assembly before getting started on the work he had been planning for so long. Actually, however, it was a poor time to be starting out on canal building—or on anything else for that matter—for on June 6, 1855, the steamship *Benjamin Franklin* had put into Norfolk Harbor from the Virgin Islands with a case of yellow fever on board. Almost immediately the contagion spread ashore, and with "appalling fury," the dread epidemic all but brought the community to a standstill during that summer. The disease reached its peak in September 1855, and it seemed to have run its course when cooler weather set in that autumn. "Long will

that period of terror and death be remembered," recorded popular Norfolk newspaper reporter "Harry Scratch," citing 1855 as "a year that will never be forgotten."[1]

During the spring of 1855 Parks involved the New York engineering firm of Courtright, Barton and Company in the affairs of the canal. A preliminary survey of the route was made under the direction of

---

[1] Burton, *History of Norfolk*, pp. 19–21. The disaster and its implications are well covered in David R. Goldfield, "Diseases and Urban Image: Yellow Fever in Norfolk, 1855," *Virginia Cavalcade*, 23, no. 2 (autumn 1973): 34–41.

their civil engineer, John Lathrop, who subsequently stayed on in Virginia in the canal company's employ as chief engineer. Milton Courtright also began a long period of identification with this area. Parks himself embarked on still another venture. On June 6, 1855, the very day that the ill-starred *Benjamin Franklin* made port, he married Sophia Jackson.

The route planned for the Albemarle and Chesapeake Canal has already been briefly cited. For this route, the actual land excavation required was slightly over fourteen miles in two separate cuts. Initially, the contractors proposed digging them to a navigable depth of six feet, with the trench forty-three feet wide on the bottom and sixty-one feet on the surface. Including the tide lock and whatever deepening of the river channels would be required, Courtright, Barton estimated a cost of $800,000 for the project. This same amount was authorized by the Virginia legislature the following year. At a canal company board meeting on June 11, 1855, the engineering firm's offer was accepted, and the contract was duly executed on August 25.

Hinshaw states:

> The contract was to be paid as follows: $400,000 in company stock at par value. $250,000 in guaranteed bonds of the company, and $150,000 in cash. Upon the completion of work worth an estimated $100,000—an estimation determined by an engineer—a like amount of stock was to be paid to the contractors. Following that payment, monthly estimates were to be made and the contractors were to receive the bonds of the company for the previous month's work until another $100,000 had been spent. After this sum of $200,000 was paid, the contractors were to receive monthly the sum due in equal amounts of bonds, cash, and certificates of stock, while the company was to retain ten per cent of the stock payment as security for the proper construction of the canal. The contractors agreed to take an additional $150,000 in stock, in lieu of cash payment, from such stockholders as desired to transfer their shares. These stockholders were to be designated by Parks and Burt.[2]

On the promise that their work would be completed within two years, Courtright, Barton began actual construction at several points along the canal in October 1855. Unlike the Dismal Swamp Canal, which had been dug by hand, Parks's contractors depended largely on steam power. By February 13, 1856, the first of seven dredges began its work. The others progressively joined in, and the last of the seven was in operation by the following May. Two more dredges of larger capacity came along the next year.[3]

Understandably, before any of the dredges could be employed, the trees of the swamp forest along the canal line had to be cut down and hauled aside. This entailed extensive logging operations, but it also in-

---

[2] Hinshaw, "North Carolina Canals," p. 46.
[3] *Busbee's Report*, pp. 10–12; Albemarle and Chesapeake Canal Company, *Second Annual Report* (1857), p. 4. Hereafter cited as A & C Canal Co.

sured a plentiful supply of wood to feed the steam excavators' voracious boilers.

However, the logistical problem of delivering this equipment to the work sites must have been considerable. The first seven dredges were placed in the following manner. Two were located at the North Carolina Cut, where—as will be explained—the digging was easiest, and two were at the east end of the Virginia Cut, whence the proposed channel would head westward from the North Landing Bridge, slated to be rebuilt with a draw.[4] These four vessels had to be towed down the Atlantic coast, brought into Pamlico Sound through one of the inlets, then towed across Albemarle Sound to Currituck Sound. Two of the dredges were then dropped off to go to work on the Carolina Cut at Coinjock, and the other two were taken on up to the headwaters of the North Landing River. The most difficult part of the excavation lay here at the eastern end of the Virginia Cut. The other three dredges reached their destinations more easily. They were towed from Norfolk up the Southern Branch of the Elizabeth River to the Great Bridge location. Two of them proceeded to dig eastward in a straight line, aiming for a reunion with the pair working towards them from North Landing. The seventh dredge, along with a powerful steam pump and a pile driver, remained at Great Bridge and was used in excavating for the tide lock to be located a half mile west of the village. When the final pair of larger dredges was obtained the next year, they were positioned midway along the Virginia Cut at a place designated as Old's Point.

An interesting contemporary description of the work of excavation is available from a famous Virginia botanist, Edmund Ruffin, sometime editor of the *Farmer's Register* of Petersburg. Ruffin made a swing through his neighboring Tarheel State in the spring of 1856 and subsequently devoted three chapters of his book, *Agricultural, Geological and Descriptive Sketches of North Carolina,* to both the Dismal Swamp Canal and the then-building Albemarle and Chesapeake.[5]

Ruffin took particular pains to visit three separate locations along the construction route, and he was considerably impressed with Parks's "excavating machines," whose operations he described in considerable detail following an account of the difficulties under which their work was undertaken. He stated:

> But this very low level of the land through the route, which so much lessens the amount of earth to be excavated, serves, in most places, to increase the difficulty of the work. The surface of the swampy ground is, in many places, so nearly level with the water, and the earth is so generally a quagmire of peat, and so full of dead roots and buried logs, under the water, and of living trees and roots over and at the surface, when but very little above water, that the difficulties of removing such obstructions are very great, and would be insuperable if by the use

---

[4] *Busbee's Report,* pp. 10–12.

[5] Ruffin, *Descriptive Sketches of North Carolina,* chaps. 7, 8, 9, pp. 137–46.

of ordinary utensils, and with hand-labor. But the means used were very different; and to me, were as novel as they seemed admirable. The excavation is effected entirely by steam-dredges of new construction, and great power. The one I saw in operation near North Landing was then in the most difficult ground, the very low swamp just above the bridge. The earth was barely above the water, and covered with heavy and thick swamp forest growth—and beneath the surface, in the former channel of the choked river, were buried numerous sound stumps and trunks of cypress trees, which had been covered deeply by the slow accumulation of vegetable soil for ages past. The cutting through and removal of this mass of living and dead (but sound) wood, imbedded in semi-fluid mire, and from beneath standing water, could scarcely have been effected at all, except by the wonderful machines in use, which derives aid from the presence of deep water, in which no hand-labor could effect anything.[6]

Ruffin then undertook to explain the dredges and told how they worked in greater detail:

The dredging apparatus is in a vessel of fifty or sixty feet long, and is worked by a sixteen horse power steam-engine. There are seven of these dredging machines and vessels at the different places, and there will be built two more of greater size and power. The excavation was begun at the edge of deep water, as enough water to float the vessel is necessary for the operation. Thence, the machines carried on the excavation regularly, to the full depth and width required for the early navigation. Two machines, one working a little ahead of the other, carry the full width of the canal. After finishing at one position, the vessel is moved forward, the head of the vessel facing the earth to be cut away, and there it is fastened to the bottom securely, by convenient appliances. An enormous beam with an iron scoop, or box, at the extremity, is thrust forward and dipped into the water just ahead of the vessel, and then drawn upward against the face of the bank to be cut away. If it be of any ordinary earth, hard or soft, the cutting edge of the scoop goes in easily and the box rises filled with its load of earth, which is forty cubic feet, the measure of the capacity of the box. The beam slowly swung around (on the crane principle), the bottom of the box is left open and the earth falls out on the bank on one side. When the digging is easy, the scoop may be dropped and lifted and will cut out and dispose of its forty cubic feet of earth, once in every minute. But while the operation, as I saw it, was very much slower, its effect was even more remarkable and surprising in reference to the difficulties. The obstacles could delay, but could not prevent the effectual operation of the machine. The living roots of great size were gradually loosened and finally torn out. The stumps are undermined by the scoop cutting beneath the main roots and then lifted up. However such obstructions may retard the progress of the work, nothing can effectually resist or defeat the monster ditcher. The thrusting out of the beam, its sundry changes of position suited to every required effort, the seizing and

---

[6] Ibid., pp. 143–45.

tearing up of the roots and earth, and finally the slow stretching out of the enormous arm and emptying of its hand—all moved by the unseen power of steam—made the whole operation seem as if it was the manual labor of a thinking being of colossal size of inconceivable physical power.[7]

Ruffin explained that this eastern end of the Virginia Cut presented the greatest challenge, and digging was easier at the western end near Great Bridge, where the ground was "also low, wet and boggy, but not much encumbered by roots, or large shrubs or bushes." The third site of excavation, in North Carolina, he said was "still of different character."[8] It was at this point along the waterway that the designers had made an important decision for—instead of continuing their course via a dredged channel southeastward through the entire length of shallow and unprotected Currituck Sound, which can get extremely rough—they decided to go on into Coinjock Bay on the west side. Then, by means of the almost-six-mile-long North Carolina Cut, they would slice across the low-lying peninsula of lower Currituck County and break through into the upper part of North River. This stream already provided sufficiently deep water behind protecting banks all the way down to its entrance into Albemarle Sound proper.

As Ruffin accurately observed, excavation at this point was entirely different and comparatively easy. The first half of the North Carolina Cut was merely chopped through marshland no more than a foot above sea level, while the second part met only sandy soil, which presented little resistance to the dredge—far different from the uprooting and removal of petrified stumps in the ancient, dense forest traversed by the Virginia Cut. Ruffin's comments continue:

> The excavation here is through a low and boggy marsh, scarcely a foot higher than the water. The marsh was covered by water grasses then (late in May) about a foot high. . . . The bog soil was about four feet deep, resting on a firm blue clay. These earths were taken up by the dredge with great ease. The great difficulty here is the liability of the miry earth to run in again after being heaped on the margins—or, by its weight, to press down the soft mud of the margin and force it into the excavation. It is earnestly hoped that neither these nor any unforeseen difficulties may prevent the speedy and perfect completion of this great work—which will give to North Carolina, for the first time, a proper outlet for, and the proper use of her noble interior navigable waters.[9]

The function of the guard lock at Great Bridge has already been mentioned. Planned for this location was what would undoubtedly be a remarkable engineering wonder, for, when completed, the chamber was 220 feet long, 40 feet wide, and deep enough to pass vessels of 8-foot draft. This made it larger than any other lock on the Atlantic coast; indeed, the only locks in North

---

[7] Ibid.
[8] Ibid.

[9] Ibid.

America that exceeded it in size were those at Sault Sainte Marie, Michigan. The Soo's two tandem locks— completed only shortly before, in 1855—were built to bypass the rapids of the Saint Mary's River flowing from Lake Superior into Lake Huron. Each measured a then-incredible 350 feet by 70 feet and had a lift of about 9 feet.[10]

The need for a reversible-head lock to accommodate varying water levels in the Elizabeth and North Landing rivers, so preventing currents from surging back and forth through the canal, has been mentioned. Along with Chesapeake Bay, the Elizabeth River is subject to moon tides ranging on the average from two feet above mean tide to two feet below. However, no lunar tidal effects are felt in any of the Carolina sounds except over the bars at the inlets to the Atlantic Ocean. Being shallow, the water level in the sounds is subject to a certain amount of variation by reason of prevailing winds. A strong nor'easter, for example, will drain the waters of Currituck Sound by forcing them southward toward the Albemarle. Conversely, southerly winds tend to push the water up into the North Landing, which would raise the level in the Virginia Cut. With this situation existing in combination with dead low tide in the Elizabeth River, a ship navigating the canal eastbound would have to be raised up in the lock in order to enter the Virginia Cut.

Naturally, when high tide in the Elizabeth River is combined with northerly winds in the sounds, the opposite would hold true, and the vessel would have to be lowered in the lock to enter the canal.

In order to accommodate this so-called reversible head, it was necessary for the lock to have two complete sets of miter gates at each end, and the lock tenders would have to be sure that the proper pairs were in use at any given moment so that the oblique angle of the closed gates was always pointed in the direction of the higher water level. The company claimed that its unique lock was "probably the first lock even constructed which would allow vessels to lock up or down either way."[11]

---

[10] C. D. Merdinger, "Canals Through the Ages," In *The Military Engineer,* no. 332 (November-December 1957), part 3, "Ship Canals," p. 86; See also *St. Mary's Falls Canal* (Detroit, Mich.: U.S. Corps of Engineers leaflet, ca. 1975).

[11] A & C Canal CO., *Fourth Annual Report* (1859), p. 10.
Although the Albemarle and Chesapeake Canal Company's presumption that their 220-foot reversible-head lock was the first ever constructed might well have applied in 1859, subsequently other reversible-head guard locks have been built along Atlantic seaboard waterways as well as on the lower Mississippi. Apparently, however, the present Albemarle and Chesapeake Canal lock at Great Bridge, built in 1932, is still the largest to be equipped with double sets of gates at both ends of the lock for daily operation. The existing Great Bridge Lock measures 600 feet in length, and the width was narrowed only slightly, from the original 75 feet to 73 feet, when a replacement north wall was constructed inside the original one in 1974. The original 1859 lock at Great Bridge survived until 1917, when the canal was widened. Then, for a fifteen-year period, there was no lock, and the currents surged back and forth in the canal unimpeded. But with boat operators and local residents bitterly complaining, the present lock was provided by the United States government in 1932. Apparently, the Great Bridge Lock is the largest of the reversible-head locks regularly serving diurnal tidal variations

Each of the eight gates was built of solid timber and measured 8 feet high by 25 feet wide, each pair meeting at an oblique angle. The gates not in use remained in their side recesses. Two feet of rise and fall would be about maximum change on what still was essentially a sea-level canal.

Unfortunately, contemporary records fail to indicate how the equalizing water was passed in and out of the lock chamber. Wickets set flush in the face of the gates with hand cranks to raise and lower them might have been used, as on the Dismal Swamp Canal locks. More likely, however, would have been buried conduits controlled by cutoff valves, as in today's Great Bridge Lock, which replaced the original work in 1932. It is also not known how the gates of the original lock were hung. The only explanation is given in the company's *Fourth Annual Report* for 1859, where it was observed that "the ordinary methods . . . could not be used, but the gates opened with as much ease as an ordinary size lock."[12]

Possibly the lock was equipped with so-called balance-beam gates, such as were then employed throughout the Dismal Swamp Canal and on the James River and Kanawha Canal running westward from Richmond. These had heavy counterbalancing timbers extending from the top of the gates out across the sides of the lock, and they provided ample leverage for a husky lock tender to swing the gates open or shut from

the shore. It is probable, however, that the gates at Great Bridge were operated by a "walking contraption," activated either by cogwheels working on a quadrant notched track, or by cables winding on a drum. These means are suggested by an 1895 photograph (fig. 6), which apparently is the only surviving view of the original locks.[13] But though the methods of gate installation are not known today, the lock itself was made of dressed stone blocks cut at the granite quarries of Port Deposit, Maryland, and barged down Chesapeake Bay to the location.

When the first annual meeting of the company was held on December 2, 1856, two miles of canal had been dug in Virginia, and considerable other progress could be reported.[14] Some 4,433 shares of the total 5,449 of company stock were represented at the meeting and, accordingly, were entitled to 1,250 of the 1,852 votes.

---

the year round. A. C. Brown, "Reversible Head Locks," *American Canals,* no. 34, August 1980, p. 3.

[12] Ibid.

---

[13] First reproduced in *Art Book of Norfolk and Vicinity* (Norfolk, 1895). Reproduced here as fig. 6.

[14] Hinshaw, "North Carolina Canals," p. 47; A & C Canal Co., *First Annual Report* (1856), pp. 8–9. No first annual report appears in the collections of canal company annual reports deposited in the Sergeant Room, Norfolk Public Library, or in the archives of the District Engineer, Fort Norfolk. The latter collection was originally the property of President Parks and bears his signatures. These publications were microfilmed by the Virginia State Library to create a full set ranging from the 1855 *Report of the Great Bridge Lumber and Canal Company* and the 1857–81 *Reports of the Albemarle and Chesapeake Canal Company* to the 1885 A & C Canal Co. *Report* (1881–84 are missing). Sets of microfilm are available at the Virginia State Library, Richmond; the Mariners' Museum, Newport News; the Chesapeake Public Library; and elsewhere.

FIG. 6. *The Albemarle and Chesapeake Canal stone guard lock at Great Bridge, looking north, shows the 1887-built stern-wheel steamboat* Comet *heading east out of the lock. Note the masonry work and the double wooden gates permitting locking up or down in either direction. (Reproduced from a photograph in* Art Book of Norfolk and Vicinity, *1895.)*

Marshall Parks now moved up to the presidency, and his directors were T. L. Skinner, B. T. Simmons, Mills Roberts, Edmund Simmons, and Jas. C. Johnson of North Carolina; Thos. V. Webb, James Gordon, and J. Cary Weston of Virginia; and Addison M. Burt of New York.[15]

Table 3 shows the financial statement of the company as of December 1856 itemized:

Table 3—1856 financial statement of the company

Capital Stock Subscribed

By individuals	$504,000.00
By Currituck County	44,000.00
	548,000.00
Received in cash, labor, materials, and county bonds on stock not paid in full	134,900.00
Installments on stock not paid in full	7,930.07

Expenditures

Construction	$ 80,000.00
Engineers	9,382.41
Office	486.34
Contingent	3,829.84
Land damage	183.65
Property, steam excavators, etc.	60,000.00
Commission	1,800.00

Source: Hinshaw, "North Carolina Canals," p. 48, quoting *First Annual Report of the President and Directors of the Albemarle and Chesapeake Canal Company*, pp. 8 9.

———

[15]Hinshaw, "North Carolina Canals," p. 47.

Apparently construction work on the canal was now in full swing despite the aftermath of the epidemic which had swept through Tidewater the year before with such devastation. Professor Thomas Jefferson Wertenbaker, quoting from the Norfolk *Argus* of April 20, 1857, relates that it had become a popular recreation of many Norfolk residents to journey down to Great Bridge and "sidewalk superintend" the operation of the "Iron Titans" pulling stumps and digging up peat and mud with loud "coughings and gruntings."[16]

The *Argus* writer also expressed the visitors' wonderment at the work in progress, echoing Ruffin's account that it "would have been considered wholly impossible" in days before steam power. Ruffin summarized that "under the guidance of Mr. Parks," he had "recently examined the work with entire approbation."[17]

On February 2, 1857, the North Carolina General Assembly undertook an entirely different procedure with respect to the Albemarle and Chesapeake Canal Company's financing, and it amended the charter accordingly. Prior to that time, the company had issued certain bonds, which the state had guaranteed by receipt of a mortgage of $250,000 dated August 12, 1856, covering the entire property.[18] Now the bonds were

———

[16] Wertenbaker, *Norfolk: Historic Southern Port*, p. 185.
[17] Ruffin, *Descriptive Sketches of North Carolina*, pp. 140–43.
[18] Deed Book 84 (1856) pp. 461–63, recorded in the Clerk's Office of the Circuit Court of the City of Chesapeake (formerly Norfolk County), Virginia.

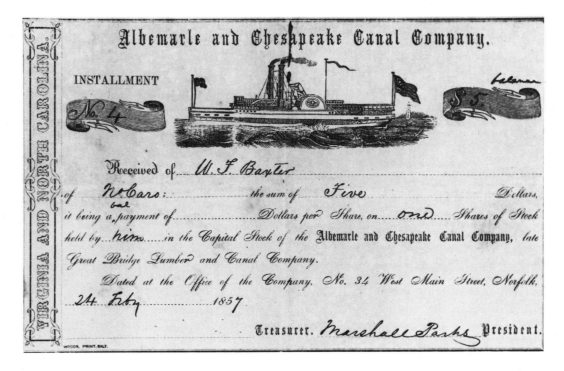

FIG. 7. *Canal Company stock certificates. (A) Currituck County Canal Company, dated January 1, 1856 (from the collection of Mrs. Elizabeth P. Sanderlin, courtesy of the Currituck County Historical Society). (B) Albemarle and Chesapeake Canal Co., dated February 24, 1857, and signed by President Marshall Parks (from the collection of the Norfolk County Historical Society).*

The vessels shown in the engravings resemble the 1848 pioneer steamboat Empire State *of New England's Fall River Line, a far cry from any vessels suited to Virginia canal navigation.*

withdrawn and canceled, thus annuling the mortgage. The state then subscribed to $250,000 worth of company stock and announced its intention of further subscribing $100,000 when the canal was open for the passage of vessels. "Thus the Board have the satisfaction of stating that the Company is free of debt and its property wholly unincumbered"[19] exulted President Parks. Reproduced here (fig. 7B) is an official receipt, signed by Parks, of a share of stock payment dated February 24, 1857.

These financial arrangements were cited in the company's *Second Annual Report* issued following the stockholders' meeting held November 11, 1857. A progress report on construction was also provided in detail. It was stated that the lock pit was excavated as far as it was possible without damaging the cofferdam, and one-third of the piles were ready to receive the foundation stone, which had already been delivered to the site. In the Virginia Cut, a total of five miles had been dug to full width. Parks also announced that it was an "intention of the company to carry on the business of steam towing," and the revenue he expected to receive thereby would, he felt, equal the amount coming in from toll collections.[20]

Parks was reelected president, and the number of directors was reduced to six—J. Cary Weston, Thos. V. Webb, L. H. Chandler, and James Gordon of Virginia; B. T. Simmons of North Carolina; and A. M. Burt of New York. Some 2,007 of the total 2,482 votes were represented at the meeting.[21] Table 4 shows the financial statement of the company dated October 1, 1857.

---

[19] A & C Canal Co., *Second Annual Report* (1857), p. 3.
[20] Ibid.
[21] *Busbee's Report,* p. 13; Hinshaw, "North Carolina Canals," p. 49.

Table 4—1857 financial statement of the company

Subscription by individuals	$515,400.00
Less individuals unpaid	393,109.93
	$122,290.07
Subscription from North Carolina	$250,000.00
Subscription from Currituck County	44,000.00
	$416,290.07

Source: Hinshaw, "North Carolina Canals," pp. 49–50, citing A & C Canal Co., *Second Annual Report* (1857), p. 7.

During the ensuing year another articulate visitor to the then-building Albemarle and Chesapeake Canal was the Virginia artist and writer Edward Caledon Bruce.[22] Accompanied by some friends, Bruce made two separate excursions from Richmond to South Side counties, thence on to the Albemarle, later recording his experiences in an interesting two-part article which was published in *Harper's New Monthly Magazine* in 1859 and 1860. These accounts were illustrated by a number of Bruce's excellent woodcuts, providing rich detail.[23]

Bruce took the James River steamer down from Richmond to Norfolk, and then, at Norfolk, "one fine

---

[22] Moody Simms, Jr., "Edward Caledon Bruce: Virginia Artist and Writer"; Alexander C. Brown, "Edward C. Bruce Recorded Tidewater Scene."
[23] Edward C. Bruce, "Loungings in the Footprints of the Pioneers."

morning in late May, 1858," he and his party engaged a wagon, a driver, and a team of bay horses for the seventeen-mile drive south to the bridge at North Landing. A little over two hours later they arrived and boarded the canal company's newly acquired dispatch boat *Calypso,* a trim little steamer which was waiting there to take them on a cruise down the North Landing River and on to Currituck Village.

The *Calypso,* characterized by Bruce as a "pony steamboat," apparently was the first item of floating property acquired by the canal company, not counting the nine dredges. The little boat's principal claim to a footnote in history lay ahead, however. Later she had the honor of making the initial transit of the canal. The date and place of building of the *Calypso* are unknown, but the purchase price of $1,199.84 is recorded under expenditures in the company's *Third Annual Report* of 1858.[24]

The *Calypso* measured fifty feet long and nine wide and was equipped with a high-pressure oscillating steam engine which turned side paddle wheels, giving her a speed of ten miles an hour. "Cabin accommodations for (in a pinch) ten" were cited by Bruce, and his spirited woodcut of the cabin interior (fig. 8) shows a convivial group of seven assembled around a table at the far end. Other views depicted the boat moored near North Landing Bridge, (fig. 9) then under way descending the curving river, (fig. 10) and later, negotiating the wooden drawbridge at Pungo Ferry—which

had evidently replaced the nautical accommodation implicit in the place-name.[25]

---

[24] A & C Canal Co., *Third Annual Report* (1858), p. 5.

---

[25] Bruce's drawing of the Pungo drawbridge (fig. 12), which appeared in the May 1859 *Harper's* (p. 755), is of considerable interest. Evidently, at this location—a short distance above where the North Landing River widens out into Currituck Sound—a crossing was established which gave the place the name of Pungo Ferry. It is impossible now to date just when this ferry began service, although undoubtedly it must date back to the early part of the nineteen century, if not earlier. From the beginning of the Virginia colony, the General Assembly had devoted much of its deliberation to the questions of locating and regulating ferries, specifically what tariffs might be charged, and other such matters. That no mention of the Pungo Ferry appears in volumes of Hening's Statutes covering acts of the colonial assembly as well as those of the early years of the republic does not necessarilly rule out earlier origins for Pungo Ferry.

In any event, the ferry which provided the place-name was replaced sometime during the mid-nineteenth century by the wooden drawbridge depicted by Bruce. Evidently this rickety structure did not last long after the Albemarle and Chesapeake Canal was opened, and probably it was easier to reinstitute ferry service than to rebuild a drawspan with sufficient width to handle the increased traffic on the river brought about by the opening of the canal. In any event, ferry service continuted through the nineteenth century and for the first half of the twentieth.

The actual Pungo Ferry was cited by Samuel Ward Stanton in 1892 as "an old flatboat for ferrying horses or passengers." (*Steam Navigation on the Carolina Sounds and the Chesapeake,* p. 14). A similar barge craft poled or pulled across the river by ropes or cables survived through the acquisition of the country road it served by the Virginia State Highway Department in 1940. (See fig. 25) At length, on March 23, 1954, the present steel swing bridge serving Route 726 replaced the ferry (see fig. 26), then

FIG. 8. *Cabin interior of the "pony steamboat" Calypso owned by the canal company, showing the artist, Edward C. Bruce, and his friends about to start out on a cruise from North Landing Bridge to Currituck, N.C. Woodcut by Bruce from* Harper's New Monthly Magazine, *May 1859.*

FIG. 9. *"Sail Ho!" is the title of Edward C. Bruce's woodcut showing him and his party at North Landing Bridge. Woodcut from* Harper's New Monthly Magazine, *May 1859.*

powered by a Model-A Ford engine. This bridge is presently in service, although it has suffered occasional collisions with errant vessels and was out of commission for a month in the autumn of 1978 (See figs. 68–72). However, the old ferry barge apparently survives also and it lies hauled up out of the way, abandoned in a little slough near its former west-shore landing place. Despite the existence of the drawbridge, Pungo Ferry retains its original picturesque name. An 1878 map indicates also a place designated Devil's Half Acre at a bend in the river just below Pungo Ferry.

Before they started out on the river trip as guests of "Mr. Meadows, a hale, cherry-faced gentleman . . . high in office in the Albemarle and Chesapeake Canal Company," some of Bruce's party boarded a rowboat at

FIG. 10. *Steamboat* Calypso *descending the North Landing River. Woodcut by Edward C. Bruce from* Harper's New Monthly Magazine, *May 1859.*

North Landing Bridge and rowed up the mile and a half of channel then completed along the east end of the Virginia Cut to the point where two of the dredges were at work. In his inimitable style, Bruce penned a flowery picture of the scene:

Our passage thither, if not altogether as imposing as Cleopatra's rows on the Nile, led through a finer colonnade of Nature's architecture than Thebes or Luxor could have matched. Our path was an avenue of water, a hundred feet wide, straight as an arrow, walled in with cypresses of primeval growth, their enormous boles sustaining at the summit a mass of the most delicate, feather-like foliage; the black but perfectly clear water overhung by varieties of flowers, grasses, and shrubs innumerable. The blue flag, the coral honeysuckle, the magnolia-like and richly

FIG. 11. *Newly invented steam dredge excavating the Virginia Cut of the Albemarle and Chesapeake Canal in 1858. Woodcut by Edward C. Bruce from* Harper's New Monthly Magazine, *May 1859.*

perfumed blossoms of the laurel conspicuous. Animal life was less profuse. Now and then a moccasin would glide under the shore, or a gray-colored lizard dodge rapidly round a stump. The mockingbird, its cousin the ubiquitous cat-bird, the blue jay, a stray heron, and—*horresco referens*—the buzzard, constituted the powers above. The great dredges, brandishing their black arms among the fallen Titans of the wood, and dragging up the remains of long departed vegetable giants, saluting the while, as if in derision, the surviving patriarchs with rapid puffs of steam, contributed more than anything else to give life to the scene. More efficient and powerful pioneers never invaded the virgin wilderness. They work in pairs, one machine a little in advance of its mate. Each cuts a path forty feet wide and eight feet deep, piling up the black chaos of mud and stumps on either hand in long ramparts.[26]

Returning from the canal excursion into the swamp—with an excellent picture of one of the dredges at work to record it (see fig. 11)—the party regained North Landing to await the arrival of an "auncient marinere," a native of the area, who would pilot the *Calypso* down the river to Currituck. With Captain Perse on hand, at length they set out. "[The *Calypso*] commenced operations by thoroughly sprinkling, in two or three well-directed puffs, a solution of soot over the clothes of the passengers. This preliminary through, she struck down the center of the canal-like

---

[26] Bruce, "Loungings," (May 1859), pp. 751–52.

FIG. 12. *The cantankerous draw-bridge at Pungo Ferry took a lot of persuasion to open. Woodcut by Edward C. Bruce from* Harper's New Monthly Magazine, *May 1859.*

stream, the overhanging branches almost brushing her wheel-houses. The water having the color of brown stout, the sensation was somewhat that of navigating the torrent that swept away a London street some years ago when one of Whitehead's vats gave way."[27]

---

[27] Ibid., p. 752.

The *Calypso* continued on down the twisting, amber-colored, juniper stream, apparently devoid of all human habitation on the banks save for one shack they encountered during the first dozen or so miles of travel. Although they saw only two people, apparently there were plenty of muskrats. "They dived under our bows with a calmness that savored more of philosophy than

FIG. 13. *"Shifting ballast." The slanting top deck of the steamboat* Calypso, *shown crossing Currituck Sound. Woodcut by Edward C. Bruce from* Harper's New Monthly Magazine, *May 1859.*

fright and perhaps more contempt than either," the observant Bruce reported.[28]

Two hours steaming brought the *Calypso* to Pungo Ferry and the drawbridge he sketched (fig. 12), which took more than an hour of persuasion before it opened so that the little steamboat could continue on its way.

"The two leaves of the draw, from long and undisturbed association, stuck so closely that the divorcing of them sufficiently to let the smoke-pipe slide through, was a work of time and patience," Bruce reported, while apparently the locals greatly enjoyed the spectacle of the city slickers struggling to open the apparatus. Undoubtedly such delays were eliminated when, not much later, the canal route opened and traffic through the bridge became a daily occurrence.

Once the obstacle of the bridge was eliminated, the *Calypso* continued southward as the North Landing River gradually widened out into shallow Currituck Sound (fig. 13). Later that afternoon, the boat reached her intended port of call at the village of Currituck (fig. 14), anchoring a hundred yards offshore, however, in deference to the mosquitoes. A horse and cart then "navigated" through shallow water and reeds to meet the passengers and take them to land.

"The town comprises but five houses independent of the courthouse and jail," Bruce allowed, continuing: "grass-grown streets are familiar things, even in many parts of our young country, but grass-grown harbors are seldom heard of." Evidently Currituck was such a place.[29]

Work on building the canal continued industriously throughout the remainder of 1858—the company's *Third Annual Report*, dated November 13, stating that the "Contractors have prosecuted the work with great energy and perseverance." Some 3,600 feet of land

---

[28] Ibid., p. 756.

[29] Ibid., p. 758.

still remained to be excavated, however. Expenditures cited in the report included $569,382.41 for canal construction and $1,199.84 for the purchase of the little *Calypso*.[30]

The Great Bridge guard lock was virtually finished by the end of the year, and barring some additional masonry work, it was expected to be completed by February 1859. When this happened, there would be a continuous navigable channel through the entire route, so permitting passage of shoal-draft vessels. Bringing the channel down to full depth was not contemplated for still another year, however.

In accordance with the February 2, 1857, North Carolina law, the company had by this time obligated itself to provide an even deeper canal than had been originally envisaged, so enabling it to handle vessels drawing as much as 7½ feet. At the November 13, 1858, meeting, therefore, the directors passed a resolution requesting the managers to renegotiate with Courtright, Barton and Company for enlarging the facility. At that meeting also, a formal request was made to the United States Treasury Department asking the Fifth Lighthouse District to survey and install various much-needed aids to navigation in upper Currituck Sound and the North Landing River. These would include lights and buoys to define the canal channel approaches.[31]

Calypso's rendezvous with destiny occurred early in the ensuing year. On January 9, 1859, she had the dis-

FIG. 14. *Currituck, N.C., with its "grass grown harbor," as described in Edward C. Bruce's article relating his trip on board the* Calypso *in 1858. Woodcut by Bruce from* Harper's New Monthly Magazine, *May 1859.*

tinction of making the first canal passage, when towing the large iron barge *Enterprise* of Wilmington southbound through the channel's full length.[32] It is likely that the *Enterprise*, a new vessel with a capacity of 600 bales of cotton or 10,000 bushels of grain, was then being delivered to her new owners, Messrs.

[30] A & C Canal Co., *Third Annual Report* (1858), p. 5.
[31] Ibid., p. 4.

[32] Burton, *History of Norfolk*, p. 31.

Richard Smith and J. H. Anthony of Halifax County on the Roanoke River. Later, the *Enterprise* became a frequent user of the canal.[33]

Obviously, deepening the canal was going to cost more money than originally anticipated and following company engineer John Lathrop's report of June 29, 1859, a new contract was let to Courtright, Barton specifying an eight-foot channel throughout the entire sixty-five mile line of navigation. This was to cost an additional $250,000. The contractors agreed to take seven percent mortgage coupons at 87½ cents on the dollar, payable in monthly installments as the work progressed. Despite the added expense of an enlarged canal, the cost of the fully dredged waterway was still running a quarter of a million dollars below the company's authorized capital of $1,500,000.[34]

While the question of increased cost was before the 1858–59 North Carolina legislature, Hinshaw reports that a joint committee from that body made a trip from Raleigh expressly to view the canal at first hand. In its findings, the committee recorded widths from 30 to 60 feet and depths from 6 to 8 feet in the Virginia Cut, while the upper North Landing River provided a channel from 110 to 120 feet wide running down the middle of the river, which itself averaged 300 feet in width and had a depth of 10 feet for the fifteen-mile stretch down to Pungo Ferry. Below Pungo, it widened into upper Currituck Sound, which, though more than ten miles across, varied in depth from a minimum of six feet to ten feet as far as Coinjock Bay, where the North Carolina Cut commenced.[35]

Being satisfied that a deeper cut would be both desirable and feasible, the North Carolina senate then passed a bill providing for the state to make a further subscription of $150,000 worth of canal company stock. Unfortunately, lack of sufficient time prevented the bill from reaching its third reading in the house, and accordingly it failed.[36]

Because of this setback, the canal company directors had to adopt other means of raising the money they needed. Instead of going at it piecemeal, however, they elected to make a single large mortgage in the amount of $400,000. Accordingly, on July 1, 1859, a deed to Messrs. William T. Hooker and Parker Handy of New York and R. H. Chamberlaine of Norfolk was executed, conveying the entire company property to them in trust as security for the $400,000 mortgage. Some $200,000 worth of bonds were then put on the market. A total of $136,000 was disposed of at eighty cents on the dollar, and $40,000 of this sum was immediately applied to the new work.[37]

[33] *Busbee's Report,* p. 19.
[34] Hinshaw, "North Carolina Canals," p. 49.
[35] Ibid., p. 52; North Carolina, General Assembly, 1858–59 sess., doc. no. 66, *Report of the Joint Select Committee on the Albemarle and Chesapeake Canal,* pp. 1–3.
[36] *Busbee's Report,* p. 16.
[37] Ibid., pp. 16–17. A holograph copy of the Hooker, Handy, Chamberlaine deed of July 1, 1959, is on file at the Clerk's Office of the Circuit Court of the City of Chesapeake: Deed Book 86, pp. 546–50.

By October 1, 1859, $909,400 had been subscribed to the company's capital stock, with $101,300 still unpaid. This made an aggregate receipt from all sources of $824,829. Hinshaw states that this latter amount was not much greater than the original contract, since the total cost of the project was expected to amount to $1,150,000 anyway. He points out that, "It was this lack of subscription and the failure to secure more funds from the State of North Carolina that necessitated the issuance of the seven-per-cent mortgage coupon bonds."[38]

The company's *Fourth Annual Report* issued in November 1859 contained a large, folding map of southeastern Virginia and northeastern North Carolina, showing the Atlantic coast from Cape Charles to Cape Lookout and extending westward from Cape Hatteras inland to Halifax County, North Carolina (fig. 15). All waterways, both natural and artificial, were delineated, as well as all sounds, back bays, rivers, and inlets. This map, drawn by John Lathrop, the company's civil engineer, is of considerable significance in presenting the requirements for adequate water transportation for the area and the arguments justifying the various canals.

The text of the *Fourth Annual Report* stated proudly: "There is now a continuous channel throughout the entire line."[39] However, although the full sixty-one foot width was now attained, there was only sufficient depth in some places to allow vessels of no more than five-foot draft, and the dredges were still required to continue working unremittingly. Three swing drawbridges had been completed—at Great Bridge, North Landing, and Coinjock—but houses for the bridge tenders were still to be finished. The first two were located on the sites of the original fixed bridges of colonial days. After the Virginia Cut was finished, both these existing low crossings at the heads of the Elizabeth and North Landing rivers would have to be converted to drawspans so that masted vessels could pass unimpeded. The Coinjock drawbridge was required at the point where the North Carolina Cut sliced across the solid land of Currituck Peninsula. Since the canal company employed the bridge tenders, providing on-the-spot living quarters for them was also required.

Meanwhile, the first of the company's planned fleet of steam tugs, the *Wasp*, was acquired at a cost of $2,850. She was almost new, having been built at Philadelphia in 1856, and she measured sixty-seven tons. In the report of expenditures as of October 1, 1859, the *Wasp* appears, together with the *Calypso*, as an investment of $5,019. Other items cited include $769,-850 for construction and engineering and $16,000 for real estate. The report also stated that it was "making arrangements for other necessary steamboats in order to be ready for the fall and winter business."[40] Ob-

---

[38] Hinshaw, "North Carolina Canals," p. 53.
[39] A & C Canal Co., *Fourth Annual Report* (1859), p. 4.

---

[40] Ibid., p. 7. Curiously, the *Third Annual Report* (1858) gives the cost of the *Calypso* as $1,199.84, and *Busbee's Report* gives the cost of the *Wasp* as $2,850.00. Lumping the cost of both vessels to-

viously the coming year of 1860 was envisaged as the one which would at last put the canal in profitable business.

Private steamboat operators were also getting ready to inaugurate services. The January 29, 1859, issue of Norfolk's *Southern Argus* announced the contemplated formation of the Currituck and Norfolk Steamboat Company to run between these points via the canal. Later in that year, the September 8 and 14 issues of the Norfolk *Herald* stated that the new steamer *Reindeer*—commanded by Captain Cline and intended to carry passengers and light freight—had come to Norfolk from Philadelphia and that she would "ply on the Albemarle and Chesapeake Canal . . . between Norfolk and North Landing." The newspaper reported "our friends in Currituck and along the line of the canal will find this neat little steamer just what they want to have."[41] The *Reindeer* made a pioneer trip down to Currituck on September 14, coming back with thirty passengers. Dr. E. Morton of Currituck was named president pro tempore of the new steamboat line.

Despite the fact that it started out with the canal "frozen end to end," 1860 proved a banner year for the canal company. When the canal thawed, at long

last ships were passing through and tolls were being collected. In fact, by July some 1,655 vessels totaling 6,600 tons had been clocked through the Great Bridge lock, where the money was taken. One of them was again the barge *Enterprise*.[42]

For a while, opening the waterway proved a mixed blessing, however. Ship traffic tended to impede the work of the dredges, and there were still shallow spots in the rivers and in Currituck Sound that needed attention. The houses for the bridge tenders were now completed and occupied, while the company's fleet had grown to five vessels with the addition of the towboats *Roanoke* ("purchased for $2,800" and "almost entirely rebuilt") and *Younaluska*[43] ("bought new" at Philadelphia) and of the barge *Cleveland* to the *Calypso* and the *Wasp*. It was planned that the company would start its daily towing line as soon as possible, with tugs picking up their tows at each end of the canal. Floating property expenditures amounted to $20,940 for the three tugs and the *Calypso* and $558 for the *Cleveland*. Expenses of running the boats were given at $6,947.[44]

Meanwhile, Congress had partially complied with

gether, the *Fourth Annual Report* cites an expenditure of $5,019.00, which is about a thousand dollars off. Possibly the greater amount includes operational costs as well.
[41] Norfolk *Southern Argus*, January 29, 1859; Norfolk *Herald*, September 8 and 14, 1859; and Norfolk *Southern Argus*, September 17, 1859. Transcripts in Emmerson, comp., "Steamboats, 1837–1868," pp. 426–27.

[42] *Busbee's Report*, p. 19.
[43] A & C Canal Co., *Fifth Annual Report* (1860), p. 3. the *Younaluska* is the name given here for the vessel reported acquired. This seventy-nine ton tug built in 1860 is recorded as the Confederate States Ship *Junaluska* in 1861. (William L. Lytle, comp., and C. Bradford Mitchell, ed., *Merchant Steam Vessels of the United States, 1790–1868: The Lytle-Holdcamper List*, p. 235. Hereafter referred to as the *Lytle-Holdcamper List*.)
[44] A & C Canal Co., *Fifth Annual Report* (1860), p. 12.

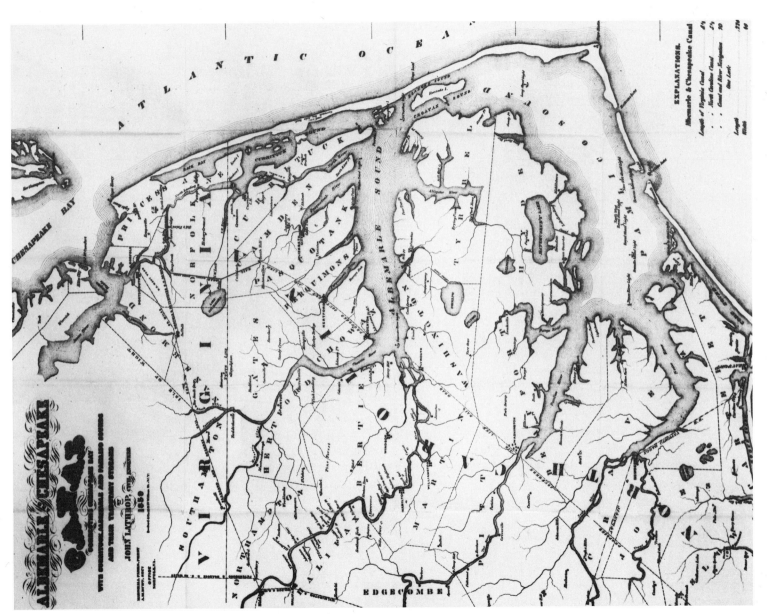

FIG. 15. *Map by civil engineer John Lathrop (1859) of the area served by the Albemarle and Chesapeake and the Dismal Swamp canals in eastern Virginia and North Carolina—from the Albemarle and Chesapeake Canal Company's Fourth Annual Report, 1859. (Courtesy the Mariners Museum.)*

the request for navigational aids, and two small light-houses had by then been built—one at the north end of the North Carolina Cut in upper Currituck Sound, and the other at the mouth of the North River in Albemarle Sound. The year before, the company had smugly reported that building the canal "has relieved the General Government from making a channel to the ocean which they had commenced at Nag's Head."[45] As might be expected, the cost of two little lighthouses was trivial compared to the contemplated five million it would have taken to cut through the inlet.

Captain Barton's "neat little steamer" *Reindeer*'s monopoly on the passenger trade through the canal was short-lived. Local newspapers of August 1860 proudly announced the completion at Graves Shipyard in Norfolk of the forty-four ton steamer *Currituck* designed to ply the canal serving "numerous landings on North [Landing] River, Currituck Sound and [K]notts Island." Built for the "wealthy and enterprising firm" of Belk and Lindsey of Norfolk, the *Currituck* apparently made an excursion to Nag's Head as its first voyage, after which she settled down to "run regularly" on the canal.[46]

Again the area was visited by a literate observer. Inasmuch as the company property, of which the state of North Carolina was such a large shareholder, had

been mortgaged to out-of-state financiers, Governor John W. Ellis, with a view to protecting the interests of his state, decided to undertake a thorough investigation of the affairs of the company, for which he had the enthusiastic support of President Parks. Accordingly, Ellis appointed an attorney, Quent Busbee, reading clerk of the state senate, to visit the organization's headquarters at Norfolk and begin an examination. Busbee arrived from Raleigh on March 1, 1860, and during the course of his inspection, he made a three-day round-trip canal voyage—down by the Albemarle and Chesapeake Canal to Albemarle Sound and back up via the Dismal Swamp Canal.

Busbee's observations have been cited above on several occasions, and it was obvious that he was much impressed by the works and the "cheerful willingness to assist" him extended by Messrs. Parks and Lathrop, "as well as by all the other gentlemen in the employment of the Company."[47]

Table 5 shows the financial statement for the company as of October 1, 1860, presented in the *Fifth Annual Report*. It was possible here to include for the first time the volume of freight carried on the canal. For the year ending September 30, 1860, the report specified commodities arranged by categories for both northbound and southbound traffic. It is amusing to contrast them with President Parks's cargo estimates presented in his prior report of 1855 to the North Carolina Senate Committee on Internal Improve-

---

[45] A & C Canal Co., *Fourth Annual Report* (1859), p. 5; *Fifth Annual Report* (1860), p. 4.

[46] Norfolk *Southern Argus,* August 16, 1860, cited in Emmerson, comp., "Steamboats, 1837–1860," p. 443.

[47] *Busbee's Report,* p. 2.

ments.[48] The new waterway's potential was still far from being fulfilled, for the canal was still unfinished and it had not yet even been open for a full year. Meanwhile, the handwriting was on the wall as far as the affairs of the Dismal Swamp Canal were concerned. Its financial troubles were just beginning. The extent and variety of products transported through the Albemarle and Chesapeake Canal are well shown by table 6.

Table 5—1860 financial statement of the company

Capital Stock

Amount subscribed	$ 909,400.00
Amount paid	873,903.00

Receipts

From state of North Carolina	$ 350,000.00
From Currituck County	44,000.00
From individuals	484,903.00
From interest on state and county bonds	10,020.00
From bills payable	29,745.00
From tolls and towing	16,644.00
From sale of mortgage bonds	111,800.00
Total Receipts	$1,047,112.00

Expenditures

For construction, purchases, etc.	$1,022,493.00
Leaving on hand	26,619.00

Source: Hinshaw, "North Carolina Canals," pp. 53–54, quoting A & C Canal Co., *Fifth Annual Report* (1860), p. 7.

[48] See chapter 4, table 2

Table 6—Volume of northbound traffic and volume of southbound traffic on the A & C Canal for the year ending September 30, 1860

volume of northbound traffic

Barrels of cotton	6,632
Barrels of fish	859
Barrels of flour	5
Barrels of naval stores	2,215
Bushels of corn	200,453
Bushels of peas	226
Bushels of flaxseed	419
Bushels of beans	1,138
Bushels of potatoes	6,341
Bushels of wheat	30,488
Kegs of lard	46
Pounds of bacon	6,950
Feet of lumber	356,294
Three foot shingles	222,400
Two foot shingles	586,475
Twenty-two inch shingles	243,475
Bunch shingles	7,455,700
Hogshead staves	816,894
Barrel staves	24,700
Pipe staves	3,235
Cubic feet of timber	17,004
Cords of wood	953

volume of southbound traffic

Barrels of bread	139
Barrels of beef, pork	928
Barrels of beer, cider	44
Barrels of flour	2,052
Barrels of fish	1,287
Barrels of molasses	203
Barrels of liquors	1,588

Table 6—(cont.)

southbound traffic (cont.)

Barrels of sugar	381
Hogsheads of molasses	96
Bags of coffee	278
Boxes of hats, shoes	155
Boxes of soap, candles	465
Boxes of tobacco	104¼
Cubic feet of dry goods	6,302
Cubic feet of hardware	856
Kegs of nails	509
Crates of wire	40
Casks of lime, cement	1,878
Bushels of salt	3,488
Sacks of salt	1,279
Pounds of iron	60,188
Tons of guano	2,000

Source: Hinshaw, "North Carolina Canals," pp. 54–55, quoting A & C Canal Co., *Fifth Annual Report* (1860), p. 13.

This was a good beginning. But then the fateful year of 1861 dawned. As far as the Albemarle and Chesapeake Canal was concerned, however, its prospects for the future were still bright, despite talk of war. The new waterway had already begun to take away a considerable amount of traffic from the Dismal Swamp Canal, and relatively little work—and that of only a minor nature—still remained before it might be declared finished.

But the proverbial "little cloud, out of the sea, like a man's hand,"[49] had already begun to darken Southern skies, and the nation's drift to civil war had inexorably reached its point of no return. By February 9, 1861, the Confederate Congress, meeting in Montgomery, elected Jefferson Davis as provisional president, and secession talk was rife throughout the land.

Then, on April 12, came the fateful shots at Fort Sumter. Five days later, on April 17, Virginia seceded from the Union, followed by North Carolina on May 20. Before it was all over, the Albemarle and Chesapeake Canal, along with much of the rest of the South, became a casualty to the nation's fratricidal strife.

---

[49] I *Kings*, 18:44.

6

Under Two Flags:
The A & C Canal in
the Civil War, 1861–65

Only a short time after North Carolina seceded from the Union, Governor Henry T. Clark, who had recently succeeded deceased Governor John W. Ellis, commenced military preparations for the defense of his state's long and exposed coast and of the vital Carolina Sounds that lay behind the barrier islands protecting an estimated one-third of the area of the state. Norfolk, of course, guarded the northern entrance to the sounds by way of the two canal routes leading south from Hampton Roads and the Elizabeth River. Since the federal government had announced its planned blockade of Southern seaports on April 19, 1861, and had then extended it on April 27 to include the coasts of Virginia and North Carolina, priority was given to building fortifications designed to prevent enemy forces from using the inlets to gain access to the interior.[1]

Accordingly, North Carolina set up two defense departments for the protection of her coastal areas. The Northern Defense Department included the shore from the Virginia line down the New River, below Pamlico Sound. The Southern Department embraced the coastline from New River to the South Carolina boundary, including the major seaport of Wilmington. In the Northern Department, plans were made to build several forts on the Outer Banks islands, cov-

---

[1] John G. Barrett, *The Civil War in North Carolina*, p. 32.

ering the navigable inlets of Ocracoke, Hatteras, and Oregon.[2]

Hatteras Inlet had gradually replaced Ocracoke as the deeper and therefore more favored channel entrance into Pamlico Sound, and accordingly, two forts—Hatteras and Clark—were set up to command the channel with their cross fire. Hatteras was the larger. Fort Oregon was built on the south side of Oregon Inlet, and Fort Ocracoke (or Fort Morgan) was constructed on Beacon Island just inside Ocracoke Inlet. As might be expected, the forts were made of earthen embankments reinforced by timber.

The difficulties that had to be overcome to build these fortifications were almost insurmountable. Vast numbers of soldiers and workmen—along with their tools, tents, arms, supplies, and even their drinking water—had to be transported out to the barren islands and unloaded over the beach on the sound side. Then there were the heavy cannon and military stores. The spring and early summer of 1861 saw a tremendous volume of shipping plying southward through the Albemarle and Chesapeake Canal for this purpose, since the city of Norfolk and the Gosport Navy Yard were the principal sources of supply for both labor and material. With commendable effort, major construction work (such as it was) on Forts Hatteras and Clark was completed by mid-June, with the Confederate colors being raised there in July.

Meanwhile, in addition to her coastline defenses, North Carolina had begun to acquire the nucleus of a

freshwater navy through the purchase of several local shoal-draft steamboats and tugs. These were hastily converted to gunboats, though the force never commanded a more respectful cognomen than the "Mosquito Fleet." In the fall of 1861 the North Carolina Navy was absorbed into the regular Confederate States Navy. Its history has been well recorded by then Acting Paymaster Adam Tredwell, North Carolina Navy, who became Assistant Paymaster, Confederate States Navy, when naval personnel were taken into that organization along with the ships.[3]

The first vessel so acquired by North Carolina was the 207-ton side-wheel passenger steamboat *J. E. Coffee*, formerly plying a Norfolk–Virginia Eastern Shore run.[4] With the boat, came her civilian skipper, Patrick McCarrick, who would serve in the same capacity as master's mate in the North Carolina Navy. Renamed the *Winslow* after Warren Winslow, chairman of the state's defense establishment, the little vessel was given the authority of a thirty-two pounder cannon and a smaller six-pounder brass rifle when outfitted at the Gosport Navy Yard under the direction of Commodore William T. Muse. She was then sent south via the Albemarle and Chesapeake Canal to commence her duty.[5]

The newly commissioned *Winslow* was followed into

---

[2] Ibid., p. 33.

[3] Adam Tredwell, "North Carolina Navy," pp. 299–313.
[4] Ibid., p. 299. Particulars on the steamer *J. E. Coffee*, registered as the *Joseph E. Coffee*, are given in the *Lytle-Holdcamper List*, p. 116. Statistics of other vessels of both Union and Confederate navies also appear alphabetically by ship name in this work.
[5] Tredwell, "North Carolina Navy," p. 300.

service by the *Beaufort,* originally the 1854-built, eighty-five ton steam tug *Calendonia* of Edenton. Then came the *Raleigh* and the *Ellis,* each mounting a single thirty-two pounder. Shortly thereafter, some of the Albemarle and Chesapeake Canal Company's tugs were requisitioned, the first being the new seventy-nine ton *Junalaska*—variously spelled both *Younalaska* and *Yunaluska.* She was equipped with a six-pounder field gun.

Quoting from a contemporary source, John Barrett, author of the definitive work *The Civil War in North Carolina,* observed that "this diminutive fleet of small river boats was manned not by sailors, but by 'soldiers, or farmers, hurriedly taught to fire a gun.'"[6]

A more scornful appraisal of the Mosquito Fleet by Confederate Brig. Gen. Henry A. Wise was possibly prompted by interservice rivalry. He stated in a letter to Maj. Gen. Benjamin Huger, CSA, on February 17, 1862: "The truth undoubtedly is that if Captain Lynch had never attempted to make the futile fleet he did make out of the canal company's tugs, we could have had them for the purpose of transportation."[7] Commodore William F. Lynch, the Confederate flag officer in charge, had been ordered to command the naval defenses of both North Carolina and Virginia and was the mentioned recipient of Wise's scorn.

The first of the Mosquito Fleet to see action was the *Winslow,* which had been sent immediately to Pamlico Sound. Taking a page out of the pirate Blackbeard's book, the little gunboat, ducking in and out of Hatteras Inlet, captured in a six-weeks period no less than sixteen prizes—unsuspecting federal merchant ships skirting the coast near the cape. The *Winslow's* career came to an untimely end on November 4, 1861. In the process of rescuing the crew of the French corvette *Proney,* wrecked on Ocracoke Island, she herself came to grief, striking the wreck of a sunken vessel nearby and going down too.[8]

Expectedly, it was not very long before the federal authorities decided that the "depot for rebel privateers" at Hatteras should be broken up. The North Carolinians, too, well appreciated that their lucrative, made-to-order harassment of enemy commerce was undoubtedly too good to last, and the defenders of the pathetic little forts of mud, logs, and sand realized that their moment of truth was not far away either. It came in August 1861, when a massive amphibious expedition was assembled at the southern end of Chesapeake Bay with the intention of neutralizing the North Carolina defenses. Leaving Fort Monroe on August 26, the force was composed of some seven major warships, including the frigate *Minnesota* as flagship, mounting a total of 143 guns. Accompanying were two chartered bay steamers, the *Adelaide* and *George Peabody,* to act as transports towing surf boats. Along with these vessels was a retinue of small craft including the tug *Fanny,* a shoal-draft screw steamer intended to cross the bar into Pamlico Sound and to be based there once the

---

[6] Barrett, *The Civil War in North Carolina,* p. 35.
[7] U.S. Navy Department, *Official Records of the Union and Confederate Navies in the War of the Rebellion,* ser. 1, vol. 6, p. 764. Hereafter cited as *Official Records . . . Navies.*

---

[8] Tredwell, "North Carolina Navy," pp. 303–4.

forts were put out of commission. (The *Fanny* was subsequently captured by three vessels of the Mosquito Fleet, including the *Junalaska*.) Commodore Silas H. Stringham USN, was in command of the union fleet, with Maj. Gen. Benjamin F. Butler in charge of land forces.[9]

The firepower this considerable force brought to bear on the little forts proved insurmountable, and by late afternoon on August 28, after absorbing a devastating bombardment, Fort Clark capitulated. Fort Hatteras followed suit the next day. Approximately seven hundred defenders surrendered, including the Confederate naval commander, Flag Officer Samuel Barron, and as prisoners of war, they were loaded on board the Union ships lying offshore for transport to New York.[10]

With less than conspicuous gallantry, the forts at Oregon Inlet and Ocracoke were quietly abandoned shortly thereafter, without any resistance at all being offered, the Confederate strategy then being to stage a major defense effort at Roanoke Island. The loss of the forts guarding the entrances to North Carolina's inland seas was a serious blow to the Confederacy. But others, even greater, were soon to follow.

Before the federal forces could press on by water to the inland regions via the Carolina sounds' riverside settlements, a further buildup of strength would have to be effected, and that meant the establishment of a shoal-draft Union navy to operate on the sounds. For the time being, the Confederate Mosquito Fleet could still come and go as it pleased with orders to intercept any federal vessels it might encounter, while building up its own strength as well as that of the Confederate army holding Roanoke Island.

This was a period of almost frenetic activity while the Albemarle and Chesapeake Canal remained still safely and usefully in Confederate hands. In addition to transports and supply ships, one of the canal company's steam dredges and the pile driver used at the Great Bridge lock—requested of President Parks to aid in building up defenses for Roanoke Island in both adjacent Croatan and Roanoke sounds—went to the scene of action by the canal route.[11]

Parks availed himself of this opportunity to state the case for his well-used canal before the Confederate States government—specifically War Secretary Judah P. Benjamin—in a long letter dated Norfolk, December 15, 1861. Following a complete description of the canal's route and facilities, together with a lengthy review of its history—not omitting the difficulties which had had to be overcome to build it in the first place—Parks pointed out the obvious value of the waterway to the Southern cause: "After six years of unremitting toil, a larger portion of which time we worked both day and night, we were enabled to get a navigation for ves-

---

[9] Barrett, *The Civil War in North Carolina*, pp. 36–37.
[10] Ibid., pp. 40–45.

[11] U.S. War Department, *Official Records of the Union and Confederate Armies: The War of the Rebellion*, ser. 1, vol. 9, p. 142. Hereafter cited as *Official Records . . . Armies.*

sels drawing five feet. Pushing forward our work with the aid of the revenue we received from a rapidly increasing business, we were enabled by the commencement of the war to get six feet throughout the whole line, while for many miles it is completed to the depth of eight feet."[12] But eight feet, the entire canal's project depth, was still not entirely achieved, particularly in places in Currituck Sound and the North Landing River.

Parks then went on to state that the war had pretty well eliminated tollpaying traffic, and not enough money was coming in to enable construction work to be continued. He reminded the secretary that "we have afforded transportation for all heavy ordnance, have passed 184 gun-boats and army transports since September 1, for which service we have not received one dollar."[13]

Parks also testified to "the reckless manner in which Government steamers navigate" the canal in defiance of the established rules governing speed limits and right of way in the channels and in the lock. With caving banks, silting channels, and other deterioration of the still-unfinished waterway staring him in the face, Parks concluded that "suspension of the navigation" might well have to eventuate. Benjamin was also advised that the canal's "unusual expenditures, when prosecuting the work with vigor," had amounted to from $10,000 to $15,000 per month. However, for granting the Confederate government free use of the canal, Parks suggested that an allowance of at least $2,000 to $3,000 per month would not be out of order.[14]

Evidently the secretary was slow to respond, for only a fortnight later, Parks sent a similar plea for relief to Brig. Gen. Henry A. Wise, who had just been assigned the command of the military district embracing the Albemarle-Currituck area. In virtually identical language, Parks pointed out on January 1, 1862, the usefulness of the canal to the Confederacy and in particular to Wise's command. He revised his figures for military use of the canal since the end of August 1861 to include the passage of "over 200 army transports and steam gun-boats, varying in size from 50 to 300 tons each." He also reminded General Wise that "the large fleet of gun-boats now constructing at the various shipyards [presumably up North Carolina rivers like the Roanoke] will require navigation to reach Gosport dock yards for their outfits and equipment."[15]

Parks again labored the difficulties in getting the canal down to its intended depth and complained of the injuries done to the banks by unscrupulous military vessels speeding through. He also suggested that it would by only fair for the Confederacy to pay a fixed sum monthly for the use—and abuse—of the waterway. Instead of the usual individual ship tolls assessed commercial craft, this time he suggested an overall charge of $3,000 per month.[16]

---

[12] *Official Records . . . Armies*, ser. 1, vol. 51, pt. 2, pp. 412–13.

[14] Ibid., p. 441.
[15] Ibid.
[16] Ibid.

Parks was not alone in emphasizing the importance of the Albemarle and Chesapeake Canal to the war effort. On board his flagship *Sea Bird,* a former 202-ton New Jersey side-wheel passenger boat, Commodore Lynch wrote on January 10, 1862, from Roanoke Island to Confederate Navy Secretary S. R. Mallory: "Being enabled to speak from experience, I feel justified in saying that without the use of the canal, heretofore supplies from, and imperatively requisite repairs at Gosport Navy Yard could not have been received or effected. The vessels composing this squadron under my command could not without regular supplies and effectual repairs be kept together." And he concluded by "most earnestly" recommending the canal to Mallory's "fostering care."[17]

Both Park's letter to General Wise and Lynch's letter to Secretary Mallory were forwarded on to War Secretary Benjamin at Richmond, General Wise wrote Benjamin a covering letter on January 16 endorsing the proposal and stating that the canal "is indispensable to the Army and Navy" as a means of forestalling a Union attack on Norfolk and Portsmouth from "the rear of those cities." He concluded: "In a word, the work and its steam tugs and officers and all its other means are now monopolized by the orders of Government. This company fitted out all the gun-boats now employed in the defense of the Albemarle and Pamlico Sounds, and their enterprise is most worthy of Government care and patronage. They ought certainly to be saved from sacrifice and enabled to serve Government more usefully on any reasonable terms."[18]

Mallory concurred. On February 3 he wrote to Benjamin, "I regard it [the canal] of vital importance to the defense of North Carolina," stating that it was imperative that it be maintained in a navigable condition.[19]

However, neither General Wise nor Commodore Lynch then had any way of knowing that "fostering care" of the canal by Mallory, Benjamin, or anyone else in the Confederate hierarchy did not have much time left to run. Only a month later, the *Sea Bird*—and the rest of the Mosquito Fleet—were no more, and control of the Carolina sounds region had passed into Union hands for the duration of the war.

As early as the autumn of 1861, the federal government had planned, as a part of its "grand strategy" for 1862, a second amphibious operation against the North Carolina coast. This time, a considerable number of Union warships of sufficiently shoal draft to allow them to cross the bars of the Outer Banks inlets were included, so enabling the buildup of the Union's own freshwater navy to operate in the sounds. Many units of this makeshift fleet were recruited from double-ended New York Harbor ferryboats, but all were heavily armed and superior to the Confederate fleet in firepower. The overall plan was to be implemented by Brig. Gen. Ambrose E. Burnside, and the various

[17] Ibid., pp. 439–40.

[18] Ibid.
[19] Ibid., ser. 1, vol. 9, p. 427.

operations under his command came under the blanket name Burnside Expedition.[20]

Ships of the federal fleet commenced crossing the Hatteras bar in January 1862. Once safely inside Pamlico Sound, they headed north for the planned attack on Roanoke Island, in conjunction with the army embarked in transports. Successful landings were made, and despite a stalwart Confederate defense, the federal force was too powerful to resist; after battles ashore and afloat, the island was taken on February 8.

Once Roanoke Island fell, General Burnside could move with virtual impunity against any spot he selected on the North Carolina mainland, initially opposed only by Commodore Lynch's tiny seven-ship Mosquito Fleet. Having expended all their ammunition in the naval battle of February 8 in defense of Roanoke Island, these brave little ships had retired to Elizabeth City to resupply. However, a flotilla composed of some thirteen Union vessels pursued them up the Pasquotank River, and though Lynch hoped to be able to defend Elizabeth City, in the end all but two of his Mosquito Fleet were captured or sunk there on February 10.[21]

The *Beaufort* escaped upriver and made it safely through the Dismal Swamp Canal to Norfolk, but the *Appomattox* turned out to be a heartbreaking two inches too wide to enter the locks at South Mills and accordingly was expressly burned by her own men to avoid capture. A vessel under construction at Elizabeth City was destroyed on the stocks. So it was, then, that in a matter of only seven days the Burnside Expedition had taken the Confederate stronghold of Roanoke Island, had occupied both Elizabeth City and Edenton, and had eliminated the entire Confederate naval force in the sounds.[22]

Loss of her navy made it all too apparent that the Albemarle and Chesapeake Canal, which had been the Confederate lifeline between Norfolk and North Carolina, might now provide the enemy with an open-back-door invasion route up into southeastern Virginia. Accordingly, the Confederate hastened to plug the gap by sinking some of their vessels in the North Carolina Cut of the canal. The federals had the opposite conception of the canal's potential role, however. They were afraid that the South might now elect to send reinforcements down through it and accordingly, they decided independently to block the channel also.

Soon after the federal expedition returned from its easy capture of Edenton on February 12, following the fall of Elizabeth City, Commander S. C. Rowan, USN, dispatched five vessels to the North River—"with prize schooners in tow to obstruct the Chesapeake and Albemarle Canal"—expecting they would

[20] Barrett, *The Civil War in North Carolina*, pp. 66ff.

[21] Report of Flag Officer Lynch, CSN, given in *Official Records . . . Navies*, ser. 1, vol. 6, pp. 594ff.; Tredwell, "North Carolina Navy," pp. 307–8.

[22] Barrett, *The Civil War in North Carolina*, p. 89.

meet scant resistance.[23] Upon reaching the southern end of the North Carolina Cut of the following day, Lt. William N. Jeffers, who headed this expedition, discovered that the Southerners had already started to do that job.

Jeffers submitted his official report of this activity from the U.S.S. *Underwriter* on February 14:

> On opening the reach of the [North] River leading to the mouth of the canal, I discovered two small steamers and three schooners about a mile and a quarter up the canal, and that the mouth of the canal was obstructed.
>
> Pickets stationed near the mouth fired their muskets to give the alarm, and a large body of men, whose muskets glistened in the sunshine, got under cover at the point where those vessels were.
>
> I immediately moved up within a couple of hundred yards to the mouth of the canal, until all the vessels grounded, and ordered the *Whitehead* to open fire with her nine-inch guns. But three shells were fired, when the whole body precipitately fled.
>
> On going on shore, I found that a schooner had been sunk about fifty yards within the mouth, supported by piles, logs, etc., forming a complete barrier. I advanced a picket of 15 men, under command of Acting Master Graves, followed by the machinists of the *Louisiana*, with crowbars, mauls, etc. At the distance of half a mile, a second row of piles had been driven. They were at work on this when we surprised them. The steamers and schooners had left before we landed; but a fine large dredging-machine remained, and this we soon saw sinking. This sunk diagonally across the canal, closing it entirely for the passage of the smallest vessel being say ten feet from one bank and six from the other. The machinery was entirely destroyed by the working party, the hull above water burnt and entirely consumed.
>
> A resident named Stone, having a store near this point, was interrogated, and stated that the force near was the remnant of the Wise Legion, commanded by Wise in Person, and numbering about 600 men. Capt. Graves, with a few men, followed their rear guard to the county bridge. This is the throughfare between Currituck and the upper counties, and there was a battery of three guns placed to command the canal and main road. The guard had been removed. In their haste they left the axes used in destroying the dredging-machine, some canteens, haversacks, and clothing. In fact, as a contraband deserted from the Legion at Elizabeth City told me: "Ever since that fight in Western Virginia, in which we lost 500 men, we have been running all the time, and now they will never stop until they get back to Richmond."
>
> I completed the rebel works by sinking two schooners in the mouth of the canal and burning all that remaineed above water. The work completed, I returned to this anchorage.[24]

---

[23] Ibid., p. 88.

[24] *Official Records . . . Navies*, ser. 1, vol. 6, pp. 638–39; Frank Moore, ed., *The Rebellion Record* 4:131–32.

Meanwhile, to the north, in Hampton Roads, Virginia, the stage was being set for one of the Civil War's most dramatic and far-reaching events—the epic first battle between ironclad ships of war. While the famous "Cheesebox on a Raft"—the U.S.S. *Monitor*—was being rushed to completion in Brooklyn, New York, the Confederacy was hastening to finish the casemated ironclad ram it had reclaimed from the sunken hulk of the U.S. steam frigate *Merrimack*, left behind (presumably destroyed) when the Union forces precipitously abandoned the Gosport Navy Yard on April 20, 1861.

The celebrated duel beetweem the *Monitor* and the rechristened C.S.S. *Virginia* took place on March 9, 1862, and resulted in a stalemate, with neither vessel able to destroy, or even to seriously cripple, its adversary. The *Monitor* retired behind the safety of the batteries at Fort Monroe after the four-hour battle ended, however, and for a period of two months the lumbering *Virginia* reigned supreme on Hampton Roads, though she did not dare attempt to leave the area.[25]

In the North Carolina sounds, however, the leisurely Union takeover of the port towns located at the mouths of the rivers continued. The Burnside Expedition captured New Bern on the Neuse River on March 14, then went on to take "Little" Washington, on the Pamlico River, and Plymouth, at the mouth of the Roanoke. Not much later, Governor Clark was to ruefully report to Gen. Robert E. Lee that these three places were then "swarming with Yankees, Negroes and Traitors."[26]

During March and April 1862, however, when the *Merrimack* still posed an alarming threat to the North and the Peninsular campaign designed to take Richmond was at a standstill, the somewhat absurd fear arose again that she, or some other Confederate ironclad (there were none), might elect to sail down either the Dismal Swamp Canal or possibly the reopened Albemarle and Chesapeake Canal in pursuit of the Union vessels then commanding the North Carolina sounds.

This prompted sending an expedition under Brig. Gen. J. L. Reno from Union-held Roanoke Island to the Pasquotank with a force of 3,000 men, in an attempt to cut the banks of the Dismal Swamp Canal and to blow up the locks at South Mills. In a brief, but sharp, action in the northern part of Camden County on April 19, General Wise's Confederates were able to check the Union advance, and Reno's weary men— they had had a long, hot march already—retired, leaving the canal intact. In his memoirs, "Early Operations in North Carolina," Union Brig. Gen. Rush C. Hawkins summed up the situation neatly with the remark: "The lock the expedition was sent to destroy remains to this day [ca. 1884] intact and no ironclad has ever passed through it and for the best of all reasons that

---

[25] One of the latest and best works about the *Monitor-Merrimack* affair is A.A. Hoehling, *Thunder at Hampton Roads.*

[26] Barrett, *The Civil War in North Carolina*, p. 133, quotes a letter dated August 3, 1862, in H. T. Clark Papers, North Carolina Department of Archives and History, Manuscript Division.

none was ever built for that purpose."[27]

Shortly after the inconclusive attack was made by the Union forces on the Dismal Swamp Canal, a naval expedition was again sent up the North River, once more to attempt to block even tighter, the Albemarle and Chesapeake Canal's North Carolina Cut. Lieutenant-Commanding C. W. Flusser submitted his report of this activity from his command ship, the U.S.S. *Commodore Perry* (one of the former ferryboats) at Elizabeth City. To his superior, Commander S. C. Rowan, USN, in charge of all United States naval forces in the sounds, he wrote on April 16, 1862:

> In obedience to your orders, I left this place on the twenty-third inst., in the *Lockwood*, with the *Whitehead* and *Putnam* in company, each with an officer and a detachment of men on board, the *Lockwood* towing the wrecking schooner *Emma Slade*, with the apparatus for blowing up the banks to block up the Albemarle and Chesapeake Canal at the mouth of the North River. We were joined by the *Shawsheen*, having in tow a schooner which had been sent the day before to Roanoke Island, to be filled with sand. On the afternoon of the twenty-third, fifty men were landed on each bank, while a launch with a heavy twelve-pounder was sent up the canal, and with this force we moved up two miles, examining the banks to find the best place for operations.
>
> I concluded to place the obstructions near the mouth, that the men while at work might be under the cover of the guns of the steamers, and the enemy be prevented from removing it. The schooner was sunk just inside of the canal and with brush, stumps, rails, trunks of trees and earth, the passage was obstructed from the schooner about fifty yards above. We were occupied from noon until sunset of the twenty-third, and from half-past seven A. M. until half an hour after sunset on the twenty-fourth. Earth was thrown in by hand as far as it could be, but we had no wheelbarrows to carry it to the middle.
>
> Prof. Maillefert, of the New-York Submarine Engineering Company, and his assistants, were of the greatest assistance to me. Indeed, I was merely governed by his advice, as he is more familiar with this sort of work than I am. He is of the opinion that it will require two or three months' labor with a dredging-machine to remove what we have placed in a day and a half. He says it will be easier and cheaper to cut a new outlet than to remove the obstruction. The rebels have, I think, no thought of using the canal, as they have themselves been obstructing it above and below the bridge. It would be well to send a steamer there daily until the lumber is well water-soaked and sunk.[28]

Confederate control of Norfolk and the Tidewater

[27] Robert Underwood Johnson and Clarence Clough Buel, eds. *Battles and Leaders of the Civil War*, 1:657. Brev. Brig. Gen. Rush C. Hawkins, "Early Operations in North Carolina."

[28] *Official Records . . . Navies*, ser. 1, vol. 7, pp. 260–61; Moore, ed., *Rebellion Record*, vol. 4, p. 509.

country to the south was disappearing. On May 9, 1862, a powerful federal force was disembarked to the east of the key port-city in order to launch an attack from the flank. Realizing that their positions were now untenable, Norfolk and Portsmouth surrendered that very day, and the Confederate Navy's Gosport yard again fell into Union hands. Cut off from her base and drawing far too much water to enable her to be taken up the James in the general withdrawal to the Confederate capitol, the famous *Virginia (Merrimack)* was put to the torch by her own crew off Craney Island on May 11. The Civil War was to drag on for three more desperate years, but for Tidewater Virginia and eastern North Carolina, it was now all over except for sporadic guerilla activity.

With both ends of the Albemarle and Chesapeake Canal now in the Union's firm control, it was obvious to the occupying forces that it would be a distinct military advantage to reopen the waterway as soon as possible, so that the transportation of the enormous quantities of federal troops and supplies could now effectively take the inside water route. Hawkins immediately urged that General Burnside designate work on the canal a number one priority in order that federal forces would no longer need to use "the sometimes dangerous and always unreliable channel of Hatteras Inlet."[29]

Accordingly, work parties and equipment were rushed to Currituck County and began to clear out the obstructions placed by both sides in the North Carolina Cut. Despite the opinion of Lieutenant-Commanding Flusser's expert that it would "require two or three months' labor with a dredging-machine to remove what we have placed in a day and a half," the work proceeded quickly, and as a dispatch sent from Fort Monroe to Washington, D.C., on May 30 proudly reported, the side-wheel steamer *Port Royal* had just arrived there from Roanoke Island via the canal, with "Colonel Hawkins and a company of his gallant Zouaves" embarked. "By this movement we can dispense with all seaward transportation and forward supplies, etc., in a safe and rapid manner to our troops in that vicinity," the account concluded.[30]

This accomplishment did not meet with immediate acclaimation, however. Union Flag Officer L. M. Goldsborough, commanding the North Atlantic blockading squadron, petulently advised Navy Secretary Gideon Wells in a letter dated June 9 sent from his flagship, the *Minnesota*, at Norfolk, that the president of the canal company had just reported to him that the "Currituck Cut" was cleared out and was again navigable and that General Burnside and his staff had come through the canal the night before.[31]

"The clearing away of these obstructions [by authority of Generals Wool and Burnside] has been done without the slightest consultation with me," Goldsborough complained, and "I can not but regard the pro-

---

[29] Hawkins, "Early Operations in North Carolina," p. 657.

[30] Moore, Ed., *Rebellion Record*, 4:509.
[31] Hawkins, "Early Operations in North Carolina," pp. 657–58.

ceeding as strange and inconsiderate."[32] But at least the canal was now open and has remained so ever since, except for brief interruptions in the wake of accidents or when repairs were being carried out.

Though southeastern Virginia and northeastern North Carolina were now theoretically in Union hands, and patrols to insure the safety of the Federal occupation and the use of both the Albemarle and Chesapeake and the Dismal Swamp Canals had been instituted to protect and operate the waterways, there was actually a considerable amount of unorganized, hit-and-run guerilla activity going on throughout the area, which very much needled the occupying forces. Particularly embarrassing was the easy capture of two small federal mail steam boats, the *Arrow* and the *Emily*, on May 16, 1863, in Currituck County. These unarmed vessels, modest craft by any standards, measured sixty tons for the propeller steamer *Arrow* and ninety-four tons for the side-wheeler *Emily*. Both had been summarily appropriated by the Union army from their former Southern owners, so their return to the services of the Confederacy had a nice justification. Apparently retaking them was the work of some thirty members of the Pasquotank Guerillas, who merely jumped on board the *Arrow* as she was going past the drawbridge at Coinjock, quickly subdued the surprised crew, and then proceeded on a couple of miles to take the *Emily*, unsuspectingly waiting for the *Arrow* in the North River to transfer the mails.

---

[32] *Official Records . . . Navies*, ser. 1, vol. 7, p. 467.

Although the word of this soon got back to Union headquarters, valuable time was lost before an expedition was manned by the federals to attempt to find and retake the steamers. It was not until May 17 that the U.S. gunboats *Commodore Perry* and *Valley City* of Captain Flusser's squadron set out from Plymouth with a hundred and fifty infantrymen embarked to try to track them down.

Thinking that the Confederates might have hidden the boats in some backwaters of the North River near where they had seized them, the Union warships first searched various nooks and crannies there and in the Pasquotank, but without success. Meanwhile, with two-days head start, the captured boats, having put some of their passengers ashore, boldly steamed up Albemarle Sound and then ascended the Chowan and Blackwater rivers, going up the latter as far as Franklin, Virginia, where the larger federal vessels could not follow.

An official account of the proceedings was contained in a letter dated May 17, 1863, from Union Capt. W. Dewees Roberts to Maj. F. A. Stratton. It stated:

> About 4 o'clock they [the Confederate guerillas] captured one of the above named boats [*Arrow* and *Emily*] in Currituck Canal and with her [the *Arrow*] pushed out into the North River where they captured the other boat, taking the crew prisoners. . . . The captured boats seem to have been taken down the Albemarle Sound and up the Chowan River. The rebel crew declared their intention of so doing, but if overtaken by our forces they would then de-

stroy the boats. . . . The party capturing the boats seem to have been about 40 of the Pasquotank Guerillas, Captain Elliott commanding. . . . I have received this information from several persons living in the vicinity of Currituck Bridge.[33]

More colorfully related, however, was Confederate Capt. E. T. Elliott's own official report to Governor Zebulon B. Vance, as printed in the May 23, 1863, issue of the semiweekly *Raleigh Register*. Elliott, who actually led a force of thirty Partizan rangers, had arrived with his thirteen prisoners at the state capital only the day before. Under the headline "One of the Most Daring and Brilliant Feats of the War," the commander's account stated:

> I have the honor to report the capture of the steamers *Emily* and *Arrow* yesterday [May 16, 1863], the former a fine sailing sidewheel steamer, and the other a propeller, used on the canal between Norfolk and Albemarle Sound, Roanoke Island and other points. I had conceived a plan of capture sometime ago, and yesterday found an opportunity to execute it. About six o'clock P.M., at the usual hour, the *Arrow* hove in sight in the Currituck Canal. I made the proper distribution of my men, thirty in number, and when she came alongside, we halted her and demanded a surrender, which was complied with without resistance. After capturing the *Arrow* and knowing that the *Emily* was lying about two miles below awaiting the arrival of the *Arrow*, I took twelve men aboard, determined if possible to secure this prize, and believing that it would require a great deal of caution, I placed the captain of the *Arrow* in the wheel house and required him to steer up along side of the *Emily* as if nothing unusual had happened. My plan succeeded, and she surrendered without resistance. We captured on board the *Arrow* the officers and men, numbering seven, and thirteen on *Emily*. Among those captured on the *Arrow* was a Surgeon, U.S. Navy. The great haste required gave me no opportunity of reporting their names. We found no guns on the boats, but a lot of mail bags which are forwarded to you.
>
> After eight o'clock I started for some port to secure my prizes. We steamed all night, passing a large gunboat (the *Whitehead*) mounting six guns; we passed Edenton about daylight, the people believing we were Yankees. In passing up the Chowan, five Negroes hailed us, believing us their Northern allies. I received them on board and immediately dispatched them to their owners, who no doubt have them in a more available and certain shape.[34]

Captain Elliott then related the rest of his journey

---

[33] *Official Records . . . Armies*, ser. 1, vol. 8, pp. 355–56; *Official Records . . . Navies*, ser. 1, vol. 9, pp. 23–25.

[34] *Raleigh* [N.C.] *Register*, May 23, 1863, p. 2, col. 2, presents a transcript entitled "A Brilliant Achievement—Two Steamers Captured in North Carolina Waters—All Honor to our Partizan Rangers." (Provided by Historical Publications Section, Department of Cultural Resources, Raleigh, N.C.)

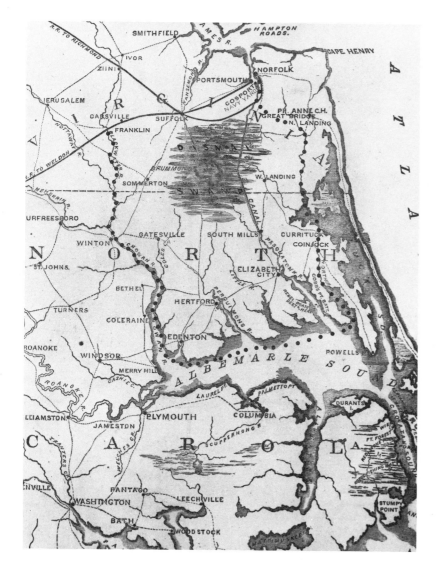

FIG. 16. *This "General map of Albemarle and Pamlico Sounds showing the theatre of operations of the Burnside Expedition" appeared in* Harper's Weekly, *March 1, 1862. Superimposed are the routes taken by the federal steamboats* Emily *and* Arrow—*the* Emily *from Norfolk to capture by the Confederates at Coinjock, N.C., thence both vessels to Franklin, Va., May 16, 1863.*

(see fig. 16) up the Blackwater River, where he arrived at South Quay about one o'clock on the eighteenth and was met by a Major Boggs and a Captain Dobney, "an old officer of the Navy," who took command of the boats, while the prisoners were sent up to Franklin and ultimately on to Raleigh. Elliott concluded his report: "The *Arrow* is valuable on account of her machinery, which is said to be fine by the engineer who was assigned me by Major Boggs. The *Emily* is valuable for her machinery as well as hull, which in my opinion and that of officers stationed here, would make a valuable gunboat."[35]

Thirty years later this story of the capturing of the vessels was related to Samuel Ward Stanton, maritime feature writer and editor of *Seaboard Magazine*, by Capt. Thomas M. Southgate, veteran master of the Old Dominion Line steamboat *Newberne*, as they were passing Coinjock on a routine voyage from Norfolk to

---

[35] Ibid.

New Bern early in 1892. Stanton subsequently retold it in one of his *Seaboard* articles.[36] Substantially, it is similar to the two official reports quoted above. However, Captain Southgate stated that the leader of the venture was "a dashing cavalry officer by the name of Burrass," a member of the Pasquotank Guerillas, and "most of his company was made up of watermen—who had spent most of their lives on the sounds, either in steam or sailing vessels." He reported that before the officers and crew of the *Arrow*: "could turn around they were all secured. Then he [Burrass] placed a soldier on either side of the engineers of either vessel, and with the Stars and Stripes still flying, he ran right down to the Union fleet, left the mails and then went up Albemarle Sound and so on to the Chowan River and ascended to Franklin where he hauled down the Union Flag and hoisted the Confederate colors. The *Emily* was afterwards captured by the Union forces."

Regrettably, nothing further is known about the "dashing" Burrass, and no records for a North Carolina officer by that name may be found in the state Division of Archives and History. Since, by the official reports, there is no question but that Captain Elliott led the raid, undoubtedly Captain Southgate was mistaken on that point, and certainly the part concerning their going ahead and delivering the mail directly to the Yankees was apocryphal. One may be certain, however, that the daring exploits of Captain Elliott did not endear him to the Union high command. Although it was the *Arrow* which was recaptured by the federal gunboat *Whitehead* on July 29, 1864—the vessel she had so blithely eluded the year before—apparently no word of the fate of the *Emily* has come down. Undoubtedly, she too was taken before the ultimate collapse of the Confederacy.[38]

Meanwhile, the horror of federal occupation was intensified in this unpacified region of eastern North Carolina by the activities of pillaging "bands of armed Negroes who domineer the homes of their masters and spread terror over the land."[39] In addition to the rampaging blacks, native Union sympathizers known as Buffaloes terrorized the countryside, perpetrating every type of crime and violence. When the Southerners reacted in an attempt to defend themselves and their property and to break up the roving bands that preyed on them, General Butler considered that the sparsely settled countryside needed pacifying and elected to send Brig. Gen. Edward A. Wild and two regiments of Negro troops to scour the land and to teach the inhabitants a lesson.

Wild's raid, lasting from December 5 to 24, 1863, achieved a new low in military deportment and was

---

[36] Stanton, *Steam Navigation on the Carolina Sounds and the Chesapeake in 1892*, p. 16.
[37] Ibid.

---

[38] *Official Records . . . Navies*, ser. 1, vol. 18, 321; A popular account of the capture of the *Emily* and the *Arrow*, drawn from this chapter of *Juniper Waterway*, was published in 1978: Alexander C. Brown, "The Runaway Steamboat Caper: A Daring Wartime Feat. . . ."
[39] Barrett, *The Civil War in North Carolina*, p. 174.

marked by burning houses, barns, and crops, appropriating livestock, pillage, rape, terrorizing women, children, and old men, and carrying away hostages. The supplies for Wild's troops were intended to follow them along the line of march south from Virginia into North Carolina via the road flanking the Dismal Swamp Canal, but they were diverted by mistake to the Albemarle and Chesapeake Canal, so arriving late at Elizabeth City. The men did well enough living off the countryside, however. This orgy had one positive benefit, though, for horrified Confederate authorities urged eastern Carolinians to abandon all resistance. Even notorious "Beast" Butler had to admit that General Wild had done his job "perhaps with too much stringency."[40]

Meanwhile, the reopened Albemarle and Chesapeake Canal continued to serve its federal masters as well as it had the South for the previous thirteen months. Soon after Norfolk was occupied, President Lincoln appointed Milton Courtright, a civil engineer from Pennsylvania and head of the New York contracting firm that had built the canal in the first place, to serve as general agent of the company. As a Southerner, Parks was then ineligible. Courtright advanced the necessary funds to pay for repairing the damage to the canal, and he put the works in efficient operation again. Indeed, President Parks was to admit later on, when he again became acting head of the canal company, that "but for this prompt action on his [Court-

right's] part, it is believed the navigation would not have been preserved in its present condition."[41]

Though no annual reports were published by the company during the war years, records were kept, and in the printed cumulative *Tenth Annual Report* terminating with the fiscal year ending September 30, 1865, various figures were given on a yearly basis. For example, total tolls credited amounted to $23,407.70 for 1861; $4,435.51 for 1862; $19,686.15 for 1863; $42,715.67 for 1864; and $70,421.16 for 1865.

These covered the passages of 2,569 vessels in 1861; 1,297 in 1862; 950 in 1863; 1,291 in 1864; and 2,617 in 1865, for a grand total of 8,824 craft. Broken down by types of vessels, steamers were in the preponderance with 3,844 passages. Schooners amounted to 1,690; sloops to 438; lighters to 1,044; barges to 474; rafts to 16; and "boats" to 1,318.

Expenditures are listed in table 7.

It is impossible to determine precisely the number of military vessels which transited the canal, first in the service of the Confederacy and then, subsequent to the reopening of the canal in May of 1863, for the Union. However, one of the latter—possibly even the smallest—was to have considerable significance on the outcome of the war by thwarting the South's last, desperate effort staged in the North Carolina sounds area. Though defeated there early in 1862 and later denied the use of Hampton Roads, the South did not give up on its navy. Counting on the invincibility of ironclads—

---

[40] Brown, *Dismal Swamp Canal*, p. 105.

[41] A & C Canal Co., *Tenth Annual Report*, (1860–65) p. 5.

Table 7—1861–65 expenditures for running the canal

Engineers expenses	$ 1,885.50
Canal repairs and expenses	62,958.89
Interest and legal expenses	11,761.25
Currituck County	2,056.09
Steam tow boats and contingent expenses	36,329.90
Bills payable and exchange account	14,234.57
U.S. revenue tax	1,116.97
Steam dredges and repairs	10,364.32
Construction	43,802.43
	$184,508.92

Source: A & C Canal Co., *Tenth Annual Report* (1860–65), pp. 7–9.

as tellingly demonstrated by the *Virginia*—and surmounting incredible logistical difficulties, she contrived to build, well up the Roanoke River, a powerful shoal-draft imitation of the vessel which has forever gone down in history as the *Merrimack.* Thus eventuated the brave C.S.S. *Albemarle,* which, like the *Virginia,* had a sloping armored casemate and carried two 100-pounder English Armstrong guns mounted at bow and stern.[42]

Assembled in a "cornfield shipyard" improvised at Edwards Ferry, near Hamilton, North Carolina, between April 1863 and April 1864, the *Albemarle* proved a formidable weapon indeed, measuring 152 feet long by 45 feet wide, but drawing only 8 feet of water. She was powered by two steam engines of two-hundred horsepower each. By the spring of 1864, the *Albemarle* was nearly completed and hopefully would soon again command the Carolina sounds for the Confederacy by retaking Plymouth, guarding the mouth of the Roanoke River, ultimately defeating the Union freshwater navy, and bringing on a great victory for the South.

By April 17, the Confederate army in the area under the command of twenty-seven year old Gen. R. F. Hoke—who had been assured of the assistance of the then all-but-finished *Albemarle*—confidently put his forces in motion for the recapture of Plymouth. Meanwhile, the untried ironclad descended the river, engaged in a running battle with federal gunboats defending the town, and turned the balance in favor of the Confederacy in the ensuing land battle. With the Union's surrender of Plymouth on April 19, the *Albemarle* had gained a base at the head of Albemarle Sound, from which she might now, with luck, drive all enemy warships from the inland seas. The South rejoiced.

Naturally the Union was well aware of the new threat to federal supremacy which the *Albemarle* now posed as a one-ship fleet-in-being, and the federal officers were in agreement that somehow the new Confederate Goliath must be destroyed. Young Lt. William B. Cushing, USN, came up with a plan to play the role of David. He proposed to sneak up on the Confederate ironclad under cover of darkness in a tiny vessel carrying a spar torpedo. Approval was given, and Cushing found two thirty-foot steam launches in the Brooklyn Navy Yard

---

[42] Maurice Melton, *The Confederate Ironclads* (New York: Thomas Yoseloff, 1968), pp. 183–86.

which he considered suitable for his possibly suicidal mission.[43]

A twelve-pound howitzer and a long spar with a complicated explosive device fastened to the end were provided for each of the little open boats. So equipped, they started south, bound for Roanoke Island, in the middle of September 1864. One of them sank on the way down, but, nothing daunted, Cushing with his six-man crew set out from Norfolk in the remaining launch on October 20, via the Albemarle and Chesapeake Canal. Arriving at Roanoke Island three days later, the little craft then proceeded immediately up to the head of Albemarle Sound to join the Union fleet guarding the mouth of the Roanoke River and blockading Plymouth—ever ready to do battle with the *Albemarle* should she emerge.

Fortunately for Cushing, the night chosen for the attack was dark. Carefully stalking the unsuspecting quarry moored to a wharf in Plymouth, the crew of the launch soon spotted the *Albemarle* in the gloom and went in for the kill. A barking dog and then sentries gave the alarm, but Cushing, undaunted, called for full steam ahead, and in a hail of bullets, the launch rammed a heavy log boom floating around the ironclad to protect her. Incredibly, the little vessel contrived to slide over the logs, and as soon as he was close enough to the hull of the ironclad, Cushing was able to set off his spar torpedo underneath her.

The little Union launch was itself destroyed by the enormous explosion that followed, which rent the *Albemarle*, sending her down with "a hole in the bottom big enough to drive a wagon." Cushing managed to kick off his shoes and swim ashore, and he ultimately gained the safety of a Union picket vessel, the *Valley City*. Of his six companions, one also escaped, two were drowned, and three were taken prisoner.[44]

As a result of this daring exploit, Plymouth was recaptured by the federals on October 31, and the hopes of the Confederacy faded once more. By now the war was almost over anyway. Less than six months later, on April 9, 1865, General Lee surrendered at Appomattox, and the broken South set about the difficult task of picking up the pieces under the crushing burden of Reconstruction.

The Albemarle and Chesapeake Canal had itself come through the war comparatively undamaged, although most of its equipment—dredges, lighters, and pumps—and all of its steam tugs had been destroyed, not excepting the jaunty little *Calypso*, whose fate it may well have been to be sunk to help block a channel. The company did not greatly suffer financially either. Milton Courtright, as general agent, reported in a "statement of affairs" as of January 1, 1864, that nearly the entire amount of stock was held by its original holders, "who are all loyal Northern men, and the small balance, held in Norfolk and vicinity, is, so far as we know and believe, in the hands of parties who have taken the oath of allegiance to the Government of the United States.

---

[43] Barrett, *The Civil War in North Carolina*, pp. 227–28.

[44] Ibid., p. 230.

The bonds are substantially all held by parties constituting the firm of Courtright, Barton & Company, who took them in payment for work done."[45]

At length President Parks was reinstated, and with

commendable understatement, he reported to the stockholders in the *Tenth Annual Report* that, "Circumstances beyond our control have prevented your regular annual meetings since November, 1860. . . . Many changes have occurred since last we met."[46]

---

[45] A & C Canal Co., *Fifth Annual Report* (New York, 1864), pp. 9–10.

[46] A & C Canal Co., *Tenth Annual Report*, 1860–1865, p. 1.

Ten Years of
Reconstruction, 1865–75

From the very beginning the Albemarle and Chesapeake Canal had no towpaths or flanking roads and was entirely dependent upon mechanical power to convey ships through the narrow cuts. For this reason, the first consideration after the Civil War ended was an attempt to reassemble a fleet of steamboats and tugs to transport people and freight throughout the North Carolina sounds market area upon which the canal depended for its trade. The federal government's military vessels, which had been so busily using the waterway all through the war, were withdrawn upon its conclusion, and virtually no commodities could move until new vessels were brought upon the scene. Prior to the war, an estimated three hundred craft of all classes had regularly plied the sounds, going up and down the new canal, but only about a dozen were said to be available at the end. "Farmers and lumbermen have no way to send their products to Market," the canal company's *Tenth Annual Report* lamented.[1]

Although following the war there was some ocean-going traffic originating from sound-side cities like Edenton and New Bern that plied through the inlets en route to various east-coast seaports, a far greater number of the vessels which had formerly navigated the Carolina sounds either had been built on them or, having once entered by way of the canals or ocean in-

---

[1] A & C Canal Co., *Tenth Annual Report*, (1860–65), p. 3.

lets, had remained for the rest of their careers in these virtually landlocked seas. As far as steam vessels were concerned, it would be some time before any began to be constructed locally, and the first little steamers to ply the sounds took their chances sailing down the coast during good weather and coming in by way of either Hatteras or Ocracoke inlets.

In the beginning although Robert Fulton's partner, John Stevens of Hoboken, New Jersey, had been granted the exclusive privilege of operating steamboats in North Carolina waters by the state legislature as early as 1812,[2] he still had not introduced a steam vessel within the two-year period required by the legislature, and his monopoly had lapsed accordingly. The first steam craft actually to run in North Carolina was the *Norfolk,* a 222-tonner built in Norfolk in 1817. She was brought down the coast the next year and after a stormy voyage arrived at New Bern in April 1818.[3] Her owners intended that she ply between New Bern and Elizabeth City via settlements bordering Pamlico, Croatan, and Albemarle sounds, carrying passengers for a fare of fifteen dollars and connecting at her terminal sound ports with stagecoaches—New Bern to Fayetteville and Elizabeth City to Norfolk—for an estimated four-day trip. Unfortunately, this did not work out satisfactorily, and after only a three-month trial, it was called off and the *Norfolk* returned to Chesapeake waters.

The next Carolina-sounds steamer was appropriately named *Albemarle.* An eighty-tonner built in New York in 1818, she was intended to provide daily ferry service across the upper end of Albemarle Sound on a two-hour run connecting Edenton and Plymouth, a distance of twenty-one miles. She too was scheduled to operate in conjunction with stage lines, but lack of patronage doomed the venture.[4]

After the enlargement of the Dismal Swamp Canal in 1828 provided a more accessible way to market, small steamers were able to enter the Carolina sounds via canal from Norfolk. The next year the Virginia and North Carolina Transportation Company was chartered and acquired the 142-ton steamboat *Petersburg* from the James River. Being too large for the canal locks, however, the *Petersburg* came to Albemarle Sound by the roundabout route via Ocracoke Inlet. In 1829 her function was to tow barges and schooners back and forth from the Roanoke, around and up the Pasquotank, to the south end of the canal, whence they would be tracked through by their crews. The *Petersburg* made these runs between Weldon and Elizabeth City via Milton, Halifax, Plymouth, and Edenton. She was soon joined by the *North Carolina,* a smaller vessel of only seventy tons, Norfolk-built in 1830, and also

[2] North Carolina Legislative Papers, 1812, box 263. Raleigh, N.C., quoted in Sarah Woodall Turlington, "Steam Navigation in North Carolina Prior to 1860."

[3] *Carolina Centennial,* April 25, 1818, quoted in Turlington, "Steam Navigation," p. 48.

[4] Ibid., February 13, 1819, quoted in Turlington, "Steam Navigation," p. 50.

owned by the Virginia and North Carolina Transportation Company. The little recessed stern-wheel steamer *Lady of the Lake,* sixty-three feet long and specially built in Portsmouth in 1830 to ply the Dismal Swamp Canal, was apparently the first steam vessel to navigate through it regularly.[5]

Encouraged by young Marshall Parks, a few iron canal-steamers arrived on the sounds in the 1840s. These were the previously cited *Pioneer* (1842), *Conestoga* (1844), and a second vessel named *Albemarle* (1844), this one commanded by Parks himself. These vessels regularly passed through the Dismal Swamp Canal towing barges from Roanoke River country to Norfolk. Meanwhile, upon recovery from the financial panic of 1837, the decades between 1840 and 1860 witnessed a marked increase in the number of steamers sailing all of North Carolina's inland waters. Thomas Sloan estimates that there were some forty employed on the Cape Fear River system—in no way physically connected to the more northerly sounds and hence irrelevant to this study—with twenty-five or thirty on the Neuse, Pamlico, Roanoke, Chowen, and Pasquotank (all of which fed into the sounds). Half a dozen or so plied the Dismal Swamp Canal.[6]

Despite the failure of the *Norfolk* in 1818, at mid-century regular services connected most of the principal cities of the area. Boats from Elizabeth City at the north steamed to Edenton and other river ports, and as summer seaside resorts were gaining popularity, steamboat excursions were instituted to Roanoke Island and Nag's Head in season as well. Plying this run were such vessels as the fine 343-ton iron side-wheel steamer *Curlew,* which had been built at Wilmington, Delaware, in 1856 and whose home port was listed as Edenton. Edward C. Bruce, the artist-writer who had viewed the digging of the Albemarle and Chesapeake near North Landing in 1858 and who then cruised down to Currituck Sound on board the company dispatch boat *Calypso,* came back to eastern North Carolina the next year and took passage at Elizabeth City on what he described as "an excellent iron boat with the airy name of *Curlew,*" which "winged us down the Sound" en route to Roanoke Island. Bruce had high encomiums for Captain Burbage and was astonished that, unlike on board other vessels, everything went like clockwork on board the *Curlew,* which he said was managed "with so little damage to the Third Commandment."[7]

By the end of the 1850s, as we have seen, although most North Carolina craft of the area plied exclusively within the sounds, at last the Albemarle and Chesapeake Canal was available, and larger vessels like the *Curlew* did not have to go outside, but could readily make the inland trip to Norfolk for annual overhaul. With war clouds gathering, however, the *Curlew,* like the canal company's steam tugs, was soon appropri-

---

[5] Brown, *Dismal Swamp Canal,* pp. 74–75.

[6] Thomas H. Sloan, "Inland Steam Navigation in North Carolina, 1818–1900."

[7] Bruce, "Loungings in the Footprints of the Pioneers," pt. 2, pp. 726–27.

ated for Confederate naval duty. She, along with the other units of the Mosquito Fleet, was sunk in the Pasquotank off Elizabeth City early in 1862.

As soon as possible after the war's end, then, the canal company built two small vessels for its own use in repair work and superintendence—the steam tug *Coinjock* and, to replace the *Calypso*, the little dispatch boat *Fannie*. Sad to say, the *Coinjock* did not last long, exploding its boiler and killing all on board on November 11, 1865—apparently the first canal-related deaths recorded.[8]

Shortly thereafter, however, two more steam tugs were obtained for commercial towing in the canal: the *Chowan*, a fifty-six tonner built in Philadelphia in 1862, and the *S. C. Brooks*, a sixty-two tonner which was also northern-built in 1857 and came down from the Great Lakes. Subsequently, the tug *Croatan* was acquired in 1868 for $7,500.[9] Meanwhile, more steam dredges were secured by the company to continue the unremitting task of maintaining channel depths throughout the system.

In addition to its own tugs—for towing for hire was again an integral part of the company's canal operation—the company badly needed a dock in the center of Norfolk to store freight for forwarding down the canal, for transshipping goods in and out of canal vessels, and as a place to assemble tows. Accordingly, in December 1865, the so-called railroad ferry depot was leased for a ten-year period, a spacious building on it was repaired for company offices, and a substantial three-hundred-foot wharf, twenty-four feet in width, was then constructed.

In the *Eleventh Annual Report*, Parks was gratified to record that, for the year ending September 30, 1866, there had been a material improvement in the amount of traffic moving on the canal—3,643 vessels, showing an increase of 1,026 from the year before. Tolls collected contributed $41,346.54 to the company treasury. "The eastern portion of North Carolina . . . is slowly recovering from the effects of the late war," Parks observed, continuing: "The change in the labor system has rendered a large number of plantations improductive [his euphemism concerning the abolishment of slavery] and consequently there is less corn, wheat, peas, &c. shipped than formerly."[10]

Meanwhile, several steamboat services had been established on a regular basis to move available freight—though some of the ships were "carpetbaggers" brought south to get in on the act, and Parks spoke disparagingly about "an inferior class of boats" using the canal, "many of them unfit for navigation."[11] Apparently anything that could float would suffice, since taking over the business of trading along the North Carolina rivers while the inhabitants were still pros-

---

[8] A & C Canal Co., *Eleventh Annual Report*, (1866), p. 4.
[9] Ibid., Steamboat particulars are taken from the *Lytle Holdcamper List*, pp. 36, 189. Probably the iron-hull tug *Croatan*, twenty-eight tons, of Erie, Pennsylvania, cited on page 48 of the *Lytle-Holdcamper List*, was the vessel purchased.

---

[10] A & C Canal Co., *Eleventh Annual Report* (1866), pp. 3–4.
[11] Ibid., p. 5.

trate offered an inviting prospect for out-of-state entrepreneurs.

In the 1866 *Report,* however, President Parks specifically cited approvingly the arrival of the brand new 140-ton side-wheeler *Bette,* offering service between Norfolk and New Bern (where she had been built in 1865), while the "fine propellor" *L. G. Cannon,* owned by W. L. Oswald, performed on a run to the proprietor's home town of "Little" Washington in Beaufort County. This boat, commanded by Capt. D. W. Todd, was noted with gratification as having arrived at Norfolk December 11, 1866, with a "full cargo from the Roanoke River" consisting of 264 bales of cotton, 37,000 shingles, and 22 barrels of tar.[12] Starting life prosaically as an iron-hulled barge in New York in 1845, the *L. G. Cannon* was converted to steam in 1862, then was taken in service as the U.S. Quartermaster Department transport *General Meigs* during the war, and at length was redocumented as a passenger and freight carrier and renamed *L. G. Cannon* on March 1, 1866.[13]

Parks specifically cited the following steamers trading on the Roanoke River which generally engaged in towing loaded barges as well: *Pocosin, Orient, Cotton Plant, Fairy, Roanoke, J. D. Coleman, Currituck,* and *Hackensack.* Serving on the Chowan River were the stern-wheeler *Weyenock,* the screw steamers *Maria, Our Flag,* and *Emma,* and the steam tugs *Kate* and *Bertie.* One prewar vessel, the 110-foot iron barge *Enterprise*—"the first boat built to navigate this canal, belonging to parties on the Roanoke"—had survived the conflict and was back again, carrying 1,005 bales of cotton through on a five-foot draft.[14] Cotton was to become a major northbound shipment.

The canal company president was also gratified by the "large number of steamers passing through the canal to distant ports in the south." In order to encourage such through traffic, he was successful in making arrangements with officials of both the Chesapeake and Delaware Canal and the Delaware and Raritan Canal so that products of North Carolina which had come up through the Albemarle and Chesapeake Canal might be entitled to pay only half fare on the northern canals.[15]

Commencing with its *Eleventh Annual Report* in 1866, the company inaugurated the custom of listing by name and tonnage the various vessels that used their waterway. Some 109 steamers were recorded alphabetically that year, ranging in size from 10 to 380 tons. The *Report* commented that those of the greatest capacity, "measuring 380 82 / 95 tons old measurement, or about 540 new," were the steamboats *Vineland* and *General Burnside*—the latter hardly a name to enchant the ears of defeated North Carolinians, still smarting under the depredations of the Burnside Expedition.

---

[12] Norfolk *Journal,* December 11, 1866, cited in Emmerson, comp., "Steam Navigation, 1837–1860," p. 452.
[13] *Lytle-Holdcamper List,* p. 122.

[14] A & C Canal Co., *Eleventh Annual Report* (1866), p. 8.
[15] Ibid., p. 7.

These craft were of about equal size—158 feet long, 22 feet wide, and capable of carrying some 400 tons on a 6½-foot draft.[16] The report continued: "The largest and most costly steamer on the bay—the *Thomas Kelso*—[17]draws loaded less than six feet. The *Augusta*[18] and *Savannah*, side-wheel steamers belonging to the U. S. Government, were the largest side-wheelers that have passed through this Canal, and were estimated to carry over 1,200 bales of cotton each. The *Julia St. Clair*[19] a new and large iron stern-wheel steamer, lately passed through, will carry 900 bales cotton on three feet water."[20]

A curious entry in this first canal-fleet list was that of the ten-ton side-wheeler *Calypso*, for it will be recalled that she was the original company dispatch boat, already noted in the *Tenth Annual Report*, the year before, as having been destroyed during the war. Also listed, seemingly erroneously, was the *Sea Bird*, Confederate Commodore Lynch's flagship, also destroyed—off Elizabeth City in 1862—and certainly ineligible for that reason.

However, since more than a hundred steamers were named in the 1866 *Eleventh Annual Report*, while only forty-one are listed as navigating the canal in 1867—after business had begun to pick up—it would appear that the longer list must undoubtedly include the names of a number of craft that had plied the canal prior to 1866.[21]

Obviously steamboat services throughout the area were proliferating, and the Norfolk *Journal* of December 5, 1866, contained an announcement placed by Marshall Parks of steamer sailings from the canal depot at the foot of Nebraska Street for Elizabeth City, Plymouth, Jamesville, Williamston, Hamilton, Hills Ferry, Currituck Court House, Coinjock, Windsor,

[16] Ibid., p. 8.

[17] It is highly improbably that the Baltimore Steam Packet Company's steamer *Thomas Kelso* ever navigated the Albemarle and Chesapeake Canal, however. Reference to this vessel in the *Report* was probably merely to afford a comparison with other vessels with respect to draft and cargo capacity. In any event, this iron 1865-built side-wheel steamboat's measurements were 1,439 tons, 236.9 feet long, 25.4 feet beam, and 10.4 feet depth. It had been built for the Old Bay Line's Norfolk to Baltimore overnight service just after the Civil War by Reaney, Son and Company at Chester, Pennsylvania, but unfortuantely exploded its steam drum while under way off Wolf Trap Shoal in Chesapeake Bay on December 8, 1866. Towed to Portsmouth for repairs, the *Thomas Kelso* was sold in 1869 to New York owners, leaving the Chesapeake for good. (Alexander C. Brown, *Steam Packets on the Chesapeake*. [Cambridge, Md.: Cornell Maritime Press, 1961], pp. 54, 163)

[18] *Lytle-Holdcamper List*. p. 16.

[19] Ibid., p. 118.

[20] A & C Canal Co., *Eleventh Annual Report* (1866), p. 8.

[21] Two other vessels, picked at random, which seem out of place on an Albemarle and Chesapeake Canal roster are the *T. F. Secor*, a New York steamer acquired by the U.S. War Department in 1863, and the 1857-built New York Harbor commuter steamer *Sylvan Shore*, plying the then-fashionable route between Harlem and lower Manhattan. (Alexander J. Wall, *The Sylvan Steamboats on the East River* [Salem, Mass.: Steamship Historical Society of America Reprint no. 1, 1941], p. 70; *Lytle-Holdcamper List*, p. 208.)

Gates Ferry, Barfields, Murfreesboro, Columbia, North Landing, and Northwest River.

A further event of moment in the shipping news of this immediate postwar era was recorded in the *Journal* of December 17, 1868, in the announcement of the forthcoming arrival of the "fine new light-draft iron steamer *Old North State*, James J. Swain, Master."[22] This stern-wheeler, scheduled to begin service between Norfolk and Washington, North Carolina, in 1867, and commemorated by a lithographic portrait published by Endicott and Company, New York printmakers (fig. 17), was undoubtedly the finest vessel plying the canal when she came out. However, for reasons neither disclosed nor expanded upon, she was noted in the annual-report fleet list of 1869 as "lately gone to South America."[23]

Narrow-beamed vessels like the *Old North State* with stern-wheel propulsion became increasingly popular during the latter part of the nineteenth century for southern inland waters navigation. This was owing to the fact that, with a wheel extending the entire width of the vessel, they could retain full paddle power astern without having to increase the ship's beam with sponsons to accommodate side paddles. Furthermore they did not have to operate on as deep a draft as screw propellers would require. A few of that type lasted well into the present century. Currituck Sound apparently

---

[22] Norfolk *Journal*, December 14, 1867, cited in Emmerson, comp., "Steam Navigation, 1837–1860," pp. 451–52.
[23] A & C Canal Co., *Fourteenth Annual Report* (1869), p. 16.

being one of the last Atlantic-seaboard strongholds of stern-wheelers, made memorable by many famous Mississippi River steamers.

A full description of the *Old North State* was published in the Norfolk *Journal* of January 14, 1867, as follows:

> This new iron steamer, built at Wilmington, Delaware, by Pusey, Jones & Co., for William Swaine, Esq., merchant of this city, arrived here yesterday via the Capes of Delaware.
>
> The *Old North State* was built under the direction of Captain Swaine, especially for the North Carolina trade, and is intended to run from this city to Washington, N.C. Her length is 135 feet, beam 20 feet, six inches, depth of hold six feet, three inches, tonnage 252 63/100 tons. The *Old North State* is propelled by a vertical stern-wheel, driven by a horizontal engine, having an 18-inch cylinder and six feet stroke of piston. There are ten finely fitted up staterooms, and accommodations for 26 passengers. The freight capacity of the steamer is 200 tons. There is on board a superior and well arranged hoisting engine, built in this city by the Atlantic Iron Works Company, which is intended to hoist out the cargo, thereby giving great dispatch in loading and unloading.
>
> The *Old North State* will make weekly trips to Washington, N.C., via the Albemarle & Chesapeake Canal, and we hope the patronage may be sufficient to repay the enterprising owner, who has expended nearly $40,000 in the enterprise. Freight intended for Roanoke Island, Washington, Greensville, Tarboro, and other landings on the Pamlico and Tar

ENDICOTT & CO. LITH. 59 BEEKMAN ST. NEW YORK.

"OLD NORTH STATE,"

OF SWAINE'S LINE.

VIRGINIA & NORTH CAROLINA STEAMER.

Built by
PUSEY, JONES & CO.
Wilmington, Del.
1866

Fig. 17. *Iron, stern-wheel steamer* Old North State, *built in 1866 at Wilmington, Del., expressly for travel through the Albemarle and Chesapeake Canal, was 135 feet in length and measured 252 tons. From a lithograph by Endicott & Company in the Elwin M. Eldredge Collection. (Courtesy the Mariners Museum.)*

Rivers, should be sent by this steamer. The iron stern-wheel steamer *Cotton Plant* is now running from Washington to Greenville and Tarboro, and will take freight beyond Washington on the arrival of the *Old North State* at that place.[24]

Still other notable 1860s-built vessels whose services were long identified with the Albemarle and Chesapeake Canal included the "new and elegant steamer *Olive*, Captain Slocum." Though in independent operation at first, the 1867 Norfolk-built screw-steamer *Olive* (fig. 18) had the distinction of becoming the first vessel of the Old Dominion Line's North Carolina division. She was a wooden steamer measuring 120 feet in length by 20 feet beam by 7 feet depth and was rated at 272 tons. Initially, she made weekly trips back and forth from the canal depot to "Little" Washington. A few years later, commanded by the same Capt. T. H. Southgate, noted in the previous chapter as master of the *Newberne* in 1892, she was switched to serve New Bern, and then in June 1872 she was acquired by the Old Dominion Line, continuing on that run for many years thereafter.[25]

These new owners, the Old Dominion Steamship Company, founded by a merger in 1867 of existing lines, began that year to provide passenger and freight service down the coast from New York to Norfolk with the oceangoing side-wheel steamships *Hatteras* and *Albemarle* and, by the middle of that year, with the *Niagara* and *Saratoga* also. It was not long thereafter that the new company began to acquire some smaller steamboats that, sailing out of Norfolk, served as feeders to the main line at its southern end. These services, in which ultimately a considerable number of vessels were involved, plied the lower Chesapeake estuaries, Mobjack Bay, Hampton Roads, and the James River, as well as Virginia's Eastern Shore and the North Carolina sounds by way of the Albemarle and Chesapeake Canal.

The Norfolk *Journal* of August 25, 1868, contained an interesting accouncement covering the construction of a new iron side-wheel steamer at Norfolk's Atlantic Iron Works as promoted by Marshall Parks, the "enterprising president of the Albemarle and Chesapeake Canal." The boat would be 100 feet long, 22 feet in overall width, and powered by a forty-horsepower engine. Its function was to be "carrying fish alive from the sounds to northern markets," and also to providing

---

[24] Norfolk *Journal*, January 14, 1867, cited in Emmerson, comp., "Steam Navigation, 1837–1860," p. 458.

[25] Ibid., September 30, 1869, cited in Emmerson, comp., "Steam Navigation, 1837–1860," p. 472; Richard E. Prince, *Norfolk Southern Railroad, Old Dominion Line and Connections*, p. 207–47. (Particulars on steamboat *Olive*, p. 225); see also John L. Lochhead, "Steamships and Steamboats of the Old Dominion Line." John Lochhead was for many years the knowledgable librarian

of the Mariners' Museum, Newport News. An Old Dominion Line historian as well as a former purser on its steamers, he states sadly that "early records of the Old Dominion's Virginia and Carolina Divisions are meager," though citing the *Olive* as first of the southermost division's vessels. More will be recorded about these operations in the following chapter.

FIG. 18. *Wood, screw steamboat* Olive, *built at Norfolk in 1869, became the first vessel of the Old Dominion Line's Carolina Sounds division. She originally ran from Norfolk to ["Little"] Washington, N.C., and New Bern. She was acquired by the Old Dominion Line in June 1872 and was finally abandoned as the* Hertford *in 1924. (Photo courtesy the Mariners Museum.)*

"for the comfort of a limited number of passengers." Quite likely this vessel turned out to be the *Astoria,* noted in the *Journal* of March 17, 1870, as "lately built at the Atlantic Iron Works of this city," and "placed by its enterprising owners, Messrs. C. W. Grundy and D. D. Simms, on the Roanoke River through the Albemarle and Chesapeake Canal."[26] No further mention about transporting fish appears, however.

Another canal steamer of the time which should be noted was the little Currituck Sound iron paddle-wheeler *Cygnet.* She was first advertised in the *Journal* in 1869 "for Princess Anne and Currituck;" later that year as being well suited for "pic-nics and private excursions;" and also mentioned as sailing "frequently for all points of Currituck Sound and the duck area."[27] That duck hunting was an increasingly popular diversion of people coming from far away is attested by the November 5, 1868, advertisement announcing the departure of the steamer *Gazelle* from Norfolk on a "Ducking Excursion bound for Currituck Sound with a party of New York sportsmen."[28] Year after year, the *Cygnet*—appropriately named, since her cargo was so frequently barrels of wildfowl bound for northern markets—enjoyed the distinction of having made a greater number of passages through the locks at Great Bridge than any other canal traveler.[29]

Though the four-miles-per-hour speed limit enforced for vessels plying the canal cuts insured against disastrous collisions, there were plenty of untoward experiences to which a canal steamer was prone—running aground or impaling itself on a snag, not to mention being delayed by engine breakdown or the transit of unwieldy tows. However, one of the worst accidents in the canal's history occurred on May 10, 1872, from still a different cause. Like the canal company's tug *Coinjock* seven years earlier, the little steamer *Rotary,* a regular canal traveler, experienced a boiler explosion. The boat's engineer was killed along with some of his family, who happened to be on board as passengers. Capt. William Y. Johnson and several members of the crew were injured to varying degrees, and the canal was blocked by the wreck for some time before the *Rotary* could be hauled clear.

As its name implied, the *Rotary* was equipped with a

---

[26] Norfolk *Journal,* August 25, 1868, and Marsh 17, 1870, cited in Emmerson, comp., "Steam Navigation, 1837–1860," pp. 467, 474. The *Astoria* was evidently completed too late to receive mention in the *Lytle-Holdcamper List,* p. 14.

[27] Norfolk *Journal,* February 26, August 29, and December 22, 1869, cited in Emmerson, comp., "Steam Navigation, 1837–1860," pp. 470, 473.

[28] Norfolk *Journal,* November 5, 1868, cited in Emmerson, "Steam Navigation, 1837–1860," p. 468.

[29] Duck Shooting became a major industry of market gunners in the Currituck–Back Bay area—today performed without mass slaughter to protect the species. Customarily the birds would be loaded on local sharpies and sailed to such rendezvous points as Buck Island, partway up the North River, and there they would be loaded on board the *Cygnet* or another steamer or, along with as many as a dozen other sailing craft, be made up into a tow and hauled thence through the canal to Norfolk in tandem by a steam tug. In season, this practice continued down into the present century. (Jack Baum, "A History of Market Hunting in the Currituck Sound Area," p. 14.)

novel steam-turbine engine. Built in Brooklyn, New York, in 1859, the 196-ton screw vessel had been brought south after the war and was then running regularly down the canal to the Albemarle Sound, thence up the Chowan and Meherrin rivers to Murfreesboro. The explosion occurred without warning early in the morning while the boat was steaming along halfway through the Virginia Cut, Norfolk-bound. A lurid account appeared in the Norfolk *Journal* the next day:

Yesterday morning, Marshall Parks, Pres't of the A & C Canal Co., received a letter through Mr. D. C. Crowell of this city from Capt. Wm. Y. Johnson, of the steamer *Rotary*, which runs up the canal to Murfreesborough and other points, stating that the boiler of the steamer had exploded and killed the engineer, and that the engineer's wife and child and sister were drowned. He asked that a doctor and coroner be sent up at once. . . . Mr. Parks embarked on the steamer *Chowan* [the company tug], Capt. Ives, at 12 M. for the scene of the disaster. . . . Shortly after passing through the locks at Great Bridge, late in the afternoon, the party arrived at Old's Point, the scene of the disaster, which is about 17 miles from Norfolk and about three up the canal.

Here a horrible sight presented itself to the view. The *Rotary* was a shattered mass of splintered wood and distorted iron lying half way across the canal, preventing the egress of no less than six steamers, while three other steamers and several sailing vessels were prevented from passing through on their way up.

Lying partly in the water at the base of the bank opposite the *Rotary*, [were] the dead bodies of the engineer, his wife and child and sister; and on board the steamer *Lynnhaven*, which lay at the stern of the *Rotary*, were the captain, mate and crew. The steward who was badly hurt, lay under the awning in the forward part of the boat.

The captain, although suffering from a very painful bruise on his right leg, was seated on a chair, and willingly gave the reporters all the information in his power. He says that the steamer left Murfreesborough last Friday night, but had been delayed by getting aground, and did not reach Old's Point until 7 o'clock yesterday morning. On board the boat, beside his regular crew, were his son, and the engineer's wife, child and sister. The captain and a Negro man named Isaac Knox were in the pilot house forward. Suddenly they heard the crashing of timber and the next moment they were hurled into the water. Swimming to the shore, the captain found that his son and several of the crew had preceded him and were already on the bank. He heard some one say: "Oh Captain! save that lady." He looked around, but saw no one.

The assistant engineer immediately plunged overboard and swam to the wreck, but was too late to save the unfortunate woman, whose death struggles had attracted his attention. . . . The bodies of Mrs. Wm. Walke, wife of the engineer, Mrs. Elizabeth Crane, his sister, and that of the child were found in the canal under the wreck of the cabin. The engineer's body was found in the canal several yards above the place.

The captain had no idea of the cause of the explosion. He says that he heard one of the firemen say, since the disaster, that the engineer said that there was a small hole in the top of the boiler, but that it would last until they got to Norfolk. He thought that the engineer was carrying 40 pounds of steam at the time. . . . The forward head of the boiler was blown out. The freight house, engine house, pilot house and, in fact, nearly everything on the deck was blown off. The forward part of the boat was literally blown to splinters. Barrels of fish and pieces of wreckage were floating in the canal for miles. Such was the force of the explosion that a yawl boat was blown over the bank 50 yards into the woods and we saw a piece of timber lodged in a tree 60 feet above the ground. . . . The crew consisted of Capt. Wm. Y. Johnson; the captain's son, temporary clerk; Wm. Walke, engineer; Jefferson Lee, assistant engineer; Wm. Bowser, steward; William Miller, fireman; Isaiah Hooper. The engineer's wife and little girl, about 18 months old, were returning to their home on Ferry Point from a visit to relatives in Currituck County.

The *Rotary* was owned by Capt. Johnson, who bought her about a year ago, and was insured for $4,000 in the "Andes" of Cincinnati. During the war she was used by the Federals as a water boat in the harbor and Hampton Roads. She had a rotary engine, hence her name.

The dead were placed in the steamer *I. A. Waters* and sent to Currituck County, and the others were brought to Norfolk on the *Lynnhaven*.[30]

Through the greater part of the decade following the Civil War, use of the Albemarle and Chesapeake Canal had been increasing at a commendable rate, though admittedly this continued to be at the expense of the more seriously war-damaged Dismal Swamp Canal. Actually, however, the latter had found itself in dire straits from the moment the larger and more expeditiously navigated Albemarle and Chesapeake Canal had been opened. Following the nationwide financial panic beginning in September 1873, traffic fell off on the new waterway as well. Fortunately, the depression—though severe—did not last very long; business revived again, and with it, the canal's prosperity returned.

Figures given in the yearly summaries for 1867 through 1875 have been taken from company annual reports.[31] On occasion, the figures do not balance out correctly, but no attempt has been made to verify the numbers given, even though different totals often appear even in the same report. The year ending September 30, 1866, has already been cited. Tolls, towing, and wharfage provided $57,379.47, and the total number of transits through the canal by vessels of all types came to 3,643, an increase of 1,026 over 1865—which was, of course, only a partial year for navigation, following the war.

---

[30] Norfolk *Journal*, May 11, 1872, quoted in Emmerson, comp., "Steam Navigation, 1837–1860," p. 480. The appearance of a steamer named *Rotary* (official no. 21471, 186 tons), registered in Norfolk in 1877 (U.S. Treasury Department, *List of Merchant Vessels of the United States*), suggests that the vessel was salvaged and rebuilt following its canal accident. The *Rotary* was no longer registered after 1883.

[31] A & C Canal Co., *Tenth Annual Report* through *Twentieth Annual Report*, (1866–75).

For the succeeding year, ending September 30, 1867, the *Twelfth Annual Report,* gave a total of forty-one steam vessels plying the canal, of which the largest listed were the 262-ton stern-wheeler *Orient,* the 250-ton lighthouse-tender *Heliotrope,* and the brand-new, 252-ton *Old North State.* Vessels of all varieties made a total of 4,243 passages through the canal in 1867—an increase of 600 trips over the previous year. Tolls paid by northbound craft amounted to $38,186.77 and southbound to $10,495.24, for a total of $46,682.01. Towing fees collected by company tugs were $6,653.53 northbound and $4,157.30 southbound, totaling $10,810.83. Along with payments amounting to $3,530.51 from miscellaneous sources including wharfage, this gave a grand total of $60,023.00 in receipts for all operations of the company in 1867.

For the year ending September 30, 1868, there were 2,385 northbound craft and 2,345 southbound totaling 4,730 and producing $61,089.19 in full earnings for tolls, towing, and other services—only a slight increase from the previous year, even though many more ships transited the canal. The *Thirteenth Annual Report* listed the names of 121 vessels, this year broken down by types into 39 steamers, 52 schooners, 15 sloops, and 15 barges. As might be expected, all but the 39 steamers —some 82 named vessels—went through on the end of towlines. In comparison with today's costs, it is interesting to note, that among other expenses for operating the canal a little more than a century ago were $5,360 for the combined salaries of president ($2,000), secretary ($1,200), and collector ($1,000),

plus other modest stipends for lockkeepers, bridge-tenders, and a lighthouse keeper.

For the year ending September 30, 1869, the *Fourteenth Annual Report's* list of vessels passing through the canal had risen to 44 steamers, 136 schooners, 46 sloops, and 22 barges: a total of 242 vessels of all kinds. Of these, 204 were unpowered and had to be towed, and 44 went under their own steam. Some 4,488 passages were recorded—242 more than in 1868—but total receipts were down to $56,894.91.

The following year, 1870, saw a total of 4,382 vessels passing through, almost equally divided between northbound and southbound. Of the 1,487 trips made by steam craft (who paid $24,896.92 in tolls), the little *Cygnet* again headed the list with 210 trips, for which her owners paid $1,025.40. Next came the company's own tugs, *Chowan* and *Croatan,* with 181 and 116 passages respectively. Fifty-six named steamers were recorded. For the five-years period 1866–70, total tolls were computed at $235,822.70, and total towing fees at $53,828.97.

Toll receipts for 1871 mounted to $55,778.72—a gain of $8,116.16—with 4,900 transits. However, towing was down $2,760.79 from the previous year. Of fifty-one steamers cited by name, once more the little *Cygnet* made the greatest number of trips, 219, and the towboat *Chowan* had the second highest number, 165. The steady increase in the company's business was noted in the *Sixteenth Annual Report* and a summary from another source commented: "The freight brought to Norfolk by the canal embraced large quantities of cotton, salt, fish, turpentine, lumber, shingles, staves, railroad ties, wood, juniper logs, bacon, peas and beans, wheat, fresh shad, watermelons, etc. Forest products of timber amounted to over 60 million feet of board measure."[32]

Cumulative totals for eleven-year active life-span of the canal—1860–71—recorded a grand total of 35,050 ship transits of the waterway since it first opened. This was broken down to 11,292 steamers, 6,832 schooners, 2,030 sloops, 5,812 lighters, 1,991 barges, 209 rafts, and 6,002 boats. Receipts from all sources were listed at $523,796.16. By any standard, this was an impressive amount of business, producing more than half a million dollars and well justifying a century of dreamers and planners' beliefs that the canal would be successful. Even so, the management confessed that it was still "astonished at the progress" that the canal had made.[33]

Toll and towing receipts went up again in 1872 and amounted to $60,846.64 and $10,251.58 (or $10,859.61—both figures are given) respectively. In any event, there was an increase from both sources of more than $6,000 from the year before. Some 4,808 transits were made through the canal, and the list contained the names of 57 steamers. One of the hazards of canal navigation is indicated by the notation in that year's report of $3,000 spent "for a large float for clearing the canal of logs."[34] In a waterlogged state,

they could readily punch holes in the bottoms of un-suspecting vessels.

The *Eighteenth Annual Report* for 1873 indicated that total receipts from tolls and towing had reached the commendable height of $84,084.40—some $12,000 more than the year before. This issue of the *Report* also presented cumulative totals, citing 45,799 ship passages between 1861 and 1873. Money collected each year was given as follows, but these totals vary from those already given from year to year. The $84,084.40 above becomes $84,839.04 in the yearly list below.

1866—$	50,588.29
1867—	59,492.84
1868—	58,270.57
1869—	56,525.86
1870—	58,230.17
1871—	64,585.59
1872—	71,098.22
1873—	84,839.04
Total:	503,630.48[35]

The year 1874 reflected the effects of the depression, but only partially. Total transits amounted to 6,283, of which 2,214 were made by steamers. Tolls generated $71,657.34 and towing, $12,430.06—for a total of $84,087.40. Apparently the company elected at this time to give up the towing business, for reasons

---

[32] Jedediah Hotchkiss, *Virginia: A Geophysical and Political Summary*, p. 231.

[33] A & C Canal Co., *Sixteenth Annual Report* (1871), p. 9.

[34] A & C Canal Co., *Eighteenth Annual Report* (1873), p. 16.

[35] Ibid.

unexplained, and to let commercial interests handle it entirely. In any event, the *Nineteenth Annual Report* noted that the tugs *Chowan* and *Croatan* were both sold in August 1874, for the seemingly modest sum of $1,209.00. They might well have been worn-out, however. Total company receipts from all sources are given in the treasurer's report at $97,788.50, leaving a balance of $4,033.81.[36]

The *Twentieth Annual Report* for the year ending September 30, 1875, recorded 2,408 passages made by steam vessels with the total toll charges produced standing at $76,055.27. Towing, "by *Chowan, Croatan, Virginia,* etc." gave $19,576.46. Elsewhere in the *Report* is the notation: "towing transferred to purchaser of tugs, $20,115.37." The company treasurer's report gave total receipts and disbursements as $100,670.71, showing a balance of $3,692.00. In its "Statement of Affairs," the company's authorized capital at this time was still a million and a half dollars. Total liabilities were $1,303,034.34, of which the greatest amount was $350,000.00 in stock held by the state of North Carolina.[37]

As has just been pointed out, financially the Albemarle and Chesapeake Canal was doing well and had made commendable recoveries both from the Civil War and from the subsequent depression. Physical aspects of the canal were to give continual concern, however. Unfortunately, serious troubles began to develop in the area of the Great Bridge lock in the immediate postwar period. This situation became critical when it was feared that leaks in the floor of the chamber might well threaten "the whole structure."[38]

To get to the source, company engineers built temporary earthen dams across the canal at both ends of the lock, which was then pumped dry. The management spared no expense in order to get the job accomplished as quickly as possible, even importing skilled labor from New York. But even at that, the lock remained inoperative from November 16, 1865, until January 24 of the next year while the leaks were located and stopped. Though they determined that the "foundation, floor and masonry [was] in good condition," when the lock was empty, it was also observed that the gates were "much decayed" and their replacement would soon have to be carried out as well.[39]

Further trouble near the lock occurred the following year, necessitating the construction of a "new dam across the ravine running into the mill pond near Great Bridge."[40] In 1865, the company, "at great expense," had built a wasteway in that area to relieve the lock of excess pressure when storms backed up water in the Elizabeth River. This structure was carried away in July of 1867, however. Then, after a new and stronger timber-piled dam was built to replace the original one, a steam dredge was brought in to remove

[36] A & C Canal Co., *Nineteenth Annual Report* (1874), p. 10.
[37] A & C Canal Co., *Twentieth Annual Report* (1875), p. 7.
[38] A & C Canal Co., *Eleventh Annual Report* (1866), p. 3.
[39] Ibid.
[40] A & C Canal Co., *Twelfth Annual Report* (1867), p. 5.

shoals from the channel, caused by the break. A portion of the canal between the drawbridge and the lock was then sheet-piled.[41] Even this strongly reinforced dam was fated to carry away again, however, and this spot was to prove a continual headache to the company for several more years to come.

Drawbridge problems also began to develop. All three of the company's roadway swing bridges—at Great Bridge, North Landing, and Coinjock—had been destroyed at one time or another during the war and "replaced in a great hurry with inferior lumber," which soon evidenced decay. In 1867 the maintenance force was kept busy patching up the bridges until completely new ones, all with a forty-four foot swing, could be built. But during 1868, the draw at Great Bridge collapsed anyway, and an unfortunate horse was lost. Then, in the dead of winter, the Coinjock bridge was frozen, and it was carried away by a passing steamer.[42] Though in 1869 the bridges were reported as being in "good order," the one at Great Bridge had been damaged again when run into by the steamboat *Louise*. When rebuilt, "the amount expended will be collected from that vessel," the company stockholders were reassured.[43]

With the leak problem solved, the 220-foot by 40-foot lock had been pronounced in satisfactory shape in the 1868 *Thirteenth Annual Report*, and the company was obviously well satisfied with its operation in 1871 observing that, by doubling up, "rafts half a mile in length pass through the lock without being disconnected. . . . Lumbermen appreciate this arrangement."[44] Disassembling a lengthy tow only to have to put it back together again was a time-consuming process hardly appreciated by those who had to do it or by the operators of other craft waiting their turns to get on through the lock. But it was now obvious that the ten-year-old gates would require at least partial renewal during the ensuing year. "It is a question whether it would not be true economy to make them to iron—galvanized iron—and estimates will be invited," the 1868 *Report* stated.[45]

Though nothing was done about the gates right away, a firm decision to try out metal ones was reached at that time. A subsequent *Report* in 1871 boasted that there still were no gates made of this material on any existing American canals, and "if we introduce them . . . we shall be the pioneer in this as we have been in so many other improvements."[46]

Two pairs of iron gates and one new pair of wooden ones were put on order for the company in 1872 at a cost of $3,600 for the iron and $1,200 for the wooden. The next year they were installed and immediately began to give satisfactory service. The *Seventeenth Annual Report* noted that "having erected two pairs of

[41] Ibid.
[42] A & C Canal Co., *Thirteenth Annual Report* (1868), p. 8.
[43] A & C Canal Co., *Fourteenth Annual Report* (1869), p. 8.

[44] A & C Canal Co., *Sixteenth Annual Report* (1871), pp. 6–7.
[44] A & C Canal Co., *Thirteenth Annual Report* (1868), p. 9.
[46] A & C Canal Co., *Sixteenth Annual Report* (1871), p. 7.

wood and two pairs of iron gates at the same time, and in the same lock, will at least test their respective merits." "To provide against disaster, one pair of old [spare] gates have been repaired and made ready for any contingency," the next *Report* noted.[47]

From the very beginning shoaling was a continuing problem for the canal engineers, for the surge of water rising in the wake of passing vessels produced waves which washed up the banks and brought sediment back down into the canal bed. Where to dispose of dredged material —for if deposited too near the edge of the canal it would slide right back in the channel—was a taxing problem. Since the banks did not have to be kept clear, as in a towpath canal, planting vegetation down to the water's edge to hold the earth was encouraged.

Except for the overland cuts, which obviously were the canal company's own obligation to maintain, there were several places along the line of navigation in public waters, particularly Currituck Sound, where it might well be argued that the federal government had the major responsibility. Such a place was a six-mile-long stretch known as Blackwater Flats Channel, which supposedly had a nine-foot depth of water but where, it the area where the Blackwater River discharged into Currituck Sound at the upper end near Faraby Island, shoaling was a perpetual nuisance. Silt brought down by the river was the culprit, and the company had hoped that Congress would appropriate funds for its removal. Since the government persisted in dragging its feet, however, the company was at length forced to undertake the work itself, employing one of its own dredges there from July through November 1868. Unfortunately, a violent gale capsized and sank the dredge, which took several thousand dollars to raise and repair. Meanwhile, it remained out of service until July of 1869. Faced by continual slides of sand, however, and since its own "steam dredge was not deemed sufficient," the company was forced to hire a "powerful machine of the Virginia Dredging Company."[48]

In the region where the mouth of the North Landing River expanded from half a mile to two miles in width, boats had to be guided through the 35- to 40-foot dredged channel by a line of stakes. The stakes cost the company $15,078.87 to install, and it proved difficult to keep them in place since they could readily come adrift in stormy weather or under icy conditions. Although driven log piles of thick wood would have been more durable and permanent as channel markers, the hazard of vessels running into them and injuring themselves was too great, hence the use of more limber— also more breakable—poles. The annual expense of maintaining the stakes is indicated in the *Reports* for several years thereafter. Actually, what was needed was a lighthouse on Faraby Island from which ships might take bearings, for the small stakes were difficult to see at night even under the best conditions.[49]

---

[47] A & C Canal Co., *Seventeenth Annual Report* (1872), p. 6; *Eighteenth Annual Report* (1873), p. 4.

[48] A & C Canal Co., *Sixteenth Annual Report* (1871), p. 6.
[49] Ibid., p. 4.

At the northern end of the canal, there was a crying need for dredging the headwaters of the continually silting Southern Branch of the Elizabeth River. The *Sixteenth Annual Report* of 1871 noted that at low tide there was only five feet of water up to the outboard lock gates, and many deeper-draft vessels had to wait out in the stream until a flooding tide provided sufficient depth for them to reach the lock. The dredging of federal waters was the responsibility of the government, but the Army Engineers demurred, and the company itself was forced to go to work on one bad spot in the Elizabeth River, some 350 yards in length, known as the Nicaragua Bar.

The *Eighteenth Annual Report* stated that "at several points the Company have also improved the [Elizabeth] River. A cutoff has been made through a point in the river below the lock improving the channel very much."[50] This was evidently in the area presently facing the docks of the former Richmond Cedar Works at Camden Mills. Additional straightening of the channel leading to the lock was suggested in 1875 as a project for the Army Engineers, as well as digging "a short [bypass] canal a few hundred yards in length".[51]

As previously mentioned, a number of these channel loops—or oxbows, so picturesquely termed because of their resemblance to the U-shaped harness yokes for oxen—existed in the upper reaches of both the Elizabeth and the North Landing rivers. The latter were particularly crooked for the first three miles below the drawbridge at North Landing. These river bends were also referred to in the company *Reports* as "Dutch Gaps," after the famous Civil War cutoff canal dug under fire by Union troops to eliminate a Confederate fortified loop in the James River above City Point. At length the company "caused a number of its points to be cut off," so straightening the river and leaving half-moon shaped islands behind an improved dredged navigation.[52] The then-bypassed loops soon became a burial ground for generations of worn-out derelict craft hauled into them and abandoned.

Along with believing that dredging was the government's responsibility, the company felt that it was also responsible for providing much-needed navigation lights and lighthouses along the more than fifty-mile-long river routes of the canal. Application for these installations was first made to the government prior to the Civil War, and in 1860 Congress had appropriated $10,000 for a screw-pile lighthouse for placement in Albemarle Sound at the wide mouth of the North River, as an indication of the commencement of the canal's northbound route. In addition, $500 was appropriated for buoys "on the line of navigation."[53]

The North River entrance lighthouse, one of major importance, was not built until 1867, however, and the company's application for other lights—at Mackey's Island in Currituck Sound and at Faraby Island at the

[50] A & C Canal Co., *Eighteenth Annual Report* (1873), p. 3.

[51] A & C Canal Co., *Twentieth Annual Report* (1875), p. 4.

[52] A & C Canal Co., *Eighteenth Annual Report* (1873), p. 5.

[53] A & C Canal Co., *Tenth Annual Report* (1860–65), p. 4.

A Glimpse of Norfolk, Virginia.

Fig. 19. *"A glimpse of Norfolk, Virginia"—woodcut from* The Great South, *by Edward King (Hartford, Conn., 1875).*

mouth of the North Landing River—was not acted upon for several more years. Having dredged Blackwater Channel in 1869, the company installed its own temporary lighthouse there. But the need for the light of Faraby Island continued to be cited in several more issues of the company annual reports. "It would be of great assistance to the pilots," the company bemoaned.[54] It had been mentioned earlier, however, that "experiments are now being made with petroleum gas lights which . . . burn continually without the atten-

tion of a keeper. . . . Should these simple structures prove successful, steamers may traverse the entire navigation as well in the night as the day."[55]

In 1872, these lights were referred to as Dr. S. K. Jackson's patented "self-acting lights," and the company then proposed to illuminate Blackwater Channel with three of the automatic lights, in addition to those which it had set up off Bell's Island and Mackie's Island. At Long Point, at the northern entrance to the North Carolina Cut, a large lantern was displayed on the roof

---

[54] A & C Canal Co., *Sixteenth Annual Report* (1871), p. 3.

[55] A & C Canal Co., *Twelfth Annual Report* (1867), p. 6.

of a house built there that served as the residence of the canal's section master—so, in effect, becoming a lighthouse as well.[56]

Telegraph lines had been employed successfully to the great advantage of both sides during the Civil War. In 1874 a private line for company use was proposed, running from the Norfolk office to the lock at Great Bridge, thence along the Virginia Cut to North Landing, where it could also serve the Roper Lumber Company's mill near the landing—a total distance of some twenty-five miles. This would prove useful for canal operation—as, for example, when grounded boats required help from Norfolk-based tugs. Undoubtedly the need for such instant communication was keenly felt at the time of the disaster to the steamboat *Rotary*. The same Dr. Jackson who experimented with the automatic lights was reported as supervising the work as chief electrician, and the cost of the installation was given as $1,545.35 in the *Nineteenth Annual Report*.[57]

In 1872 the canal management elected to diversify its activities, and it entered into an agreement to make available its talents and equipment to excavate a sea-level canal in low-lying Hyde County, North Carolina, on the south side of Albemarle Sound. The resultant Fairfield Canal, 4½ miles long and 6 feet deep, was intended to open landlocked Lake Mattamuskett northward to the Alligator River. One of the company's dredges worked on the new canal from January to August 1, 1872, and then quit, owing not only to it being the "sickly season," but more importantly, because the dredge failed. A new dredge, costing $22,500, was built during the remainder of the year, and during the course of 1873, work on the Fairfield Canal was resumed and was nearly completed by the year's end.[58]

In addition to draining the surrounding low, marshy countryside, so improving the land in the process, Albemarle and Chesapeake Canal Company officials expressed the not unreasonable hope that the new waterway would prove a valuable feeder for their own canal. The new steam dredge *Albemarle* completely finished the work the next year, providing navigation for vessels of six-foot draft. No locks were required. But still a few more years were to pass before even a small steamer was regularly employed to make only tri-weekly runs between Fairfield and Elizabeth City.[59]

A serious national financial panic was precipitated by the failure on September 18, 1873, of the New York banking house of Jay Cooke and Company—said to have been, as were many other banks, over-involved in railroad finance. However, the Albemarle and Chesapeake Canal contrived to weather the ensuing depression—"which came upon the company so unexpectedly," President Parks confessed. He also observed in the company's *Twenty-First Annual Report* that the "past fis-

---

[56] A & C Canal Co., *Twentieth Annual Report* (1875), p. 5.
[57] A & C Canal Co., *Nineteenth Annual Report* (1874), pp. 6–7.

[58] A & C Canal Co., *Seventeenth Annual Report* (1872), p. 4; *Eighteenth Annual Report* (1873), p. 8.
[59] A & C Canal Co., *Twenty-Fifth Annual Report* (1880), p. 9.

cal year [1875] will be long remembered," and he cited "many failures in our mercantile community." He also noted that the nation's railroads had drastically reduced their rates "to keep up a show of business" but that the nation's canals have "fallen off but little during the year."[60]

On September 30, 1875, Parks had proudly reported that the canal had experienced "not a single day's interruption during the entire fiscal year." Although the lumber market was still depressed, one of the canal's mainstays—cotton—was increasing. Though

he was still trying to persuade the federal government to take a more active part in improving the route of the canal, Parks noted that "Congress at last spent some money."[61]

By and large, the decade following the termination of hostilities had seen a remarkable recovery, not only of the canal but of the entire region that it served. The waterway provided "good navigation" for 6½-foot draft throughout the line, and prospects were bright for the following ten-year period to be one of prosperity under the continuing leadership of popular Commodore Marshall Parks.

[60] A & C Canal Co., *Nineteenth Annual Report* (1874), p. 4; *Twenty-first Annual Report* (1876), p. 4.

[61] A & C Canal Co., *Twenty-First Annual Report* (1876), p. 4.

Shipwrecks and
Surveys, Late 1870s

The North Carolina Outer Banks had long taken a grisly toll in lives of shipwrecked mariners. In the late 1870s, two particularly grim disasters occurred, which produced a renewed public outcry and the demand that something be done about it. Although better found ships and more competent navigators apparently were the only guarantees for sailing these dangerously exposed waters without hazard, proposals were strongly advanced for the federal government to take over the Albemarle and Chesapeake Canal forthwith. Despite the fact that it would have been a physical impossibility to convert it to an oceangoing ship canal—thus eliminating the necessity for coastwise shipping to risk the heavily traveled outside route around disaster-prone Cape Hatteras—it was argued that under government auspices, the existing canal could be materially enlarged and deepened for the benefit of a greatly increased amount of traffic.

The first of the two highly publicized shipwrecks of late 1877 and early 1878 was the U.S. iron steam barkentine *Huron*, which came to grief near Kitty Hawk on November 24, 1877. She was followed ashore on January 31, 1878, by the bark-rigged auxiliary screw steamer *Metropolis*, wrecked at Nag's Head.[1]

---

[1] These two shipwrecks are well described in David Stick, *Graveyard of the Atlantic*, pp. 73–85 (*Huron*), and pp. 86–194 (*Metropolis*). See also John C. Emmerson, Jr., comp., "Wrecks on the Outer Banks: A Series of Articles from Various Newspapers," typescript (Portsmouth, Va., 1956), chaps. 6–7, pp. 35–57 (*Huron*) and pp. 58–74 (*Metropolis*).

The *Huron* was a well-manned naval steamer. Her commanding officer felt no particular anxiety in setting sail despite existing bad weather, and the steam barkentine left Hampton Roads bound for Havanna on November 23. An angry southeast gale was blowing, and at 1:30 the next morning, the *Huron* unexpectedly grounded and was immediately gripped by the sand. With the wind driving her onto this dangerous lee shore, her engine was powerless to pull the 541-ton vessel free. Of 132 officers and men on board, only 34 made it ashore alive through the pounding surf, and her skipper, Commander George P. Ryan, USN, was not one of them.

According to a contemporary account: "The night was intensely dark," and unsuspected variation in the ship's magnetic compass was held to blame for the vessel straying in too close to the beach in the first place. Delay in the men reaching the scene from the Kitty Hawk Lifesaving Station, a dozen miles away, and setting up a breeches buoy, was said to account for the heavy loss of life.[2]

———

[2] *Frank Leslie's Illustrated Newspaper* (New York), supplement, December 8, 1877, pp. 233–36 (cited hereafter as *Leslie's Weekly*); *Harper's Weekly*, December 15, 1877 pp. 979, 986–89, and December 29, 1887, p. 1024. The latter reference depicts a bitter full-page cartoon showing Uncle Sam overlooking dead bodies washed up on a beach, with the *Huron* wreck in the background. Entitled "Death on Economy," Uncle Sam is quoted. "I suppose I must spend a little on Life-Saving Service, Life-boat Stations, Life-boats, Surf-boats, etc; but it is too bad to be obliged to waste so much money."

Those of the *Huron* survivors who reached land were escorted to the Roanoke Sound side of the banks island, and there they embarked on board the little 100-foot Currituck Sound side-wheel steamboat *Bonito*, a regular canal traveler of the Norfolk and Princess Anne Steamboat Company, and were taken on up the waterway to Norfolk.

Two months later, the wooden-hulled auxiliary screw steamer *Metropolis* was lost in the same general area, under virtually identical circumstances. The 879-ton, bark-rigged vessel, bound from Philadelphia to Brazil, was old, and it was subsequently determined that she was not particularly seaworthy, since she had been lengthened without adequate reinforcement during a recent overhaul. This hastened the vessel's subsequent breakup in the surf. Despite this dangerous condition, however, the *Metropolis* was carrying a heavy deadweight cargo consisting of a thousand tons of building materials destined for a railway in Boliva. Early in the morning of January 31, 1878, the *Metropolis*, like the *Huron*, grounded on Currituck Beach, and nearly 100 of the 248 people on board—mostly construction workers going down to build the railroad—were drowned during what survivors described as a terrific gale, which totally wrecked the ship.

Captain Ankers, who survived, denounced "the conduct of the men attached to the life-saving station" at Kitty Hawk, but did not comment on the fact that his unseaworthy vessel was overloaded and apparently incompetently navigated. In any event, it was six hours after the ship went ashore before the first of the too-few lifesavers arrived on the scene.[3]

As with the *Huron* survivors, the 127 bedraggled men of the *Metropolis* were also taken across the narrow banks island to a sound-side dock, this one opposite the premises of the Currituck Light Shooting Club. From there, they were brought to Norfolk by the faithful little canal steamer *Cygnet,* running mate of the *Bonito*—described by a reporter sent down from New York by *Frank Leslie's Illustrated Newspaper* as "a very small steamer used on the Albemarle and Chesapeake Canal principally for the conveyance of wildfowl." A spirited woodcut, depicting the night arrival of the overloaded steamboat at Norfolk, shows the castaways disembarking Saturday, February 2, (fig. 20). The next day the same reporter boarded the *Cygnet,* "freighted with coffins for the dead washed ashore," for her return to the Outer Banks so that he might see just where the wreck occurred.[4]

Then, less than a month after that, on a stormy February 21, 1878, a German bark—not, at that time, identified by name—was driven ashore on Hatteras Beach, and all sixteen men on board perished. The event wrung the following editorial comment from a Dare County writer in the *Economist:* "Oh, why won't Congress, without delay, stop this frightful sacrifice of life by going around the Hatteras horrors through an inland communication? One year's losses on the coast will pay every expense."[5]

Although criticism of the shortcomings of the Albemarle and Chesapeake Canal was certainly undeserved when applied to these grim ocean catastrophies, President Parks was constrained to refer to 1878 in his *Twenty-Third Annual Report* as an "eventful year," stating that the offshore wrecks had "created a great sensation," and again directing congressional attention to the "inland route free from the dangers of Hatteras."[6]

Since Secretary Gallatin first proposed his now sixty-year-old plan for creating a continuous inland water channel from north to south along the Atlantic seaboard, there had been several attempts at reviving that idea. By an act of May 3, 1836, Congress had appropriated money to continue surveys along this "grand internal line of water communication," the idea being

---

[3] *Harper's Weekly,* February 16, 1878 p. 127; February 23, 1878, p. 158; March 9, 1878, p. 204; and April 20, 1878, p. 315.
[4] *Leslie's Weekly,* February 17, 1878, pp. 411–13; February 23, 1878, pp. 428–29; and March 2, 1878, pp. 448, 451. *Leslie's Weekly* gave full coverage to this disaster, sending a reporter to Norfolk to interview survivors brought there by the steamboat *Cygnet* and then to visit the wreck site. Three woodcut illustrations appeared in the magazine on the dates cited above. Seventy-five years after the shipwreck, Mariners' Museum curator Robert H. Burgess, accompanied by Museum librarian John L. Lochhead, visited the beach at Currituck and identified timbers surviving from the vessel, later contributing an interesting article, "The *Metropolis* on Currituck Bank," to the Norfolk *Virginia-Pilot* Sunday feature section, January 31, 1954.

[5] Dare County (N.C.) *Economist.* March 5, 1878, quoted in John C. Emmerson, Jr., Comp., "Shipwrecks along the North Carolina and Virginia Coasts, 1797–1939," typescript of articles from various newspapers (Portsmouth, Va.; assembled by the author, 1956), p. 359.
[6] A & C Canal Co., *Twenty-Third Annual Report* (1878), p. 3.

FIG. 20. *The 1869-built side-wheel canal steamer* Cygnet *of the Currituck Line brought the survivors of the shipwrecked steamship* Metropolis *from the Carolina Outer Banks to Norfolk on the night of February 2, 1878. Woodcut illustration from* Leslie's Weekly, *February 23, 1878. (Courtesy the Mariners Museum.)*

to open an inside channel running from the Chesapeake all the way down to Charleston, South Carolina, and thus to avoid the twin hazards of Cape Hatteras and Frying Pan Shoals. Topographical Engineer Maj. James Kearney undertook partial surveys to cover the route from Dismal Swamp down to Winyaw Bay near Georgetown, South Carolina. These were carried forward in 1838 by his successor, Col. J. J. Abert.[7]

The task had never been completed, however, and interest on the part of the federal government had waxed and waned without any tangible work on the project being done. In the meantime, the building of the Albemarle and Chesapeake Canal was being carried out by private interests.

In 1875, however, prompted by the receipt of a memorial from the Norfolk and Portsmouth Cotton Exchange addressed to the Chief of the U.S. Army Engineers (Brig. Gen. A. A. Humphreys), the project had once more been given attention. The Exchange's memorial, passed on to Secretary of War William W. Belknap, was received too late for congressional action that year, but its principal resolution—that a channel be constructed "from the waters of Pamlico Sound to Cape Fear River, by such route as may be practicable, and from said river to Georgetown, South Carolina"— was a reasonable one. By extending southward the protected-waters navigation already gained by access to the Carolina Sounds via the Albemarle and Chesapeake Canal at Hampton Roads, the memorial stated that the improvements would connect "the principal cities on the Atlantic coast with the corn, cotton, and timber regions of the Southern States. . . . furnishing at all times a cheap and ready means for the transportation of the products of the country to market. . . ."[8]

A report dated February 21, 1876, by the Chief of Engineers had covered the *Survey of a Line to Connect . . . the Waters of Norfolk Harbor,* made by U.S. Civil Engineer S. T. Abert.[9] The Neuse River is the principal southernmost tributary of Pamlico Sound. New Bern, the largest settlement, is located at the confluence of the Neuse and its tributary Trent River.

In 1878, the same year that the second of three major ship disasters occurred on the Outer Banks, Congress, by the River and Harbor Act of June 18, appropriate $20,000 for the project of making thorough surveys along the Carolina coast and rivers. This was intended not only to reexamine properly the lines of the existing Dismal Swamp and Albemarle and Chesapeake Canals with an eye to improving them but also to determine an appropriate outlet to the Atlantic south of Cape Hatteras, so as to afford navigators of the freshwater Carolina sounds access to salt water at both ends.

[7] U.S. Congress, House, 25th. Cong., 2nd sess: *Harbor and River Improvements,* doc. 90, January 12, 1838, and *Survey Norfolk, Va., to Winyaw Bay, S.C.,* doc. 445, May 26, 1838; Brown, *Dismal Swamp Canal,* p. 87.

[8] U.S. Congress, House, *Navigation from Chesapeake Bay to Pamlico Sound,* 44th Cong. 1st sess., exec. doc. 45, pp. 1–2.
[9] U.S. Congress, House, *Survey of a Line to Connect . . . the Waters of Norfolk Harbor,* 44th. Cong., 1st sess., exec. doc. 35.

FIG. 21. *Capt. Charles B. Phillips, U.S. Army Corps of Engineers, was Norfolk district engineer from July 1, 1879, to June 14, 1881. (Photo courtesy U.S. Army Corps of Engineers, Fort Norfolk, Va.)*

This task was assigned to Capt. Charles B. Phillips of the U.S. Army Corps of Engineers (fig. 21), and with government approval of his plans for conducting the survey, work got under way on August 10, 1878. A year and a half later it was completed, and the results were forwarded to Brig. Gen. H. G. Wright, Chief of Engineers, on January 15, 1880. It subsequently appeared in print as Senate Executive Document Number 73, on February 7, 1880.[10] Phillips was the first incumbent of the post of District Engineer, whose present headquarters at venerable Fort Norfolk, overlooking the east bank of the Elizabeth River, were first occupied in June 1923. Phillips served as Norfolk District Engineer from July 1, 1879, until June 14, 1881. On an average, the post has been rotated every three years.

Captain Phillips had produced an impressively comprehensive report consisting not only of forty-seven pages of finely printed text but also of nine new detailed maps (one reproduced here, fig. 22), together with tracings of maps from previous surveys, copies of Coast Survey charts, and sections and profiles of canal routes (existing and planned) comprising thirty-seven additional sheets.

---

[10] U.S. Congress, Senate, *Water Routes from Norfolk to the Atlantic Ocean*, 46th Cong., 2nd sess., Senate exec. doc. no. 73. (Letter from [Alex. Ramsey] the Secretary of war, transmitting report of Capt. C. B. Phillips, Corps of Engineers, in relation to inland water routes from Norfolk, Va., to the Atlantic Ocean, south of Cape Hatteras, dated February 9, 1880.) Hereafter cited as "Phillips Report."

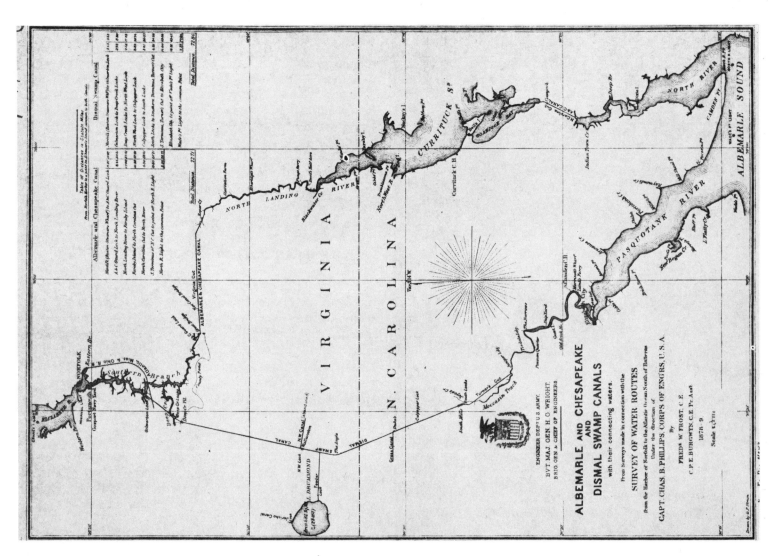

FIG. 22. *Map showing the Albemarle and Chesapeake and Dismal Swamp canals as surveyed under the direction of Capt. Charles B. Phillips, by Frederick W. Frost, 1878–79. (U.S. Congress, Senate, 46th Cong., 2nd sess., 1880, exec. doc. no. 73.)*

At the outset, Phillips had divided the men into two field parties. His plan was first to complete the examination of the existing canals north of Albemarle Sound, and then to take up the Pamlico–Cape Fear area. On September 4, 1878, a survey of the Pasquotank River was begun by one group; the next day the other commenced its work in Currituck Sound. Before leaving the Dismal Swamp Region, the engineers made what was, up to that time, "the only survey of the lake [Drummond] of which there is any record."[11]

The routes of both canals have been cited in sufficient detail in chapter one to render further descriptions unnecessary. In summary, the government surveyors first planned major and expensive improvements to the Dismal Swamp Canal—at that time, as already observed, in a depressed condition—by replacing its seven existing small locks with four new and larger ones, 220 feet long by 40 feet wide, exactly the same size as the Great Bridge lock. They also suggested lowering the Dismal Swamp Canal's summit level by more than 3 feet, deepening the feeder ditch, and improving the river approaches at both ends. This rebuilt canal, 80 feet in width on the bottom, would provide a depth of 9 feet at an estimated cost of $1,483,646.

An alternate plan covering a narrower 60-foot canal with 30-foot-wide locks was also submitted at a slightly lower figure.[12] Curiously, when the Dismal Swamp Canal Company was finally reorganized and outside financing was brought in to cover its modernization

from 1896 to 1899, the summit level was reduced 8½ feet to its present level. This required only two locks, one at each end of the elevated portion. These locks measured 250 feet long, by 40 feet wide, with a 9-foot depth over the sills.[13]

The complete upgrading of the Albemarle and Chesapeake Canal provided the engineers with a "less difficult problem to solve," for the newer waterway was already a busy, going concern of demonstrated utility. In addition to widening and deepening both land cuts, the river approaches, and the dredged route across Currituck Sound and Coinjock Bay, however, a supplementary guard lock, similar in all respects to the existing Great Bridge lock (which was still considered entirely adequate in size), was proposed for installation at the east end of the Virginia Cut at North Landing. It was felt that this would better control varying elevations caused by winds and "by this means we would be enable to keep the water on this section of the route at nearly the same level as the water in the Elizabeth River or in the North Landing River, selecting, of course, the higher of the two." (The settlement at North Landing, incidentally, was cited by the survey party as "a place of no very great commercial importance, being simply a suburb of Roper City, which takes its name from its proprietor" as the location of "a large steam sawmill" whose products were shipped out from there via the canal.)[14]

[11] Ibid., p. 3.
[12] Ibid., pp. 5–6.
[13] Brown, *Dismal Swamp Canal*, pp. 140, 143.
[14] "Phillips Report," pp. 6, 27. The Baird-Roper Lumber Company was founded in 1867 when Capt. John L. Roper, late of the Pennsylvania Militia, joined forces with the Baird family.

To keep sand dredged from the bottom of the canal cuts from sliding back in again—a perennial nuisance—the engineers proposed that virtually the entire length of the Virginia Cut be sheet-piled on both sides. They were scornful of the original design of the cut, citing "three bends . . . that might have been avoided" and concluding that "the construction of this cut is faulty, and cannot be considered respectable engineering." When the suggested improvements were completed, the revamped Albemarle and Chesapeake Canal would be nine feet deep and would carry a bottom width of eighty feet, all at an estimated cost of $509,702.[15]

As proposed in the company's 1873 *Annual Report,* in addition to the improvements to the canal proper, an ultimate goal for the sinuous North Landing River would be to have five separate cutoffs—eliminating oxbows in the river and so straightening the channel by getting rid of tight bends which slowed navigation and risked grounding ships in transit. With the exception of the proposed additional lock, which was a new concept, all the other problems had been recognized by the owners and were being handled as funds permitted. However, an additional eighteen inches added to the project depth would be very much welcomed, according to the company reports, as a means of enticing larger and deeper vessels to use the canal.

Captain Phillips's report of 1878 mentioned the 1871 survey of the Elizabeth River made by Col. W. P. Craighill, plus the expenditure there of $40,000 in congressional funds since 1872. He also cited two additional appropriations aggregating $45,000 which had been made by Congress for improving the channel through Currituck Sound and the North Landing River.[16]

These and other congressional appropriatings provided by the terms of the River and Harbor Act pertaining to Virginia and North Carolina waters totaling $352,000 were subsequently listed in the company's *Twenty-Fifth Annual Report* (1880), with the following items directly benefitting the Albemarle and Chesapeake Canal:

1873–78—$40,000 for Southern Branch of the Elizabeth River
1878–79—$35,000 for Currituck Sound and North River
1879   —$25,000 for North Landing River

and finally $20,000 for beacon lights in Currituck Sound, "which have been long waited." Indeed, only in 1877, the annual report had bemoaned the lack of lighthouses there, saying: "perhaps there is no portion of our country where there are 6,000 vessels passing annually so neglected."[17]

It was, however, at the previously incompletely surveyed and scantily improved southern end of the Carolina Sounds where Phillips's recommendations were

---

[15] "Phillips Report," p. 7.

[16] Ibid.
[17] A & C Canal Co., *Twenty-Fifth Annual Report* (1880) p. 8.

to have their greatest impact on the eventual extension southward of the Intracoastal Waterway as it exists today. Here, at Beaufort Inlet—a naturally deep cut through the barrier beach now dredged to a thirty-five foot oceangoing ship channel leading to the modern port of Morehead City—an adequate exit from Pamlico Sound leading into the Atlantic was sought by maritime interests, as specified in the original assignment of the 1878 River and Harbor Act.

Pamlico is the largest and most open of Carolina's inland seas, extending some seventy-five miles southwestward from Croatan to Core Sound behind the protective barrier islands of Hatteras, Ocracoke, Portsmouth, and Core Banks. Though Pamlico is reasonably deep (from seven feet over Ocracoke Bar to twenty-three feet in the middle of the sound), it becomes extremely shallow at the southern end where it merges with Core Sound. Approximately thirty-five miles long by only three miles wide, Core Sound lies on the south, or ocean, side of Cartaret County, a peninsula whose northern shore follows the mouth of the broad and deep Neuse River into Pamlico Sound.

Although Core Sound gave access at its southwestern end to Beaufort Harbor, which lies west of Cape Lookout—Hatteras's dread companion of the banks islands—the sound was bar-bround throughout, with only two of three feet of water in many places. For this reason, a better connection between Pamlico and Beaufort Inlet had long been envisaged by way of a canal cut across the fifteen-mile-wide western neck of the Carteret County peninsula.

"An Act for Joining the Navigation of Old Topsail Inlet to Neuse River by cutting a canal from the head of Harlow's Creek to Clubfoot's Creek" had been proposed as early as 1766.[18] Unpleasantly named Clubfoot Creek is a tributary of the Neuse River, while Harlow's Creek flows south in Carteret County into the Newport River and Beaufort Harbor.

With interest in canals revived in 1783, after independence had been gained, a water route to connect the heads of the two creeks—a comparatively short overland cut of only three miles—had ultimately been surveyed by Hamilton Fulton in 1820 as part of Gallatin's proposed line of canals. Work on improving the creeks and building the canal had gone slowly, but after a guard lock had been put in at the northern end, small vessels began to use the waterway in 1827.[19]

Financial troubles had progressively developed, however, and the Clubfoot and Harlow Canal Com-

---

18 Hinshaw, "North Carolina Canals," pp. 8–15.

19 One of the first regular customers was the sixty-foot steamboat *Codorus*. Built at York, Pennsylvania, in 1825 by John Elgar for use on the Susquehanna River, the sheet iron boat *Codorus* was the first metal-hulled craft ever constructed in the United States. Since the *Codorus* proved unsuitable for navigation this shallow, rock-strewn Pennsylvania river, the little vessel was brought south in 1829 to ply the thirty-five-mile route between New Bern and Beaufort, North Carolina, via the Clubfoot and Harlow Creek Canal. She disappeared from the official records after 1830. (Alexander C. Brown, "The Sheet Iron Steamboat *Codorus*," *The American Neptune*, 10, no. 3 (July 1950): 163–90. The article was reprinted as Mariners' Museum Publication no. 21 in 1950.)

pany was obliged to close the canal in 1844, though it was subsequently reorganized in 1849 to provide limited navigation again. Meanwhile, the state of North Carolina had acquired an interest in the canal to the amount of $38,000.

Curiously, on February 9, 1872, an entirely new canal entitled the New Bern and Beaufort Canal had been incorporated. Its route from Adams Creek to Core Creek which also entered Newport River would parallel that of the old Clubfoot and Harlow waterway half a dozen miles farther to the east and would naturally accomplish the same purpose of connecting Pamlico with Beaufort. The new canal was not organized until November 10, 1881, however, and this was, of course, after Captain Phillips's surveyors had concluded their examination of the region and had come out in favor of upgrading the then virtually defunct Clubfoot and Harlow's Creek Canal.

Interestingly enough, following the complete abandonment of the Clubfoot and Harlow Canal and the conveyance of its shares of stock by the state to the new New Bern and Beaufort Canal by deed of August 27, 1883, the Albemarle and Chesapeake Canal Company, because of its experience and equipment, was the firm selected to build the new canal. After performing this work using their steam dredge *Cyclops,* the Albemarle and Chesapeake Canal Company became a partial owner of the New Bern and Beaufort Canal Company. Part of the payment to the Albemarle and Chesapeake Canal Company for their construction work was made by the return of 2,500 shares of

its own stock, previously held by the state of North Carolina. It will be recalled that a similar arrangement for building and ownership had been made in 1872 with the construction of the Fairfield Canal. The Adams Creek–Core Creek canalized part of the New Bern and Beaufort waterway, now a part of the Atlantic Intracoastal Waterway, was finally opened on a five-foot depth in January 1885, and the Clubfoot and Harlow faded into obscurity. The latter's clogged channel can hardly be discerned today, though it is shown on modern charts, which record a depth of merely six inches in the old canal.

Today's Adams Creek–Core Creek Canal was cited in Army Corps of Engineers *Reports* of 1911 as "the present and only project" as already adopted by congressional approval on March 2, 1907, with plans for a ten-foot-deep channel. The canal was then progressively improved, and as late as October 2, 1910, the Norfolk *Virginian-Pilot* reported that dredges then working would have it reopened by December of that year, and so "link Beaufort with Ches. Bay." To June 30, 1911, the government had expended $496,401.64 for improvements. Completed to its projected depth in 1912, the New Bern and Beaufort Canal has been maintained by the government ever since.

Having attained their intent of providing for an outlet to the ocean at Beaufort, in 1879 Captain Phillips's men now pushed on southward and westward. Following an existing survey made by Maj. James Kearney forty years earlier, they proceeded to examine an inland route between Slocum's Creek, a tributary of the

Neuse River, and a point on the northeast branch of the Cape Fear River known as Bannermans, lying forty-seven miles from Wilmington. An alternate inland route extending westward from the Neuse's main tributary, Trent River, was also surveyed.

In the end, however, these inland routes, with elevations in some places of as much as fifty feet above sea level to be overcome, were abandoned for the far-more-practical sea-level line closely paralleling the coast and using existing back bays, river mouths, and salt marshes. The surveyors pointed out, however, that this shore route would entail the building of four guard locks: a new one for an upgraded Clubfoot and Harlow Canal; one at each terminus of a cut across from Newport River to the White Oak River; and finally one across the peninsula lying east and south of Wilmington. The distance, skirting the shore, totaled 182 miles, and the cost estimate covering all the required "locks, dykes and other necessary structures" reached the impressive figure of $5,695,000.[20]

Frederick W. Frost, the principal civil engineer in charge of this phase of the work, presented the table of distances shown here as table 8. Obviously, as this table points out, it would make virtually no difference in the amount of distance whether the Albemarle and Chesapeake Canal or the Dismal Swamp Canal was chosen for upgrading. When lockage time was considered, however, the Albemarle and Chesapeake Canal would certainly prove the more expeditious route.

---

[20] "Phillips Report," p. 12.

Table 8—Table of distances in statute miles from the harbor of Norfolk, Virginia, to the Cape Fear River, North Carolina

From Norfolk Harbor, via the Albemarle and Chesapeake Canal route, to a point in Albemarle Sound common to both canals	72.71
From Norfolk Harbor, via the Dismal Swamp Canal route, to the common point	72.84
From the common point, via the Albemarle, Croatan, and Pamlico Sounds and the Neuse River, to the mouth of Clubfoot Creek	117.80
From mouth of Clubfoot Creek to railroad bridge at Newport	19.95
From railroad bridge to channel of White Oak River off Pettiford's Creek	16.86
From channel of White Oak to New River Inlet	18.85
From New River Inlet to Masonboro' Inlet	36.75
Masonboro' Inlet, via Whiskey and Barnard's Creeks, to channel of Cape Fear River	9.79
Total distance from common point (in Albemarle Sound)	219.90
Total distance via the Albemarle and Chesapeake Canal	292.61
Total distance via the Dismal Swamp Canal	292.74

Source: "Phillips Report," p. 47.

Observing posted speed limits, an uninterrupted transit of the Albemarle and Chesapeake Canal was plotted at thirteen hours, three minutes, while on the Dismal Swamp Canal it was fourteen hours, six minutes. These time, of course, assumed no unanticipated delays while passing rafts or slow-moving vessels or while waiting at the locks.[21]

The Albemarle and Chesapeake Canal, then, not only took less time to navigate, but in the anticipated upgrading to meet required standards, it was calculated to be only a third as expensive to improve as the Dismal Swamp Canal. However, while the engineers' conclusion was that "the route via the Albemarle and Chesapeake Canal is the better one at present," they were careful not to pick sides on "which one will be the better after a proper improvement."[22]

The only positive immediate benefit of the Phillips survey was the continuance of the government's work then in progress in Currituck Sound and the North Landing River, and the Dismal Swamp Canal was thus forced to continue a hand-to-mouth existence for another fifteen years. Yet the information recorded and mapped contributed in considerable measure to the ultimate acquisition of both canals by the federal government in the early part of the twentieth century and to their present upgraded status.

Officials of the Albemarle and Chesapeake Canal Company in 1880 were naturally elated that their canal was rated as superior by the government engineers, and Parks reminded his stockholders during that year that four-fifths of the stock of the Dismal Swamp Canal had been owned by both the state of Virginia and the United States government and "it had

received for nearly a century their fostering aid." Harking back to the 1850s when the Albemarle and Chesapeake Canal was trying to get started, he said that it had at first seemed almost "futile to construct a work to rival" the existing ancient waterway. Yet this work was accomplished, and the Albemarle and Chesapeake Canal "stands today a monument to the fidelity and perserverence of its designers."[23]

President Parks was never one to hesitate giving himself a pat on the back. Even though he recognized that the stockholders and friends of the Dismal Swamp Canal "had a perfect right to seek aid from Congress," he was annoyed that they should "draw insideous comparisons and endeavor to show the superiority of their line of navigation" over the obviously superior Albemarle and Chesapeake waterway.[24]

In any event, the Albemarle and Chesapeake Canal was described in the Tenth (1880) United States Census Report, which briefly cited the route of the canal and stated that its total cost then amounted to $1,641,362. Though originally intended for vessels of no more than 250 tons and drawing six feet of water, the report concluded that it had been progressively deepened and that, as of the date the census figures were compiled, it could handle 800-ton vessels drawing eight feet.[25] The statement of vessels using the

---

[21] Ibid., p. 41.
[22] Ibid., p. 39.

[23] A & C Canal Co., *Twenty-Fifth Annual Report* (1880), p. 7.
[24] A & C Canal Co., *Twenty-Third Annual Report* (1878), p. 7.
[25] T. C. Purdy, "Report on the Canals of the United States," p. 20.

Table 9—Statement of vessels passed through the Albemarle and Chesapeake Canal, 1860 to 1881

Year	Steamers	Schooners	Sloops	Barges	Lighters	Boats	Rafts	Total
1860	116	393	29	67	248	136	10	999
1861	671	1,139	74	153	300	179	8	2,524
1862	453	192	88	69	275	188	—	1,265
1863	377	62	71	16	292	125	—	943
1864	953	24	15	124	96	174	5	1,391
1865	1,300	266	190	122	79	602	3	2,562
1866	1,062	739	302	256	338	921	18	3,636
1867	1,112	907	358	313	763	761	29	4,243
1868	1,093	944	442	381	778	1,066	26	4,730
1869	1,093	752	398	297	950	1,077	36	4,603
1870	1,487	859	437	167	911	486	35	4,382
1871	1,659	941	555	183	1,030	483	49	4,900
1872	1,667	1,070	523	158	752	553	85	4,808
1873	2,075	1,380	592	225	886	469	152	5,779
1874	2,214	1,607	654	338	937	411	122	6,283
1875	2,408	1,837	722	340	697	425	73	6,502
1876	2,463	1,719	720	292	639	260	113	6,206
1877	2,376	1,626	508	344	587	277	123	5,841
1878	2,627	1,759	640	226	661	243	171	6,327
1879	2,798	1,615	569	334	552	379	186	6,433
1880	3,209	1,537	392	496	570	362	288	6,854
Total	33,213	21,368	8,279	4,901	12,341	9,577	1,532	91,211

Source: T. C. Purdy, "Report on the Canals of the United States," p. 20.

canal . . ." shown as table 9 covered a twenty-one year period from 1860 to 1880.

Financially, the Albemarle and Chesapeake Canal Company was in good condition too. The twenty-year mortgage of property and possessions for $400,000 which had been effected on July 1, 1859, in the names of William T. Hooker and Parker Handy of New York and of Richard H. Chamberlaine of Norfolk had matured, and the directors elected to institute a new mortgage with the Union Trust Company of New York as trustee, this in order once more to borrow a substantial sum—in this case half a million dollars.

INLAND NAVIGATION.

THE

ALBEMARLE AND CHESAPEAKE CANAL,

TOGETHER WITH THE

Chesapeake & Delaware Canal & Delaware and Raritan Canal,

FORM THE GREAT INLAND NAVIGATION FROM

NEW YORK, PHILADELPHIA AND BALTIMORE

TO

NORTH CAROLINA AND THE SOUTH,

BY CANALS AND INLAND NAVIGATION FOR STEAMBOATS, SAILING VESSELS, RAFTS, &c., AVOIDING THE DANGERS OF HAT-TERAS AND THE COAST OF NORTH CAROLINA—SAVING TIME AND INSURANCE.

DIMENSIONS OF CANALS AND LOCKS:

CANALS.	MILES.	LOCKS. Length. Feet.	Width. Feet.	Depth Feet.
Albemarle and Chesapeake Canal	14	220	40	7
Chesapeake and Delaware Canal	14	220	24	9
Delaware and Raritan Canal	43	220	24	7
Erie, of New York	345	110	18	7

☞ Light-draft steamers bound to Charleston, Savannah, Florida and the West Indies take this route.

Steam tug-boats leave Norfolk, towing sail vessels, barges, rafts, &c., to and from North Carolina to Baltimore, Philadelphia and New York.

Freight steamers leave Norfolk for the following places: Edenton, Elizabeth City, Hertford, Plymouth, Jamesville, Williamston, Hamilton, Hill's Ferry, Palmyra, Scotland Neck, Halifax, Weldon, Columbia, Fair Field, Windsor, Winton, Gatesville, Murfreesboro, Franklin, Currituck, Coinjock, Roanoke Island, Washington, Greensville, Tarboro, Indiantown, Bay River and Newberne.

☞ For rates of tolls, towing, maps and charts, &c., apply to

H. V. LESLIE, Treasurer C. & D. Canal Co.,
528 Walnut Street, Philadelphia.

M. COURTRIGHT, Esq.,
Room 69 Coal and Iron Exchange, New York.

Or to MARSHAL PARKS,
President Albemarle and Chesapeake Canal Co., Norfolk, Va.

Dismal Swamp Canal Company.

NORFOLK, VA.

(RE-ORGANIZED DECEMBER 1st, 1880.)

Connecting the Waters of Chesapeake Bay with Albemarle and Pamlico Sounds, N. C.

The recent extensive improvements by dredging and otherwise, securing a uniform depth of water throughout, recommend this route as a desirable medium of transportation between the waters of Virginia and North Carolina.

OFFICERS.

JNO. B. WHITEHEAD, President.

CAPT. HENRY ROBERTS, Superintendent.

S. W. GARY, Collector.

H. C. WHITEHEAD, Secretary and Treasurer.

DIRECTORS.

W. H. C. ELLIS,   C. W. NEWTON,

JAMES Y. LEIGH,   CICERO BURRUSS.

NORTH CAROLINA
STEAM LINES.

STEAMER HARBINGER,
Captain M. E. CREGG,

Leaves the Wharf foot of Commerce Street, every MONDAY and THURSDAY, at 6 A.M., for HERTFORD and BELVIDERE, N. C.

STEAMER ENTERPRISE,

Leaves the Wharf foot of Commerce Street, every MONDAY, WEDNESDAY and FRIDAY, at 6 A. M. for ELIZABETH CITY, N.C. and Intermediate Points via Dismal Swamp Canal.

STEAMER CURRITUCK,
Captain J. J. JONES,

Leaves the Wharf foot of Commerce Street, every THRUSDAY EVENING for WINDSOR and all points on the Cashie River, N. C.

Freights received daily. For further information apply to

W. Y. JOHNSON, Agent.

FIG. 23. *Advertisements promoting the Albemarle and Chesapeake and the Dismal Swamp canals, appearing in Cary W. Jones,* Guide to Norfolk as a Business Centre, *1881. (Courtesy Sargeant Memorial Room, Norfolk Public Library.)*

In the deed, dated July 1, 1879, it was stated that the company "desires to make certain improvements in the canal" and would issue five hundred numbered $1,000-bonds maturing in thirty years and, as before, to secure them, it would mortgage "its entire estate real and personal, rights, franchises, and property of every kind . . . together with all the buildings, bridges, structures, fixtures, steamboats, dredges, machinery and appurtenances belonging to or appertaining to said canal." The deed was signed by Marshall Parks and B. F. Tebault, president and treasurer of the canal company, and by Edward King and James H. Ogilvie, who held the same offices in the Union Trust Company.[26]

The following year a formal release of the original lien dated December 1, 1880, was given the canal company by Parker Hardy in behalf of himself and of Hooker and Chamberlaine, since these "two of the said trustees have departed this life since the execution and delivery of the said deed" dated July 1, 1859. This release stated that the company "has fully paid, discharged and satisfied the whole of the said sum of $400,000 and all the interest thereon"—paid semiannually at seven per cent.[27] Norfolk publishers were happy to promote both the Albemarle and Chesapeake and the Dismal Swamp Canals as good business for the city (see fig. 23).

[26] This deed is on file in the Clerk's Office, Circuit Court of the City of Chesapeake, Va., Deed Book 107 (1879), p. 97. The original mortgage is cited in chapter 5 of this volume, note 39.

[27] Release of lien is on file in the Clerk's Office as above, Deed Book 110 (1880), p. 281.

Impact of the Railroads
and the Heyday of the
Sound Steamers, 1875–1900

ention has been made above of the various bridges spanning the Albemarle and Chesapeake Canal and of their replacement after damage sustained during the Civil War. Now, a dozen years later, two more bridges were to be added to the system. Until this point the only public bridge crossings along the line of the waterway were those the canal company had been required to build when the canal was dug—the company-owned drawbridges at Great Bridge, North Landing, and Coinjock.

As already observed, the venerable wooden drawbridge over the North Landing River at Pungo Ferry—which had proved recalcitrant to Artist Edward Bruce's party on their 1858 excursion down the river to Currituck on board the *Calypso*—was evidently replaced by a privately owned ferry soon after the canal was opened, since the crossing is indicated on nineteenth century maps of the area as Pungo Ferry. There has been a steel swing bridge (figs. 24, 25) on Route 726 at this point since 1954, but as late as 1940, when the final Pungo cable ferryboat (fig. 26) was taken into the Virginia state highway system, a Model-A Ford engine provided power to winch a four-car flatboat across the river, a distance of about a hundred yards. Although there is a bridge there now, the little settlement on the east bank—which includes a summer pavilion and a fairly extensive marina with various docks and piers—still retains the name Pungo Ferry. In 1879, Captain Phillips's surveyors had stated that "a small settlement of two or three houses sufficiently describes its importance."[1]

_____

[1] "Phillips Report," p. 28. See note 27, chapter 5, for early descriptions of Pungo Ferry.

FIG. 24. *Pungo Ferry swing-span drawbridge over the North Landing River. A 1972 view looking north at the 1953-built assymetrical draw. (Photo by Alexander C. Brown.)*

Building another road bridge across the canal proper received mention in the company's 1878 *Twenty-Third Annual Report*. During that year an independent turnpike company had "constructed and maintained at their expense" what is presently designated the Centerville Turnpike Bridge (fig. 27), located three miles east of the canal entrance at Great Bridge. The single-lane structure on Route 604 was replaced

FIG. 25. *Drawbridge tender W. W. Lupton of Pungo Ferry Bridge, Va. A 1972 view looking west across the North Landing River shows the old ferry landing in the distance to the right of the sign. (Photo by Alexander C. Brown.)*

FIG. 26. *This crude flat barge, abandoned in a slough on the west bank just north of the present bridge at Pungo Ferry, undoubtedly was previously used for the cable ferry. (Photo by Alexander C. Brown, August 1972.)*

by the present two-lane Department of Highways swing bridge in 1955.[2]

However, bridge construction of far greater moment than these country-road bridges occurred in 1880, when a floating swing-type drawbridge built of

wood and sustained by pontoons was constructed approximately a mile and a half east along the Virginia Cut from Great Bridge.[3] This was intended to carry

---

[2] A & C Canal Co., *Twenty-Third Annual Report* (1878), p. 8; Memorandum of Albemarle and Chesapeake Canal bridges received June 29, 1977, by the author from J. Thomas Lawless, U.S. Army Corps of Engineers, Fort Norfolk, Virginia.

[3] This interesting type of drawbridge, similar to one then used by the Norfolk & Western Railroad for its crossing of the Eastern Branch of the Elizabeth River, was identified for the author as a floating draw by Richard E. Prince from a small photograph reproduced in the Norfolk Chamber of Commerce book, *Pictures of Maritime Dixie* by A.M. (1893). The draw was hinged

FIG. 27. *Centerville Turnpike swing-span drawbridge over the Virginia Cut. A 1972 photograph looking east at the 1955-built bridge. (Photo by Alexander C. Brown.)*

the tracks of the newly established Elizabeth City and Norfolk Railroad whose route is indicated on the 1880 map (fig. 28). Although chartered a decade earlier (on January 20, 1870), construction of the railroad was put off, and its first trains only commenced operating

horizontally to the south side of the canal bank, and, when needed to be closed to let a train over, it would be floated out on its pontoons, swinging like a fence gate across to its housing on the north side, and would then be lowered to rest on fixed end-piers which were able to support the weight of the train.

Locomotives then in use weighed forty-seven tons. Varying water levels in the canal had to be taken into account with the floating of the draw, since the shore track and piers remained at a fixed elevation. Unexplained, however, are the locations of the cables that, it is assumed, would have been required to swing the draw back and forth. It is surmised that the cables would have been dropped to the bottom of the canal when the draw was open, but in that position they offered the potential hazard of being snagged by a deep-draft vessel crossing over them.

Some time prior to the operation of heavier locomotives by the railroad between Berkley and Edenton (by 1910, the Norfolk and Southern engines had attained eighty-one tons), the floating draw over the canal was replaced by a second, stronger bridge. This was reported to be an iron-girder draw which provided a forty-five foot wide horizontal clearance for the passage of vessels.

The second bridge gave way in turn to the present structure in 1928. Providing the eighty-foot span required by the widening of the canal, this Scherzer rolling lift draw was constructed by the Atlantic Bridge Company of Greensboro, N.C., and was opened October 9, 1928. Today, a small diesel engine provides the power to move a giant counterweight that raises and lowers the draw for the passage of the Norfolk Southern's two daily freight trains.

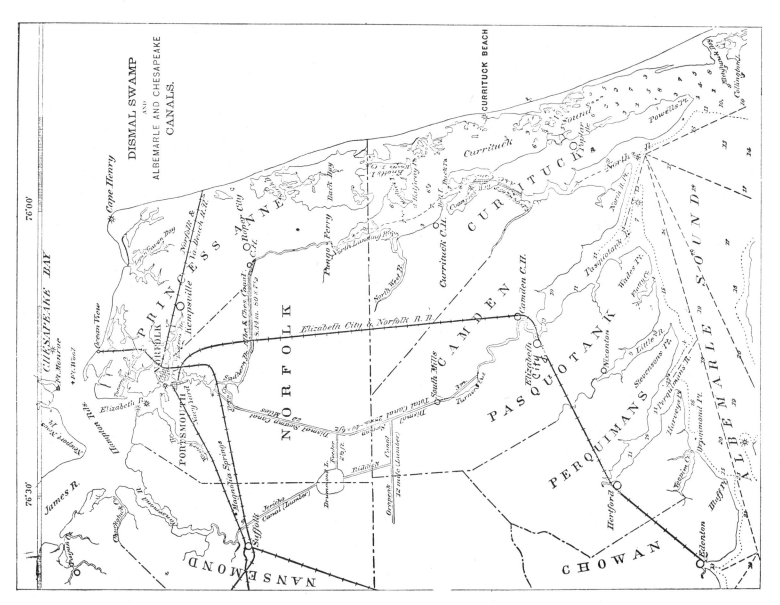

Fig. 28. *Map of the Dismal Swamp and the Albemarle and Chesapeake canals showing the line of the Elizabeth City and Norfolk Railroad. From T. C. Purdy, "Report on the Canals of the United States."*

between Berkley Terminal, south of Norfolk, and Elizabeth City on June 1, 1880.[4]

In addition to crossing the Albemarle and Chesapeake Canal, the new railroad line required two other major bridges. One spanned the North West River as the rails skirted the eastern part of Dismal Swamp on the west shore of Currituck Sound. The other bridged the Pasquotank, at what had been designated Lamb's Ferry near Camden Courthouse, a short distance east of Elizabeth City. A draw was required here, since the upper Pasquotank provided the river approach to the south locks of the Dismal Swamp Canal for masted vessels. But inasmuch as the North West Canal had been sealed off at its connection with the Dismal Swamp Canal in 1871, a drawbridge was no longer needed farther down the river at the railroad crossing site.

Despite its original corporate name, the owners of the new railroad had decided against terminating the line at Elizabeth City, and, having changed its direction to the southwest, they continued laying tracks on across the counties of Pasquotank, Perquimins, and Chowan, bridging the Perquimins River at Hertford. The rail line finally reached the shores of Albemarle Sound at Edenton on the east side of the Chowan River mouth, where a terminal was built right on the water's edge. The railroad then covered seventy-three miles from Norfolk and as early timetables indicate, constituted a 3½ hour train ride. The railroad's present bridge over the Virginia Cut is shown, open and closed, in figs. 29 and 30.

Having attained this terminus by December 15, 1881, the railroad company elected to substitute a more descriptive title for its achievement, and accordingly, two years later, it was renamed the Norfolk Southern Railroad. With minor variations to mark subsequent extensions and mergers with other lines, plus changes of corporate structure by receiverships and financial reorganization, it is so designated today.[5]

The impact of railway transportation on the North Carolina sounds area was considerable. Gradually the entire economy of the region and the functions of the waterways—particularly those of the Albemarle and Chesapeake Canal—underwent major changes. Various independent steamboat lines plying the sounds became affiliated with, and synchronized into, rail movements, with the boats serving as feeders for the trains. This, in effect, provided extension of railway services into those regions where tracks were lacking. Inevitably, however, as additional rail lines came to the area, the boats were squeezed out, surviving only on purely local runs. Improved roads and bridges would eventually drive them off the waters too.

---

[4] Prince, *Norfolk Southern Railroad*, pp. 8–9; A & C Canal Co., *Twenty-Sixth Annual Report* (1881), p. 3.

[5] The railroad's official corporate names have been: 1870–1883—Elizabeth City & Norfolk Railroad; 1883–1889—Norfolk Southern Railroad; 1889–1906—Norfolk & Southern Railroad; 1906–1910—Norfolk & Southern Railway; 1910–1941—Norfolk Southern Railroad; 1941– —Norfolk Southern Railway (Prince, *Norfolk Southern Railroad*, pp. 6–9).

FIG. 29. *Norfolk Southern Railway bascule drawbridge over the Virginia Cut, looking east. This Scherzer rolling lift bridge, built in 1928 by the Atlantic Bridge Co., is still in operation. The previous forty-foot span was replaced by this eighty-foot span. (Photo by Alexander C. Brown, 1972.)*

Until the Elizabeth City and Norfolk Railroad appeared in the 1880s, only one rail line had actually reached Carolina sounds shores prior to the Civil War. This railroad was the Atlantic and North Carolina, which by 1858 ran eastward from Goldsborough to Kinston, thence on to New Bern, Pamlico Sound's major port on its tributary Neuse River. Former-governor John Motley Morehead had been instrumental in extending the Atlantic and North Carolina southeastward from New Bern to Shepherd's Point, opposite Beaufort Inlet, where the modern port of Morehead City was established and named in his honor. Mean-

Fig. 30. *Norfolk Southern's four-unit freight train, southbound, is crossing the drawbridge over the canal's Virginia Cut on August 9, 1977. View looking west. (Photo by Alexander C. Brown.)*

while, the railroad gained the quaint nickname of the **Old Mullet Road** and adopted a jumping mullet as its emblem.

This line afforded one of the principal reasons why, from the very beginning of the Civil War, New Bern was a bitterly sought prize of the Union army. The cutting of rail lines at this point would deny the interior South one of its important interchange routes to salt water, and once captured, the railroad could well serve the Union cause in moving men and materiel for the subsequent takeover of all of eastern North Carolina.[6]

---

[6] Ibid., pp. 16–20.

With its existing rail lines running south and west, a connection with New Bern became a logical future goal of the Norfolk Southern Railroad. Making this connection by means of steamboat lines would suffice well enough for the present though, and developing these water routes was the railroad's first order of business. It was not until 1891, when the company was reorganized and renamed the Norfolk Southern Railroad, that it acquired its first additional trackage southward with the purchase of the 1887-built Albemarle & Pantego Railroad. This was originally a logging road operated by the John L. Roper Lumber Company of Norfolk, which had been organized by northern capitalists shortly after the Civil War while they were accumulating well over half a million acres of timberland in the forested coastal areas—the Tidewater low country—of Virginia and North Carolina. The Albemarle & Pantego was one of several narrow-gage roads built to serve various saw mills, one of which, at Roper City near North Landing in Princess Anne County, Virginia, has already been noted. As might be expected, the company's largest mill, at the newly named town of Roper, North Carolina, in Washington County (formerly Lee's Crossroads), lay on the Albemarle & Pantego line a short distance south of Mackey's Ferry. The railroad ran south from the ferry, located at the head of Albemarle Sound opposite Edenton and a few miles downstream from Plymouth. Thence it ran through Pantego in Beaufort County and on to Belhaven, a charming little old town on the Pungo River (not to be confused with the Pungo in Princess Anne County, Virginia), leading into Pamlico Sound—a thirty-mile-long line.

This little railroad also operated the steamboat *Haven Belle* out of Belhaven and other floating property, including the family-named steam tug *George W. Roper* and a car float. Ownership of these vessels put the Norfolk Southern Railroad in the steamboat business in its own right—a business which was to grow to very considerable proportions before the inevitable decline set in for all steamboat operations.[7]

Next came in 1899 the acquisition by the Norfolk and Southern of the ferry plying the nine-mile run between Edenton and Mackey's on the southern shore of the Albemarle, near the mouth of the Roanoke River. Ultimately, rail lines from Plymouth south to "Little" Washington were acquired, and, finally, lines from Washington on to New Bern completed the planned line in 1906.

Four years later, a remarkable five-mile-long railway trestle across Albemarle Sound equipped with a drawspan in the middle, was built to replace the big iron side-wheel double-track transfer steamer *John W. Garret,* which had been carrying full passenger trains over the sound on each voyage. The bridge now conveyed trains across without the delay of loading and unloading cars, thus providing uninterrupted rail service south from Norfolk all the way to New Bern and beyond. Expectedly, the now-parallel steamboat lines

———

[7] Ibid., pp. 7–8, 36–37. Operation of varying lumbering interests throughout the so-called Tidewater low country served by the Albemarle and Chesapeake Canal is well covered in an interesting memoir, *The Bull-Hunchers,* published by a former lumberman, Howard A. Hanlon. The largest of these timber concerns was the John L. Roper Lumber Company, formerly the Baird-Roper Lumber Company, whose holdings ultimately encompassed more than a million acres in eastern North Carolina and Virginia. These properties exceeded both those of the Camp Brothers, headquartered at Franklin, Va., and those of the Richmond Cedar Works, also giants in the industry.

Yankee go-getter John L. Roper came down to Norfolk shortly after the Civil War, first joining forces with the Baird family in a sawmill, which he promptly enlarged at North Landing to serve Princess Anne County pinelands. This was phased out when a new mill was established at the northern end of the Dismal Swamp Canal at Gilmerton on the Southern Branch of the Elizabeth River. After Baird's death in the 1880s, the company was incorporated as the John L. Roper Lumber Company. Nor-

from Norfolk via the canal serving Washington and finally New Bern were casualties to this progress, and the Albemarle and Chesapeake Canal Company suffered a decline in toll revenues as a result.

Through the 1880s, however, the Norfolk Southern placed emphasis on routing freight and passengers down its seventy-three mile line from Norfolk to Edenton, where they were turned over to, or received custom from, various existing steamboat lines calling there. Chief among these was the Albemarle Steam Navigation Company, which was to have the distinction of surviving until 1929 as the longest-lived water carrier on the sounds exclusive of barge traffic and towboats. Vessels of this pre–Civil War line plied the Chowan from Edenton up the river to its junction with the tributary Meherrin River, thence on to Murfreesboro, or else up the other tributary Blackwater River to Franklin, Virginia—the escape route, as we have

seen, of the little steamboats *Arrow* and *Emily* after their recapture by Confederate forces in 1863.[8]

The little steamer *Curlew,* patronized by Bruce on his visit to Roanoke Island in 1859, was one of the pioneer steamers of the Albemarle Steam Navigation Company, but like the Albemarle and Chesapeake Canal Company's fleet of tugs, she and her prewar sisters were all casualties of the conflict. Over the years, some sixteen vessels in all were operated by the Albemarle Steam Navigation Company's postwar fleet—extending in time on into the twentieth century with the sister ships *Virginia* and *Carolina,* built at Newport News in 1911 as the last boats expressly constructed for the line. A company schedule showing their operation as of January 1915 listed their connections as follows:

At Edenton, N.C., with Norfolk Southern R.R. Co.
At Tunis, N.C., with Atlantic Coast Line R.R. Co.

---

folk Southern Railroad interests soon became interlocked with those of the Roper Company in the development of lumbering on the south side of Albemarle Sound. The major Roper mill for the manufacture of white-cedar shingles was built at Lee's Crossroads (renamed Roper) in Washington County, N.C., in 1885. The development of logging railroad lines ensued—particularly the Albemarle and Pantego and the Washington and Jamesville (or the W & J, immediately redesignated the "Wiggler and Jolter")—with connecting boat services. The Norfolk & Southern absorbed the Roper interests in the 1890s, but though the railroad purchased all Roper Company stock in 1905, the railroad's lumbering business was maintained as a separate entity for many more years.

At the company's peak two years later, with the acquisition of the Blades Lumber Company, the Roper empire included a saw-

mill, a cedar mill, and two planing mills at Gilmerton: a sawmill and cedar-shingle mill at Roper, N.C.; a sawmill and planing mill at Belhaven; and smaller mills at nine other locations throughout the Tidewater low country. By this time, the first mill at North Landing, Va., had been abandoned;

In addition to the various mills, company holdings then included ten logging railroads of 150 to 200 miles in length, 750 heavy logging cars, 23 fifty-ton steam locomotives, 15 steam "skidders," 12 tugs, 16 barges, and 33 schooners. Mr. Hanlon's memoir concludes that "today [1970] only a few charred ruins remain of Roper's mill at Roper," in an area where "some of the finest stands of white cedar ever known" once flourished.

[8] Prince, *Norfolk Southern Railroad,* p. 213.

THE PAMLICO.

FIG. 31. *Samuel Ward Stanton's 1892 drawing for* Seaboard Magazine *of the steamboat* Pamlico, *built in 1874. (Courtesy Steamship Historical Society of America.)*

At Franklin, Va., with Seaboard Air Line Ry. and Southern Ry. Co. for the South and for Norfolk, Va., where close connection is made with Old Dominion, Old and New Bay Lines, Norfolk & Washington, Merchants & Miners Steamers, New York, Philadelphia & Norfolk R.R., Chesapeake & Ohio Ry, Norfolk & Western Ry., for Washington, Baltimore, Phila., N. Y. . . . Boston, Providence, Petersburg, Richmond and the West.

The steamboat *Olive*, which, as mentioned, was the pioneer sounds steamer of the Old Dominion Line, was acquired by the Albemarle Steam Navigation Company in 1894. She capsized and sank in the Chowan

River during a sudden terrific storm on February 13, 1903, but raised, rebuilt, and renamed *Hertford,* she continued to give good service until disposed of in December 1923.[9]

Back in the 1880s, however, the arrangement made in 1882 between the Norfolk Southern Railroad and the then ten-year-old Old Dominion Steamship Company's North Carolina feeder service was of considerable importance. By this agreement, the feeder line, which had been maintaining regular runs between Norfolk and both "Little" Washington and New Bern via the Albemarle and Chesapeake Canal, gave up the first part of its voyages in favor of the now-parallel railroad conveyance. So, instead of starting out by water from Norfolk, the boats remained in the sounds, either receiving or delivering passengers and cargo brought to them by rail at Elizabeth City or Edenton and then completing their journeys by water. This deprived the canal of two of its largest regular passenger carriers, the 1874-built *Pamlico* (fig. 31) and the 1875-built *Newberne,* (fig. 32), which at 352 and 412 tons, respectively, were averaging between 75 and 125 trips through the canal annually.

In 1882, the brand new *Shenandoah* was delivered to the Old Dominion line. This steamer was built in Brooklyn, New York, and her engine came out of the 1863-built Boston Harbor excursion boat *Nathaniel P. Banks,* which the Old Dominion Steam Ship Company had acquired in 1869 and later wished to dispose of.

---

[9] Ibid., pp. 203–6.

FIG. 32. *Iron-hull screw steamboat* Newberne, *built in 1875 for the Old Dominion Line, was 178 feet in length and measured 482 tons. She was finally converted to a barge in 1907. (Photo from a negative loaned by Harry T. Davis, North Carolina State Museum, Raleigh; courtesy of the Mariners Museum.)*

The *Shenandoah* was immediately put on the run from Elizabeth City to New Bern, but although obliged to come down through the Albemarle and Chesapeake Canal, she never used it regularly and was sold to run in New York waters in 1888. This vessel was to receive from Editor Samuel Ward Stanton the encomium:

PROPELLER NEUSE.

FIG. 33. *Samuel Ward Stanton's 1892 drawing for* Seaboard Magazine *of the propeller steamer* Neuse, *built in 1891. (Courtesy Steamship Historical Society of America.)*

"The best adapted steamboat for the navigation of the North Carolina Sounds that ever ran there."[10]

The Norfolk Southern's monopoly between Norfolk and Edenton was not to last, however, and the five-year-old contract between the railroad and the Old Dominion Line was not renewed in 1887. In that year, the New York, Philadelphia & Norfolk Railroad (the formerly well-known "Nyp-'n-N" of the Pennsylvania system)

went into full operation from New York down the Delmarva Peninsula to Cape Charles with car-float connections to Norfolk as the Old Dominion Steamship Company's oceangoing vessels' principal competitor in services between New York and Hampton Roads. Piqued by this maneuver, the Old Dominion's North Carolina division promptly put its boats back on their original canal route from Norfolk in retaliation, thus directly competing with the Norfolk Southern's rail services. At this point the Norfolk Southern entered

---

[10] Stanton, *Steam Navigation*, pp. 12–13.

into a new agreement with the Wilmington [Delaware] Steamboat Company, which put three nondescript propeller freighters on runs out of Elizabeth City. Later on, however, the Pennsylvania affiliate had expressly built (in 1891) the well-appointed iron steamboat *Neuse* (fig. 33) in order to offer stiff competition to the Old Dominion Line's existing vessels. Over the following years, the Norfolk and Southern operated a total of two dozen steamboats and tugs until well into the present century.[11]

The well-known railroad historian Richard E. Prince traces in detail the various ramifications of all this business, citing the continual jockeying for control of the services in North Carolina and Virginia waters by the railroads and their boat lines, the intricacies of which hardly need further mention here.

Meanwhile, soon after the Elizabeth City and Norfolk Railroad had gotten under way, railroad-building enthusiasm proved contagious for canal President Parks. At his company's annual meeting in September 1882, he influenced his directors to authorize a $100,000 loan to the newly founded Norfolk and Virginia Beach Railroad and Improvement Company, of which he became the first president.[12] Parks and other associates chartered the railroad on January 14, 1882, and a narrow-gage (three-foot) eighteen-mile line was laid out between downtown Norfolk and the beach front, opening July 28, 1883. At the end of the line, the railroad company had purchased the property of the Seaside Hotel and Land Company and was busy erecting pavilions and cottages, improving the hotel itself, and converting the establishment into a first-class summer resort.

Milton Courtright—the civil engineer who had built the Albemarle and Chesapeake Canal almost three decades previously, and who, as general agent, had guided its fortunes during the turbulent Civil War years while Parks, a paroled Confederate, was ineligible—had contracted to build and equip the new railroad. Courtright died before the work was completed, however, and the canal company was obliged to make further advances totaling $20,000, "so to enable the railroad company to prosecute the work until arrangements were made with other parties to complete it." In those days, locomotives were often given names as well as numbers. Of the three brought in to serve the route when it began, Number Two was appropriately named the *Milton Courtright*.[13]

The railroad got off to a good start, and *Poor's Manual*, the railroader's bible, reported that it carried 6,565 passengers over a total of 4,680 miles for the first summer session from July 28, when the line opened, to September 30, 1883. However, the road's earnings of $5,994.44 did not meet its expenses of $9,250.00, and the next year the fledgling company went into the hands of receivers. In 1884 Parks stepped down as

[11] Prince, *Norfolk Southern Railroad*, pp.189, 199, 200.
[12] A & C Canal Co., [*Thirteenth*] *Annual Report* (1885), pp. 6–7.

[13] Prince, *Norfolk Southern Railroad*, p. 10.

president of the road, with which apparently he then had no further connection thereafter. After a year in receivership, the company was restored, but was sold under foreclosure in 1887 to a syndicate that reorganized it under the same name on July 1, 1887. Charles W. Mackey then became president. One of the railroad's principal assets was the Princess Anne Hotel, built in 1885, which was to become a Virginia-Beach landmark until it burned to the ground in 1907.[14]

Meanwhile the railroad was reorganized as the Norfolk, Virginia Beach & Southern Railroad, and the track was widened to standard gage in 1898. The word *Southern* in the new corporate title had some significance in the affairs of the Albemarle and Chesapeake Canal, for a twenty-two mile branch line, leaving the main Virginia Beach line at Euclid, headed southward through Princess Anne Courthouse and on to Munden Point at the lower end of the county. Here, at the head of Currituck Sound opposite Back Bay, a steamboat wharf was built on the eastern shore of the sound at the mouth of the North Landing River, providing, for the first time, an actual direct rail connection to the canal.

Perishable products, including quantities of wild ducks, brought up the waterway to this point, could then readily be transferred to the railroad for quick delivery into Norfolk, bypassing the most constricted part of the canal route through the North Landing River, Virginia Cut, and the Elizabeth River's Southern Branch. In 1900, the forty-one miles of the Norfolk, Virginia Beach & Southern's tracks were absorbed into the widely expanding Norfolk and Southern, which established its own boat lines serving Currituck Sound out of Munden. More will be reported later on this phase of the Munden rail operations.[15] Meanwhile, the main line of the Norfolk and Southern was being lengthened and its "navy" expanded, as we have already noted, by the acquisition of tracks and connecting steamers on the south side of Albemarle Sound, in their eventual junction with the Atlantic and North Carolina Railroad at New Bern.

As observed, the final quarter of the nineteenth century saw the heyday of steamboating on North Carolina waters wax and wane. Better roads and the extension of the web of railroad lines touching their shores at various points gradually reduced travel time required to connect coastal towns. Even though the boat lines often could ply a more direct route, the greater speed of land transportation gradually won out. Then, as now, however, many people regretted seeing the boats depart.

A good idea of just how extensive their services had become can be gleaned from a statement of "the present condition of our waterways" appearing in an 1896 state of North Carolina publication. The state's 1100 miles of inland navigation were cited in *North Carolina and Its Resources* as follows:

---

[14] Ibid.; *Poor's Manual of Railroads—South Atlantic Group* (1884), p. 391

[15] Prince, *Norfolk Southern Railroad*, p. 10.

The sounds are navigated by a large fleet of light-draft and fast steamboats that furnish abundant means of transportation for passengers and freight between the numerous points where they touch. Steamboats run up the Chowan and Black Water to Franklin, Va., and up the Meherrin to Murfreesboro; up the Roanoke to Halifax; up the Neuse to Kinston; up the Trent to Trenton; up the Cape Fear to Fayetteville; up the Tar to Tarboro; up the Scuppernong to Creswell; up the Alligator to Fairfield; up the Cashie to Windsor; up the Perquimans to Belvidere; up the Little River to Woodville; up the Pasquotank many miles above Elizabeth City; up the North River to Indian Township; and up the Moccasin River and Swift Creek to the head of navigation.[16]

Several of these streams, like the Percuimans and the Little River, were comparatively short, merely draining low-lying sound-side counties. Others, however—like the Roanoke and the Chowan entering Albemarle Sound and the Neuse, the Tar, and the Pamlico entering Pamlico Sound—penetrated deeply into the interior country. In some cases they extended beyond the fall line and, as with the canal locks at Roanoke Rapids, provided access for barge traffic on into the piedmont country as well.

Steamboats serving inland areas were particularly vulnerable to improved land transport, but places closer to the outlying banks islands on the remote sides of the sounds, such as Roanoke Island and Currituck ports, of necessity required boat transport well into the present century. The same 1896 North Carolina publication gave the assessed value of property (seemingly at remarkably low assessments) of the Albemarle and Chesapeake Canal as $100,000; the Fairfield Canal, $6,453; and the Old Dominion Steamship Company's local steamers and wharves, $42,000. The Lake Drummond Canal and Water Company—the new corporation which took over the Dismal Swamp Canal after 1892—was valued at only $1,600.[17]

One of the best-known overnight passenger vessels to sail the North Carolina sounds during this final quarter of the nineteenth century was the Old Dominion Line's trim, white-painted steamboat *Newberne*, already mentioned. The *Newberne* (fig. 34) was owned by the line from the time of her construction in 1875 until she was finally sold off in 1908 to Dempsey and Sons of Philadelphia, whereupon she was converted to a barge. Though certainly small compared to the giant luxury craft then found on Long Island Sound and elsewhere in the north, the *Newberne* was typical of the larger size, shoal-draft, two-deck passenger and freight boats which plied the canal route on and off during those last, best years. Having been lengthened in 1879, with her tonnage increased from 412 to 482 tons, the *Newberne* finally measured 178.5 feet long by 24.9 feet wide, with a 9-foot depth of hold.

[16] North Carolina State Board of Agriculture, *North Carolina and its Resources*, pp. 130–31.

[17] Ibid., p. 216.

FIG. 34. *The steamboat* Newberne *was hauled ashore at the Newport News Shipbuilding and Dry Dock Co. for emergency repairs, February 20, 1894. (Shipyard photo, courtesy the Mariners Museum.)*

Chapter 6 mentions the trip made in 1892 by New York maritime writer Samuel Ward Stanton from Norfolk to New Bern and back while he was gathering material for some illustrated feature articles he planned for *Seaboard Magazine,* of which he was an editor. Though accounts of voyages taken on other lines during the late nineteenth century are legion, portions of these *Seaboard* stories provide perhaps the only surviving reminiscence of steamboating in its heyday on these southern seas and his neat little sketches of various vessels encountered on the trip, several of which are reproduced in this book, are both charming and accurate. His accounts are quoted extensively in this chapter.[18]

Having boarded the *Newberne* the night before departure, Stanton was fast asleep when the steamer set sail from Norfolk (see fig. 35) on a fine Thursday morning in February, "at the unearthly hour of four." Since our scribe was still abed, he understandably left no record of leaving the dock, arriving at Great Bridge, or going through the lock there. The *Newberne* was already well along the Virginia Cut before he first made an appearance on deck to record the passing scene.

"The *Newberne* is an excellent passenger propeller, and is well adapted to the route on which she plies," the first of a two-part article commenced. Advising his readers that the *Newberne* had been expressly built for the Old Dominion's North Carolina line by the Delaware River Iron Shipbuilding and Engine Works at Chester, Pennsylvania, in 1875, Stanton then recorded the boat's dimensions and tonnage, concluding that, "she has an engine with a 24-inch cylinder by three feet stroke. Although her propeller wheel is no more than three-fourths submerged, she makes very good time."[19]

Tracing the 225-mile course that the necessarily shoal-draft boat would take through the canals, rivers, and sounds, Stanton reported "It is undoubtedly one of the most pleasant short trips that can be made on the coast, with so little danger of sea-sickness." This was a strong recommendation for the pre-Dramamine era. This pleasant passage down the canal, rivers, and sounds occupied three days and two nights, and he stated "there is a continual diversity of scene to charm the eye and a delicious and intoxicating balminess in the air—whether it be winds from the sands of Hatteras and the Gulf Stream or the bracing and invigorating piney aroma from the forests—to delight the senses."[20]

Warming to his work, the *Seaboard* article continued:

> When I left my stateroom on the *Newberne* the morning after I had gone aboard, I found that we were in the canal, passing eastward through a forest of cypress and juniper. The sun had just arisen, and the decks were sparkling where its rays touched the dew upon them. We were passing along a cut in the forest which was so straight that the end of it was

---

[18] Stanton, *Steam Navigation,* pp. 10–18.

[19] Ibid., p. 10
[20] Ibid.

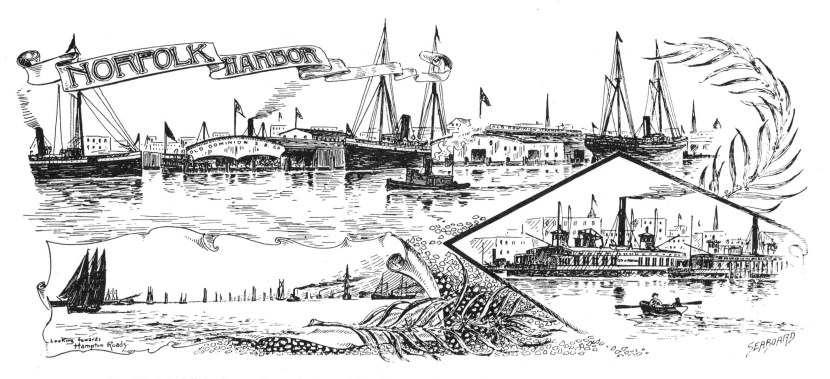

FIG. 35. *Norfolk harbor, as drawn by Samuel Ward Stanton in 1892 for his* Seaboard Magazine *article. (Courtesy Steamship Historical Society of America.)*

lost in the distance. Far ahead a tug was coming, towing a schooner, and the steam from her exhaust pipe reflected in the water.

The banks of the canal are very much unlike those of the Erie, for there is no towpath; indeed there is no path at all. The canal has been dug and the earth and trees uprooted placed on either side—the banks are composed mostly of roots and trees. Back of this extends great forests of cypress and juniper. Here and there where the bank has fallen away through the washing it receives from the waves of passing vessels, the huge trunk of a cypress tree is disclosed, half under water, as perfect and as sound as it was forty years ago when the canal was being cut through.[21]

The author proceeded to mention the various canal

---

[21] Ibid.

cuts as well as the 220-foot lock which he still had not seen, then continued:

As there is no towpath, vessels not propelled by steam have to be towed through the canal by tugs, and there are a number that are constantly employed doing this work. The rates of towing to or from Norfolk to North River are 25 cents per registered ton for light vessels, and 40 cents for loaded vessels. Those partially loaded are charged 30 cents per ton. Way towing is one cent per mile.

Tolls on the canal on vessels in ballast and without cargo are as follows: Barges, 20 cents per ton; screw steamers, 25 cents per ton; paddle-wheel steamers, 30 cents, and sailing vessels, 20 cents. If such vessels return within 30 days loaded, then the amount of tolls charged for the passage when going south not loaded will be credited on the amount of tolls due on the return cargo. Vessels are not allowed to steam at a higher rate of speed than three miles per hour. There are no obstructions to masted vessels. This route to the south is taken by all of the smaller sized steam vessels which do not draw over seven feet, and can avoid Hatteras. Those drawing less than five feet can go through the Newberne and Beaufort canal and avoid the dangers of both capes Hatteras and Lookout.

About eight o'clock the scow propeller *Ox,* loaded with cypress logs, creosoted, and towing a scow, also loaded, made her appearance ahead. When we approached and were about to pass, the *Newberne* stopped and laid by the right hand bank. After the *Ox* had passed it was found that we had grounded, and fifteen minutes were consumed in getting started again. The *Ox* is a peculiar looking boat, and has a mate in the propeller *Wemple,* which the writer saw last week at the foot of Vesey Street, New York, unloading creosoted piles for the new wharf there. . . .

There are very few cultivated spots on the canal after leaving Great Bridge where the lock is situated. For ten miles the steamer passes through a vast, unbroken forest, the tall straight trees of which stand like sentinels, so still are they. The ground beyond the bank of the canal is low and marshy, and is covered with a low mass of tangled vines, which are part of the time in water. All is still and dismal. The occasional cry of a bird is the only sound that disturbs the stillness of this mournful region. Dismal it is in the daytime; at night it is still more so.

The damp, soggy atmosphere of southern nights, the miasmatic fogs that rise from the marshes and settle like a pall over these lands, the spectral gleam of the will-o'-the-wisp, is enough to strike terror to the hearts of the most courageous.[22]

After this moody appraisal, Stanton embarked on a description of adjacent Dismal Swamp in general and its canal in particular, observing sadly that the latter had deteriorated to the extent that "vessels drawing over three feet cannot run upon it."[23] And he cited its entire fleet, which then consisted merely of the "little propellers *Dauntless,* 11 tons, and *Nellie,* 10 tons." Then, drawing on a vivid imagination, he proceeded

[22] Ibid., pp. 10–11.
[23] Ibid., p. 11.

to relate a preposterous account of how the Dismal Swamp Canal originally came into being. According to this, there were two separate groups of timber cutters working in the swamp. As they penetrated the forest, one working southward and the other northward, each dug a shallow ditch to float out the lumber.

"One day the men working far in the middle of the swamp, to which point they had dug the ditch, heard sounds issuing from the almost impenetrable glades before them."[24] And so it was—believe it or not—that the two parties met and the canals lined up right on the nose!

Possibly the originator of this unlikely tale was the *Newberne's* master, Capt. Thomas J. Southgate, apparently a raconteur of repute, for later during the voyage, his interested passenger stated: "I soon found that Captain Southgate was ready to tell me all he knew of the history" of the area.[25] In any event, the good captain had long acquaintance with the Carolina sounds country and had previously commanded on various runs and at various times such steamers as the *Olive*, the Old Dominion line's first boat, and the *Pamlico*, the *Shenandoah*, and the *Manteo*.

Continuing his recital, Stanton went on to say:

At the end of the Albemarle and Chesapeake Canal [Virginia Cut] is the first settlement. This is North Landing. It is at the head of North Landing River. The little canal passenger propeller *Helen Smith* was just leaving here as we passed. She runs between Norfolk and points on Currituck Sound. There are few houses to be seen at North Landing. The canal company has a toll house here. We soon left North Landing and were moving along at about eight miles per hour down the tortuous North Landing River. . . .

The *Newberne* has been on this route since she was built in 1876. The Old Dominion Company started the line in November, 1869, with the propeller *Olive*. She ran to Washington on the Pamlico River. There was a line of steamships—the *Ellen S. Terry, Zodiac* and *Louisa Moore*—then running between New Bern and New York via Hatteras Inlet. These latter vessels ran from the close of the war until 1870, when they stopped. After these boats ceased running, the propeller *Raleigh*—now running on the Hudson River—was placed on the route between Washington and New Bern, connecting with the *Olive*. Captain Southgate assumed command March 31, 1871. The *Olive* ran for three years to Washington, N.C., and then extended her trips to New Bern, making her first trip there March 27, 1872. In 1875 the *Pamlico* came out. She was built in Greenpoint and measured 142 feet in length, 24 feet beam, and 9 feet depth of hold. Her engine was from Harrison & Fletcher's. She left New York in June, 1875, and immediately took her place on the route to New Bern and Washington. Twelve months later the *Newberne* made her appearance. These two boats ran to Washington via New Bern, uninterruptedly, for many years.[26]

Stanton then cited the five-year contract made in

[24] Ibid, p. 12.
[25] Ibid.
[26] Ibid.

1882 between the Old Dominion line and the new Norfolk Southern Railroad. As stated, this contrived to eliminate Old Dominion boat service through the canal, and the steamers began their trips out of Elizabeth City. The contract was revoked in 1887, when the Pennsylvania Railroad began to compete directly with the Old Dominion Steamship Company's ocean service from New York to Hampton Roads ports. The return of the *Newberne* to Norfolk, along with the line's brand-new and splendid 190-foot steamboat *Manteo*, put the Old Dominion Line back as a direct competitor to the Norfolk Southern Railroad in the Albemarle Sound region.

Ultimately, the *Manteo* left to join the Ward Line and went on to Cuba. Meanwhile, the adjudged "reliable" *Pamlico* had outlived her usefulness and was broken up, her still-serviceable engine being installed in the new *Albemarle*—"a homely-looking boat with a smoke stack that resembles a bean-pole."[27] The *Albemarle* was serving as the *Newberne's* running mate at the time of Stanton's voyage.

At length, the writer resumed his personal chronicle:

> The trip down North Landing River is as an enjoyable one as could be imagined. The upper part of the river is narrow and crooked and the banks low. The latter are covered for the most part with a dense growth of cypress, juniper, gum and cedar. Here and there is seen a cleared spot, but the deserted, rude dwelling upon it tells its tale only too

> well. There are a number of these "starvation plantations" along North Landing River. . . .
>
> We passed the *Comet*, a stern-wheel boat bound for Norfolk about ten o'clock. She was on her way from Currituck Sound. The *Comet* runs regularly in W. B. Rogers' line of North Carolina steamers and is the largest local canal packet. She is 120 feet in length, 20 feet beam and 4 feet depth of hold; is of 96 gross and 73 net tons, and formerly ran on the Roanoke River.[28]
>
> The river soon began to widen and there are long stretches of meadow covered with short saw grass, back of which lie dreary forests of pine. There are no habitations in sight and the steamer courses her way around bend after bend. Capt. Southgate called my attention to a weather-beaten pole standing in the water near the right-hand bank. "Do you see that pole," said he? "I have watched it for the last twenty years, expecting every trip to find it gone. It was placed there by the hands on board the steamboat *Orient* over twenty years ago. The *Orient*, in coming around the bend here one day, swung too far to the left and, being a big boat, got stuck right across the channel. These poles marked the place where her bow was, but why they were put there I could never imagine. She was finally extricated from her position by other boats, but the poles remained. It will almost seem like losing an old friend to see the old pole go."
>
> Pungo ferry was passed during the morning. It consists of about ten houses on either side of the

---

[27] Ibid, p. 13.

[28] A photograph of the *Comet* in Great Bridge Lock taken from the *Art Book of Norfolk and Vicinity* (1885), is cited in chapter 5, note 13. It is reproduced here as fig. 6.

THE GEO. H. STOUT.

Fig. 36. *Samuel Ward Stanton's 1892 drawing of the steamer* Geo. H. Stout *for his* Seaboard Magazine *article. (Courtesy Steamboat Historical Society of America.)*

river and an old flatboat for ferrying horses or passengers across the river lies moored to a stake on one side. The propeller *Tahoma* which left Norfolk two hours later than we did, now hove in sight, several miles back. Being a small boat, she is thus enabled to steam at full speed around the bends which it is impossible for the *Newberne* to do.[29]

In the second of his two-part series, Stanton embarked on a lengthy history of the steam navigation of all the North Carolina sounds, citing its origins and describing the settlements served by the boats—Eliz-

abeth City, Hertford, Edenton, Plymouth, Roanoke Island, Belhaven, "Little" Washington, and finally his present destination, New Bern, "the City of Elms," "magnificiently situated on the Neuse River, fifty miles from its mouth, on a point of land where the Trent River joins the Neuse."[30]

Stanton then resumed the account of his voyage:

The *Newberne* increased her speed when we left North Landing River and struck the Government Channel, which runs through the head of Currituck Sound, and when the full speed bell had been rung and the familiar plash of the propeller wheel was accelerated the *Tahoma* ceased to gain on us, as she had been doing for an hour and a half. Clyde's propeller *George H. Stout* [fig. 36] now hove in sight and passed very close to us. She was on her way to Norfolk from New Bern. The tug *Jupiter*, with a raft, also the freight propeller *Flora*, with the Erie canal-boat *Scheu* in tow, both heavily loaded, were also passed about the same time.

It is not many miles across the head of Currituck Sound to the point where the Coinjock cut of the canal commences. The Government buildings where the gas for the sound lights is made is situated here, and the side-wheel lighthouse tender *Jessamine* [fig. 37] was at the dock as we passed through into the canal. The sail through this canal [the North Carolina Cut] does not consume more than an hour, but it is an interesting trip.

---

[29] Stanton, *Steam Navigation* pp. 13–14.

[30] Ibid., p. 15.

FIG. 37. *The 315-ton side-wheel lighthouse-tender* Jessamine, *built at Baltimore in 1881, was a frequent visitor to the government facility at Coinjock, where gas for illuminating the Carolina Sounds buoys and beacons was manufactured. (Photo U.S. Coast Guard Civil Engineering Office, Norfolk, Va.; courtesy Virginia State Library, Richmond.)*

Coinjock is an unimportant place. There is a bridge across the canal here....[31]

It was at this point that Captain Southgate elected to regale his passenger with the story of the Confederate capture of the federal steamboats *Emily* and *Arrow,* which had occurred at that very spot in May 1863 (see chapter 6). Stanton resumed his narration of the trip after leaving Coinjock.

The canal strikes the head of the North River and the trip down this stream was a charming one. It is wider than its brother the North Landing River, though not quite as long. We passed down this river in the afternoon and it was like a sail on an enchanted stream. And then, just before sunset, when the boat reached Albemarle Sound, it was a fitting climax to look away far to the westward, where no line of shore appeared on the horizon, the sun lighting up the waters with unfamiliar splendor while the boat glided along over this summer sea. A little melody of Hiller's seemed to float in across those waters,

---

[31] Ibid., p. 16.

FIG. 38. *New Bern harbor, N.C., as drawn by Samuel Ward Stanton in 1892 for a* Seaboard Magazine *article. (Courtesy Steamship Historical Society of America.)*

FIG. 39. *Samuel Ward Stanton's 1892 drawing for Seaboard Magazine of the raft blockade in the North Landing River. (Courtesy Steamship Historical Society of America.)*

now softly, now more loudly, but always tranquilly. To the south appeared the low-lying shores, a well marked line which gradually softened as it reached away to the west and melted into the quiet waters of Albemarle. It was a glorious and never to be forgotten scene, a picture, a poem, that would be stamped indelibly upon a gazer's memory.

Far to the west the little Fairfield boat was crossing this great sheet of water on her way to Elizabeth City, and a thin line of smoke trailed behind her. But the finest of sunset and twilight pictures will fade and as the shadows deepened, the *Newberne* continued on her way.

At eight 'oclock we reached famous Roanoke Island, famous because of the fact that upon its shores, the first white child [Virginia Dare] was born

in America and because of Burnside's expedition against this Confederate stronghold during the late War. . . .

Large quantities of fish are shipped North from Roanoke Island. The fishery business of the North Carolina sounds is the most important on the Atlantic coast. Propellers of the "nondescript" type are used for hauling in the seines, which is the chief mode of catching the fish. It is estimated that six thousand people are employed in these fisheries, and over 40,000,000 pounds of fish are taken annually.

All night long the *Newberne* continues down Pamlico Sound. Hatteras light gleams out across the waters and can be seen for about four hours, though the nearest point we go to it is twenty miles. The next

FIG. 40. *Samuel Ward Stanton's 1892 drawing of the steamboat* W. B. Rogers, *built in 1880. (Courtesy Steamship Historical Society of America.)*

morning we are steaming up the Neuse River, a broad and noble stream, not unlike the lower James.

The sail up the Neuse that morning was an ideal one and the approach to New Bern [fig. 38] a revelation. We sighted it ahead, this fair Southern city, and as we approached it looked the very picture of the lovely, quiet historical old town that it is with its incomparable situation.[32]

Stanton was evidently received as a minor celebrity, for he was given a very "cordial reception" by New Bern residents. Following this hospitality, the New York editor reboarded the *Newberne;* leaving at one o'clock for the return trip up to Norfolk, stating that it "was as enjoyable as going down." Before the journey was over, however, he was to encounter one of the principal annoyances then inherent in the canal navigation:

On the second day, while going up North Landing River, on turning a bend we suddenly came upon quite a fleet of boats. They were stopped on account of a raft in tow of the tug *Grace Titus*, which had swung across from bank to bank. [See fig. 39.] The propellers *Vesper*, *W. B. Rogers*, [fig. 40], and *Defiance* were waiting to get by. With a little help from the *Newberne*, the raft was straightened out and the boats continued on their way, the *Newberne* reaching Norfolk at six o'clock that (Saturday) night.[33] [This time he was awake to see the lock at Great Bridge (fig. 41).]

Not the least interesting part of Samuel Ward Stanton's articles was the many accompanying illustrations taken from accurate pen and ink drawings he made of sights along the way. These ranged from general harbor views of both Norfolk and New Bern, (figs. 35 and 38), to the numerous vessels of all types passed en route by the *Newberne* (figs. 31, 33, 36, 39, 40, 42). Comparable drawings were to gain a gold medal for the talented artist in 1895, when exhibited at the Chicago World's Fair.

In May of 1892, at the time Stanton was making this cruise the *Newberne's* running mates on the Carolina division were the *Accomack* (1877), the *R. L. Myers*

---

[32] Ibid., pp. 16–17.

[33] Ibid., pp. 17–18.

ALBEMARLE AND CHESAPEAKE CANAL LOCK, [GRANITE] 14 Miles from Norfolk, 220 feet long, 40 feet wide, 8 feet deep.

FIG. 41. *The steamboat* Newberne, *westbound, tied up in Great Bridge Lock. From an engraving after a photograph in* Maritime Dixie: Norfolk Port and City, 1893, *by A.M. (Courtesy Virginia State Library, Richmond.)*

[148   ]

THE ALBEMARLE.

FIG. 42. *Samuel Ward Stanton's 1892 drawing for* Seaboard Magazine *of the 1891-built steamer* Albemarle II. *(Courtesy Steamship Historical Society of America.)*

(1885), the *Virginia Dare* (1888), the *Kinston* (1890), and the *Albemarle* [II] (fig. 42) (1891). The *Newberne* continued her accustomed 225-mile route through the canal and rivers from Norfolk down to New Bern for another dozen years. In the interim, two more vessels, the *Hatteras* II (1896) and the *Ocracoke* (1898), both slightly smaller wooden-hull screw steamers, had been added to the fleet, and other boats were sold. It was not much later, however, that the entire fleet was disbanded. The *Hatteras*, *Albemarle*, and *R. L. Myers* went to the Norfolk and Southern Railroad along with the line's wharf properties. The *Newberne* went to a Philadelphia pur-

chaser in 1906, leaving only the *Ocracoke* (fig. 43) as the last survivor of the Old Dominion line's Carolina sounds fleet. By 1908, with its through rail route established, the Norfolk and Southern also gave up its overnight boat lines.

It remained for Old Dominion line historian John L. Lochhead to pronounce the line's requiem: "The round trip between Norfolk and New Bern took three days and two nights [eight hours by train as scheduled in the 1924 *Official Guide*] and was often prolonged by delays in the Albemarle and Chesapeake Canal, choked with slow moving tows or log rafts and

FIG. 43. *Wood-hull screw steamboat* Ocracoke *moored at the Southgate Terminal Corporation pier, Norfolk. She was built in 1898 at 151 feet in length, measuring 421 tons. In 1906, she was the only surviving steamer in the Old Dominion Line's North Carolina service. (Photo provided by Captain Winder; courtesy the Mariners Museum.)*

schooners which frequently ran aground and blocked traffic. The company abandoned the service without regret."[34]

It was the railroads, of course, that had administered the coupe de grace. Today, a handful of modern mini-liners annually ply the Intracoastal Waterway on spring and autumn trips back and forth between New England and Florida waters, and, of course, many yachts make the same journeys. But with the passing of such vessels as the *Newberne* following the turn of the century, the full-run overnight passenger boats sailing the length of the sounds were no longer around to display for their patrons the magnificent sunsets of Albemarle Sound, extolled by writer Stanton for those fortunate enough to have witnessed them as "stamped indelibly upon a gazer's memory."

[34] Lochhead, "Steamships and Steamboats of the Old Dominion Line," p. 53. See also *The Official Guide of the Railway and Steam Navigation Lines of the United States.* (New York: National Railway Publication Co., issued monthly).

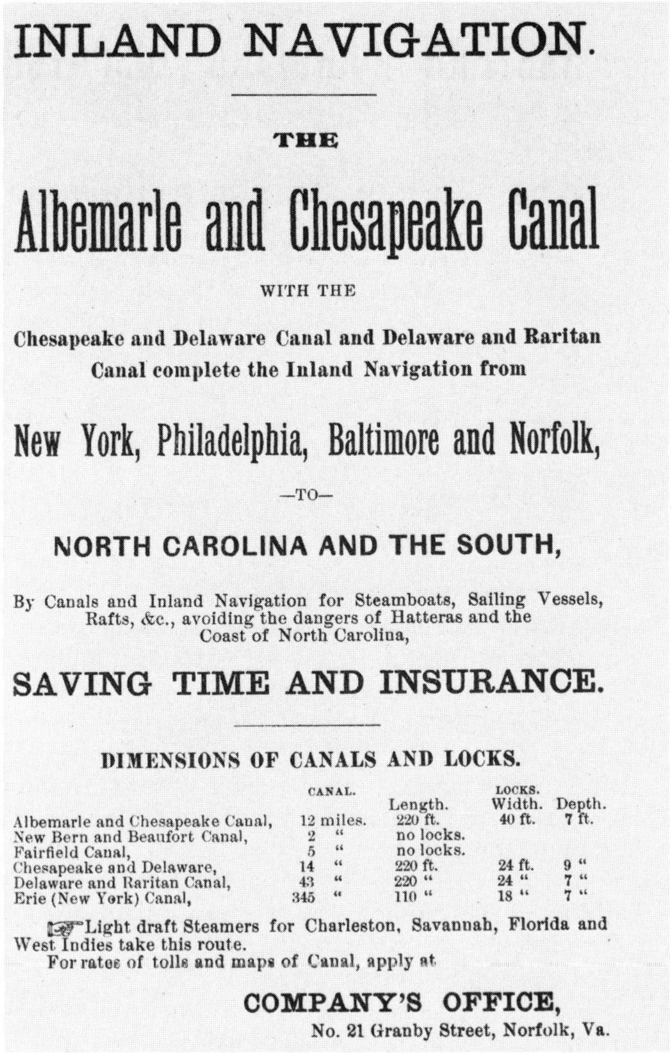

INLAND NAVIGATION.

THE

Albemarle and Chesapeake Canal

WITH THE

Chesapeake and Delaware Canal and Delaware and Raritan Canal complete the Inland Navigation from

New York, Philadelphia, Baltimore and Norfolk,

—TO—

NORTH CAROLINA AND THE SOUTH,

By Canals and Inland Navigation for Steamboats, Sailing Vessels, Rafts, &c., avoiding the dangers of Hatteras and the Coast of North Carolina,

SAVING TIME AND INSURANCE.

DIMENSIONS OF CANALS AND LOCKS.

	CANAL.	Length.	LOCKS. Width.	Depth.
Albemarle and Chesapeake Canal,	12 miles.	220 ft.	40 ft.	7 ft.
New Bern and Beaufort Canal,	2 "	no locks.		
Fairfield Canal,	5 "	no locks.		
Chesapeake and Delaware,	14 "	220 ft.	24 ft.	9 "
Delaware and Raritan Canal,	43 "	220 "	24 "	7 "
Erie (New York) Canal,	345 "	110 "	18 "	7 "

☞ Light draft Steamers for Charleston, Savannah, Florida and West Indies take this route.

For rates of tolls and maps of Canal, apply at

COMPANY'S OFFICE,

No. 21 Granby Street, Norfolk, Va.

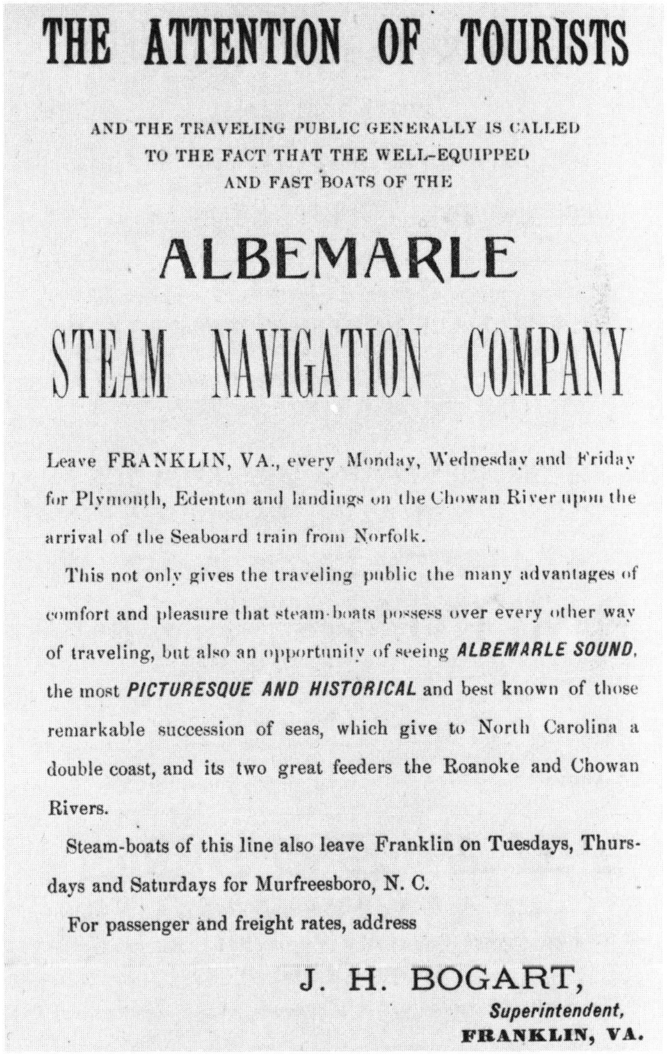

THE ATTENTION OF TOURISTS

AND THE TRAVELING PUBLIC GENERALLY IS CALLED
TO THE FACT THAT THE WELL-EQUIPPED
AND FAST BOATS OF THE

ALBEMARLE

STEAM NAVIGATION COMPANY

Leave FRANKLIN, VA., every Monday, Wednesday and Friday for Plymouth, Edenton and landings on the Chowan River upon the arrival of the Seaboard train from Norfolk.

This not only gives the traveling public the many advantages of comfort and pleasure that steam-boats possess over every other way of traveling, but also an opportunity of seeing **ALBEMARLE SOUND**, the most **PICTURESQUE AND HISTORICAL** and best known of those remarkable succession of seas, which give to North Carolina a double coast, and its two great feeders the Roanoke and Chowan Rivers.

Steam-boats of this line also leave Franklin on Tuesdays, Thursdays and Saturdays for Murfreesboro, N. C.

For passenger and freight rates, address

J. H. BOGART,

Superintendent,
FRANKLIN, VA.

FIG. 44. *Advertisements promoting (A) the Albemarle and Chesapeake Canal and (B) the Albemarle Steam Navigation Company, from Geo. I. Nowitzky,* Norfolk: The Maritime Metropolis of Virginia *(1888).*

Hard Times and
Finally the Government
Takes Over, 1885–1913

For thirty years the destinies of the Albemarle and Chesapeake Canal—from initial planning, through the turmoil of war and reconstruction, down to a position of dependability and usefulness—had been well guided by Marshall Parks. In 1885, however, the "Commodore" relinquished the presidency of the company to his associate, Franklin Weld. Weld ran the organization until 1898, when he was replaced by Warren J. Elliott. Both men had previously served as company directors and were well qualified to manage its affairs.

By the conclusion of Weld's term of office, however, the Albemarle and Chesapeake Canal came upon a period of unforseen hardship, not only by reason of increased railroad competition but also, surprisingly

enough, from a drastic loss of their business to the Dismal Swamp Canal, then completely rebuilt and modernized. These two forces resulted in severe financial troubles for the Albemarle and Chesapeake Canal Company, for, from the first, there never was enough business for both canals. Ultimately a court-ordered foreclosure sale of the entire facilities of the Albemarle and Chesapeake occurred.

At sixty-five, when he gave up running the canal, Parks still had more than a dozen years of purposeful activity ahead of him. Mention was made of the initially unprofitable railroad to Virginia Beach which he promoted in 1882. This venture came at an unpropitious time, for with the death of Milton Courtright, new engineers had to be found to complete the line, and construction expenses mounted. Then there was a financial crisis originating in New York on May 14, 1884, followed by a year-long period of industrial depression during which Parks's Norfolk and Virginia Beach Railroad and Improvement Company went into receivership.

With interests severed both from the canal and the railroad, Parks still kept busy, and during President Grover Cleveland's first administration (1885–89), he was appointed Supervising Inspector of Steam Vessels. His district extended from Baltimore down to Florida, with headquarters in Norfolk. This was Parks's last public position or active business pursuit, however. His health began to fail, and he died June 10, 1900, and was widely mourned for his "genial and kindly disposition."[1] Obituary notices praised him extravagantly, citing his many contributions to the community; perhaps the most meaningful, however, was an unconscious tribute to the success of his life's work which appeared routinely in the shipping columns of the Norfolk *Virginian-Pilot*. On the day he died, a score of vessels, from steamers to barges plying their normal rounds, were cited by name in the newspaper as transiting in both directions the canal he had planned long before and had brought to useful reality.

The unexpected competition from the Dismal Swamp Canal had its background (as noted at the end of chapter 8) in the older waterway's attempt in 1880 to extricate itself from the post-Civil War slump from which it had never truly recovered. It was generally appreciated that the rivalry provided from the very beginning by the new Albemarle and Chesapeake Canal was the contributing cause of the Dismal's continued decline. Indeed, this was not unanticipated, for an entry in the minute book of the Dismal Swamp Canal Company made back in 1857 stated that "the threatened completion of the Albemarle and Chesapeake Canal menaces us with a dimunition if not a total absorption of our business."[2] The foundering Dismal Swamp Canal Company was reorganized December 1, 1880, however, and as a result got "a little new blood in its old veins."[3] More than a dozen years were to pass before it was completely reborn, however.

The initial respite proved but temporary. In 1880, the Dismal Swamp Canal was recorded as having transported 6,731 tons of freight, contrasted to 400,000 tons moved the same year on the Albemarle and Chesapeake. After 1880, however, with some new and larger locks installed and a certain amount of dredging performed along the line of the canal, regular steamboat services were improved, and brand new canal packets such as the 1880-built *William B. Rogers* and the *Thomas Newton* (1881), each ninety-six feet in length and of similar design, joined the older and smaller passenger

[1] Norfolk *Public Ledger*, Monday, June 11, 1900.

[2] Quoted in Joseph C. Platt, *Examination into Proposal of Improving and Enlarging the Dismal Swamp Canal now Owned by the Lake Drummond Canal and Water Company*, p. 5.
[3] Cary W. Jones, *Guide to Norfolk as a Business Centre*, pp. 36–37.

steamers—actually little more than glorified tugs.

Recognizing that improvements to their own canal were a continuing necessity, the directors of the Albemarle and Chesapeake Canal company adopted a resolution at their annual meeting on November 8, 1888, which authorized them "to issue, negotiate and sell" some $50,000 worth of new company bonds guaranteed by a second mortgage on the property. This mortgage was also negotiated with the Union Trust Company of New York, the firm which had granted the canal company its $500,000 first mortgage ten years earlier. Plans now were to issue fifty $1,000 bonds paying six percent interest dated January 1, 1889.[4]

Meanwhile, by 1886, the condition of the Dismal Swamp Canal had worsened again, and once more it was "practically closed to business." This downhill trend continued, but a futile attempt at company reorganization was made in 1889 with the emergence of the Norfolk and North Carolina Canal Company as operators.[5] That year the freight-tonnage ratio be-

tween the two canals had improved slightly insofar as the Dismal Swamp Canal was concerned, with 78,211 tons carried by the Dismal in contrast to the Albemarle and Chesapeake's 316,783 tons. However, the Dismal Swamp Canal was still far behind its younger rival.[6]

The Dismal Swamp Canal continued to deteriorate, however, until the new, larger steamboats of the 1880s could no longer use it. Stanton's account of his 1892 trip on the *Newberne* noted that at the time he was visiting the area, the channel was reduced to handling vessels drawing no more than three feet. By then, he said, only two little shallow-draft steam tugs, the forty-five foot *Dauntless* and the fifty-two foot *Nellie,* regularly plied the old canal from Norfolk down to Elizabeth City.[7]

Despite the existence of the new Elizabeth City and Norfolk Railroad, which already was seriously cutting into the tolls the canals could collect, many travelers and shippers preferred—or, because of geography, were dependent upon—water transport. To accommodate them, the owners of the larger Dismal Swamp Canal steamers then were obliged to send them to Elizabeth City by the longer journey around—down the Albemarle and Chesapeake Canal to the mouth of the North River, and then up the lower Pasquotank— an over seventy-five mile trip in contrast to forty-five

---

[4] Deed Book 149 (1889), p. 417, recorded in the Clerk's Office of the Circuit Court of the City of Chesapeake (formerly Norfolk County), Va. Twenty years after this trust was instituted, the Union Trust Company of New York resigned as trustee, and T. Catesby Jones of Norfolk was appointed the substitute trustee by the Albemarle and Chesapeake Canal Company president, R. St.P. Lowry. This transaction was certified December 31, 1909, and is recorded in Deed Book 349, p. 335.

[5] Platt, *Examination into Proposal of Improving and Enlarging the Dismal Swamp Canal,* p. 5; Brown, *Dismal Swamp Canal,* p. 128.

[6] U.S. Bureau of the Census, *Transportation by Water, 1906* (Washington, D.C.: special report, Department of Commerce, 1908), p. 43.

[7] Stanton, *Steam Navigation,* p. 11.

miles by the direct canal route through Dismal Swamp.

As has been observed, except for the vessels of the Albemarle Steam Navigation Company plying the Chowan River, the passenger carriers serving Albemarle and Pamlico Sounds on longer routes gradually gave up their canal service in the face of railroad competition. However, a virile, if somewhat informally conducted, navigation continued serving isolated Currituck Sound villages and the Banks islands and persisted well into the twentieth century—when in the World War I period, improved country roads finally spelled these vessels' doom as well.

In the summer of 1890, an observant Methodist minister, the Reverend David Gregory Claiborne Butts, embarked on the little side-wheel steamer *Bonito* (already mentioned for her role in aiding the castaways of the U.S.S. *Huron*) for passage to the Outer Banks, where his family was vacationing. In a volume of reminiscences, the minister referred to a "memorable trip" he made through the Albemarle and Chesapeake Canal on board the "majestic craft" that was the eighty-five ton *Bonito*. The boat was employed, he reported, "for the transportation of passengers and freight from Norfolk to the landings on Currituck Sound as far south as 'Church Branch' in North Carolina . . . touching at North Landing, West Neck, Munden Point, and Knotts Island and so on until night overtook the boat. Then she spent the night and made the trip back to Norfolk the next day, if the captain and crew felt like doing so." Paying only a quarter for his dinner (which

subsequently disagreed with him), the Reverend Mr. Butts observed that "the saloon . . . was not large enough for more than five passengers to move about in unless the big fat female cook stayed out."[8]

Steamboat services in the Currituck area were expanded somewhat when the Norfolk, Virginia Beach and Southern Railroad inaugurated its line to Munden Point in 1896. (See figs. 45, 46.) But with the Virginia Cut bypassed from the route, tolls collected by the canal company suffered accordingly. This new railway—giving fast freight service for perishable goods bound for Norfolk and for forwarding on—ultimately acquired several steamboats, which it passed along to the Norfolk and Southern when the little Princess Anne County line was absorbed by the larger system in 1900.

These vessels included the stern-wheeler *Comet* (see fig. 6), built in 1887 for the Roanoke River trade—which Stanton mentioned, and sketched, while passing on the North Landing River during his canal trip in 1892. The *Comet* then plied a thirty-three mile run from Munden to Poplar Branch in lower Currituck County. Another Currituck Sound stern-wheeler was the 1872-built *Undine* (fig. 47), similarly acquired. Other vessels were the iron screw freighter *Lucy*, built in 1872 at Norfolk; the *Thomas Newton* (1881); the *C. W. Petit* (1895); and the then-venerable *Harbinger* (1869). All of them had been driven off the Dismal Swamp Canal by reason

---

[8] D. Gregory Claiborne Butts, *From Saddle to City by Buggy, Boat and Railway*, pp. 229–30.

FIG. 45. *Evening view of the pier and warehouses of the Norfolk, Virginia Beach and Southern Railroad at Munden, Va., established in 1896. This sole direct rail connection to the Albemarle and Chesapeake Canal was located on the east bank of the North Landing River just above Currituck Sound. Photographed about 1915 by Thomas J. Wood, former Munden station agent.*

of the canal's deterioration.

Owners of these small steamers included William B. Rogers, Charles W. Petit, and, later, the Bennets. Their vessels first plied the old waterway, but transferred to the Albemarle and Chesapeake as the Dismal Swamp Canal shoaled, and these men were the principal boat operators until the railroad virtually absorbed all services.[9] However, ownership of the boats changed frequently, providing a kaleidoscopic picture of their operation and control.

An important upswing in the pendulum-like existence of the Dismal Swamp Canal began in 1892, when the company was bought by the self-styled Lake Drummond Canal and Water Company. At first the

---

[9] Alexander C. Brown, "The Passenger Steamers of Dismal Swamp."

old canal's new owners seriously considered abandoning it entirely for navigational purposes and instead, selling the water to the growing communities of Norfolk and Portsmouth to augment the increasingly insufficient supplies available to them. Portsmouth Ditch, a narrow canal leading northward from Lake Drummond, was actually dug through the swamp, but, in the end, was never used for supplying water. Fortunately for today's yachtsmen, the 1892 owners' counsel of despair did not prevail. Instead, the Lake Drummond Company, after much soul-searching, decided to rebuild the canal entirely and to make its facilities equal, if not superior, to its rival, the Albemarle and Chesapeake Canal.

Despite the plethora of federal government surveys and recommendations already available, in 1894, the Lake Drummond Company engaged the services of a

FIG. 46. *The railroad terminal at Munden, Va., as seen from the pier, was photographed about 1915 by former Munden station agent Thomas J. Wood.*

New York civil engineer, Joseph C. Platt, to look over their situation. Platt visited the area in March of that year and traveled through both canals on board a tug. A month later, on April 20, 1894, having thoroughly reviewed both physical and economic considerations, his *Examination into Proposal of Improving and Enlarging the Dismal Swamp Canal* was published.[10]

Encouraged by Platt's report, the canal owners then elected to proceed on a grand scale, which would ultimately cost them in excess of a million dollars. Baltimore bankers funded the venture, and the United States government cooperated by dredging and straightening Deep Creek, converting it to a three-mile-long, hundred-foot-wide, and ten-foot-deep channel. Once more Deep Creek would provide the canal's northern entrance, and the Gilmerton division with its narrow tide lock on the Elizabeth River could be eliminated. Its gates were constantly giving trouble, since they were being eaten by toredo worms.

The contract for rebuilding the Dismal Swamp Canal was awarded to the Philadelphia firm of P. McManus, and work began February 15, 1896. Parts for three complete steam dipper dredges and four hydraulic dredges were assembled at the midpoint of the summit level of the canal. Then, working outward in both directions along the line and also up the feeder ditch to Lake Drummond where a new spillway was built, these monsters contrived to cut 17½ feet below the previous summit level. As the dredges advanced,

---

[10] Platt, *Examination into Proposal of Improving and Enlarging the Dismal Swamp Canal.*

FIG. 47. *The stern-wheel steamboat* Undine, *42 tons and 84 feet in length, was built in 1872 at Petty's Island, N.J., and was long employed carrying passengers and freight on Currituck Sound—where, at length, she struck a log and sank on March 3, 1912. (Photo from Mrs. W. A. Ryder; courtesy the Mariners Museum.)*

suction pipes spewed out the mud, sand, and chopped-up roots for a distance of 60 feet on either side.

At length, three years later, the trunk of the canal had been both lowered and widened to provide a 10-foot-deep channel, 60 feet wide on the surface and 40 feet wide on the bottom. This reduced the former elevation of the canal by 8½ feet and required only two locks, one at each end of the twenty-one mile elevated section running through the swamp. All in all, more than 3,500,000 cubic yards of material had been excavated. The new timber-lock chambers were 250 feet long—30 feet longer than the Albemarle and Chesapeake's guard lock at Great Bridge—by 40 feet wide and provided a 8-foot depth over the sills.

With considerable pomp and circumstance, including a parade of flag-bedecked vessels, the canal was officially opened October 14, 1899. Immediately, fickle navigators, weary of the frequent log jams in the North Landing River, abandoned the Albemarle and

Chesapeake Canal and began using the new Dismal Swamp Canal, which could now handle vessels of comparable size.[11]

Freight transported by the Albemarle and Chesapeake Canal had attained a peak of 403,017 tons in 1890, but subsequently declined on account of the railroads. In 1906, however, with the Dismal Swamp Canal a going concern, less than a quarter of that amount, only 95,169 tons of freight, was recorded plying the Albemarle and Chesapeake. Meanwhile, the rebuilt Dismal completely outstripped its rival, with an impressive 340,135 tons.[12]

A letter from Maj. Gen. W. H. Bixby, Chief of Engineers, to Jacob M. Dickinson, Secretary of War, summed up the situation in other terms, citing that

---

[11] Brown, *Dismal Swamp Canal*, pp. 140–51, traces the reconstruction of the Dismal Swamp Canal, 1896–99.

[12] U.S. Bureau of the Census, *Transportation by Water*, p. 43.

the average annual gross income of the Albemarle and Chesapeake Canal was estimated at $31,000 for the years 1901 to 1909. During the same period, the Lake Drummond Company's gross income averaged $72,000. For the first time, it had forged well ahead of its younger rival.[13]

Although, for the moment, the Dismal Swamp Canal was in a superior position, nothing could be done about either its customary lack of water to operate the locks during dry seasons or the rapid silting up of its channel during the rainy seasons. Some old dry-dock pumps were acquired from the Newport News Shipbuilding and Dry Dock Company for use at South Mills to pump water back up into the lock in cases of dire emergency, but fuel consumption by the pumps was heavy and the effect slight for the effort expended.

In the face of seriously curtailed toll receipts to pay operational costs, the Albemarle and Chesapeake Canal Company's financial position now became increasingly precarious. At length, having defaulted on payments to its bondholders, the point of no return was reached, and the company was hauled into court on October 1, 1910, on complaint of the Union Trust Company of New York as trustee. The court gave the company five days in which to pay a sum sufficient to "satisfy and discharge" the complainant's mortgage

dated July 1, 1879—and then about to mature—together with all costs and expenses. In the probable event the company would be unable to settle up and to pay the money to satisfy this thirty-year, half-million-dollar bond mortgage, jointly held by the Union Trust Company and the Central Trust Company (also of New York), then a foreclosure sale would eventuate.

As anticipated, the beleaguered company was unable to come up with the funds specified in time. Accordingly, November 10, 1910, was set for the date of sale and duly advertised in the newspapers. Percy S. Stephenson of Norfolk, the canal company's vice-president, and Henry W. Anderson of Richmond were named "Special Masters" by Judge Edmund Waddill, Jr., in the United States Circuit Court for the Eastern District of Virginia to oversee the foreclosure. The real estate firm of Stephenson and Taylor was retained to handle the details.

As specified, the sale was held on the steps of the Norfolk County Courthouse in Portsmouth on November 10. Sole bidders for the facility consisted of a holding company acting in behalf of the first mortgage-bond holders. Members of this committee consisted of James M. Edwards, Robert L. Harrison, and Henry T. Cutler, all of New York City. Their bid of $300,000 for all assets of the Albemarle and Chesapeake Canal Company was successful, and with the sale officially confirmed on January 30, 1911, by Judge Waddill, the newly formed canal company—reversing the sequence in its original name—became redesignated the Chesapeake and Albemarle Canal Com-

[13] U.S. Congress. *Intracoastal Waterway . . . Boston, Mass. to Beaufort, N.C.*, 62nd Cong., 2nd sess., January 5, 1912, pp. 100–109 (letter from Secretary of War Jacob M. Dickinson transmitting report of Chief of Engineers Maj. Gen. W. H. Bixby).

pany. Major Edwards was named president. The now-defunct Albemarle and Chesapeake Canal Company's president, R. St. P. Lowry, was not present when the papers were notarized. P. S. Stephenson signed twice—in his capacity as vice-president of the defaulting company and also as the court's Special Master. D. S. Burwell signed as company secretary.

The extent of the property and assets were detailed in the legal instruments as follows:

(*a*) Two canal cuts connecting natural waterways between the Elizabeth River, in Virginia, and the Albemarle Sound, in North Carolina. The Virginia Cut extends from the Elizabeth River to North Landing River, eight and a quarter (8¼) miles, and the right of way is one hundred and fifty (150) feet on each side, measuring from the centre of the canal, with the exception of a portion of the right of way extending through the lands of I. N. Hall, which is one hundred (100) feet on either side of said center line. The North Carolina Cut is two (2) miles long and the right of way is one hundred and fifty (150) feet on either side of said centre line, and extends from Currituck Sound to North River.

(*b*) Houses: 1 House for Collector, 2 Houses for Clerks and Foreman, 2 Houses for Lockkeepers, 3 Houses for Bridgekeepers, 1 House for Stores, 1 House for Office, 1 House for Shop, 3 Sheds.

(*c*) Land:

1.	State of Virginia, Norfolk County, Va.	877 acres
	to	
	Canal Company	July 3, 1875
2.	Norfolk County, Norfolk County, Va.	17 acres
	to	
	Canal Company	April 11, 1856
3.	Addison Burt, Norfolk County, Va.	5,773½ acres
	to	
	Canal Company	November, 14, 1857
4.	William Martin, Currituck County, N. C.	174 acres
	to	
	Canal Company	February 27, 1879
5.	White et als, Currituck County, N.C.	Doubtful
	to	
	Canal Company	July 9, 1879
		6,841 acres

A survey of these lands, made by A. C. Freeman, Surveyor, shows 2,266 acres in dispute from encroachments and other adverse claims.

(*d*) Telephone line: Private line built by the Canal Company from the locks to North Landing, ten (10) miles long.

(*e*) Machines, lighters, etc.: 1 Dredge, 2 Lighters, tools and office furniture.

(*f*) Other assets: Two hundred and seventy-five and

one-half (275½) shares of the stock of the Fairfield Canal and Turnpike Company. Also the accounts and bills receivable described in the inventory of the said P. S. Stephenson and Henry W. Anderson, Special Masters.[14]

The document concluded:

This conveyance is made expressly subject to all valid taxes, valid assessments or valid liens superior to the lien of the mortgage of the said complainant, the Union Trust Company of New York, as Trustee, existing in favor of any person or persons, corporation or corporations, as required by Paragraph Eight of the decree of October 1, 1910. The said Union Trust Company of New York, as Trustee, party of the third part, and the Central Trust Company of New York, as Trustee, party of the fourth part, for the purpose of releasing their interest in the property hereinbefore described, release and quit claim unto the said Chesapeake & Albemarle Canal Company, party of the fifty part, their several interests, whatever they may be, in all of the property and franchises, wherever the same may be, of the Albemarle & Chesapeake Canal Company.
IN TESTIMONY WHEREOF, the said P. S. Stephenson and Henry W. Anderson, Special Masters, have hereinto set their hands and seals, and the Albemarle & Chesapeake Canal Company, the Union

Trust Company of New York, as Trustee, have caused their names to be signed hereto by their respective Vice President, and their corporate seal to be affixed and attached by their respective secretaries.[15]

The newspaper account of the transaction published the next day, November 11, 1910, quoted Major Edwards as stating that if Judge Waddill confirmed it, the canal would continue to be operated until such time as it could be offered for sale again to some company "willing to take hold of it."[16] It would certainly be reasonable to assume that Edwards and the other bondholders were fully aware of the continuing interest on the part of the national government in obtaining the canal as part of its planned continuous inland waterway line from Norfolk to Beaufort. Indeed, the River and Harbor Act of June 25, 1910, specifically authorized Secretary of War Henry L. Simpson "to enter negotiations for the purchase as part of the said inland waterway of the Albemarle and Chesapeake Canal, or the Dismal Swamp Canal, together with all property, rights of property, and franchises appertaining thereto. . . ."[17]

In view of this, obtaining the canal by the bondholders' company at a comparatively modest price at the

---

[14] Clerk's Office of the Circuit Court of the City of Chesapeake, Va., Deed Book 360 (1919), pp 333–37.

[15] Ibid., p. 335.
[16] Norfolk *Virginian-Pilot*, Friday, November 11, 1918, p. 4.
[17] U.S. Congress, House, *Chesapeake and Albemarle Canal Company*, 62nd Cong., 2nd sess., House doc. no. 589, March 4, 1912.

foreclosure sale was certainly an astute piece of business. Two years later, the sale of the then-designated Chesapeake and Albermarle Canal to the government was consumated at the cost of $320,000 for the Virginia part of the canal right-of-way and $55,000 for the company buildings, vessels, and equipment. The Carolina Cut, in a separate sale, cost $180,000, thus netting a nice little profit in the transaction. The Army Corps of Engineers subsequently reported in excess of a half million dollars as the agreed purchase price for the entire package.[18]

Various nineteenth-century investigations on the part of the federal government into Atlantic coastal canals have already been covered here in some detail. Still further interest was shown early in 1904 in the "Waterway from Norfolk, Va., to Beaufort Inlet, N.C.," and the route was reappraised with an eye to possibly deepening it to a sixteen-foot channel—twice the depth that then existed. Need for such a larger channel was cited by an examination of the records of the U.S. Lifesaving Service covering the previous twenty-five year period of disasters recorded along the Atlantic coast. This reported the loss of sixty-seven lives and $3,000,000 in property damage off the Outer Banks and the Hatteras shoals. The proposed plan for a deep channel was outlined in a letter from Brig. Gen. A. Mackenzie, Chief of Engineers, to acting Secretary of War Robert Shaw Oliver dated February 18, 1904. Estimated cost of excavating the 16-foot, 68.6-nautical-mile route was given as $4,780,000 not counting the purchase price of the Albemarle and Chesapeake Canal itself.[19]

Evidently such an expenditure seemed more than was then feasible, and two years later, General Mackenzie, in a letter dated September 27, 1906, observed that "this waterway has been under discussion for a number of years and numerous reports have been submitted" and now recommended a more reasonable ten- or twelve-foot project depth. It was stated that if the Albemarle and Chesapeake Canal route were chosen in lieu of the other options and if the cost of the canal itself did not exceed half a million dollars, it would represent a big saving to the government. In due course this letter was transmitted by the Secretary of War to the Speaker of the House of Representatives, and it appeared in print as House document no. 84 of the 59th Congress.[20]

Though the Albemarle and Chesapeake Canal route was given as first choice for an improved north-south channel, the engineers did not eliminate the Dismal Swamp Canal from their deliberations, and they also came up with two brand-new projected routes leading through Virginia and North Carolina forested lowlands. These two did not entail purchas-

---

[18] Ibid.

[19] U.S. Congress, House, *Waterway from Norfolk, Va., to Beaufort Inlet, N.C.*, 58th Cong., 2nd sess., House doc. no. 563, February 18, 1904.

[20] U.S. Congress, House, *Norfolk–Beaufort Inlet Waterway, Virginia and North Carolina*, 59th Cong., 2nd sess., House doc. no. 84, 1908.

ing existing canals, except, as will be explained, for the Carolina Cut part of the Albemarle and Chesapeake. The new lines proposed would cross Dismal Swamp in the area lying between the already operational canals.

A so-called Cooper's Creek Route started out from a point on the Southern Branch of the Elizabeth River, proceeded southward on a line paralleling the Dismal Swamp Canal but eastward of it, and joined the upper Pasquotank River below Turner's Cut. This plan proposed, at a cost of $2,730,280, a brand-new 12-foot deep, 26.9-mile canal which, since the government would charge no tolls, would obviously completely incapacitate the Dismal Swamp Canal.

Use of the Dismal Swamp Canal—with further deepening of it to the suggested depth throughout the river approaches—was estimated by the Engineers at $2,901,660 for a twelve-foot channel. The purchase price of the then only recently improved Dismal Swamp Canal, which it had cost the Lake Drummond Company more than a million dollars to rebuild in 1899, would obviously be high, however, since the owners could not afford to let it go for nothing.

The fourth route was called the Blackwater Route. It proposed a new land cut running fourteen miles southeastward from the Elizabeth River to the mouth of Blackwater Creek, followed by improvements extending to the North Landing River and so proceeding on down to the lower end of the North Landing River and into Currituck Sound. This route, however, predicated purchasing the Carolina Cut from the Albe-

marle and Chesapeake Canal Company and employing it for the line out of Currituck Sound on down into the North River and Albemarle Sound—the established course of the existing Albemarle and Chesapeake Canal.

Since whichever waterway the United States government ultimately acquired and operated would be toll free, as are all the nation's federally maintained rivers and harbors, it is apparent that building either of the two brand-new routes would contrive to seriously cripple both the Dismal Swamp and the Albemarle and Chesapeake canals. Also, if the choice fell to either of those two existing privately owned canals, it would be equally obvious that the selection of either one would practically sound the death knell for the other.

Recapitulating the estimated cost to the government for all four of the possibilities for a federal inland waterway (and figured for either a sixteen-foot, a twelve-foot, or a ten-foot depth of channel), it was obvious that even with an anticipated half-million-dollar purchase price, the Albemarle and Chesapeake Canal would be the best bet. Exclusive of the cost of the canal, the reconstituted Albemarle and Chesapeake route planned by the government would cost $3,390,000 for a depth of sixteen feet, $1,892,230 for twelve feet, and $1,777,540 for ten feet. Though the engineers noted certain disadvantages to the Albemarle and Chesapeake Canal route—particularly the potentially rough seas in exposed and shallow Currituck Sound and the depression of the water surface in the North Landing

River caused by northerly and easterly winds—its advantages over the others were material, and in the end, the Army Engineers gave their endorsement to this route, with a project depth of twelve feet.

The impact of the engineers' selection was clear. Although the rebuilt Dismal Swamp Canal was then only in its seventh year of operation, when the Corps of Engineers took over the Albemarle and Chesapeake Canal in 1913 and made it free, the Dismal Swamp Canal immediately lost vast numbers of its previous customers. When it too was finally acquired by the federal government in 1929, it had become virtually bankrupt once more as a private company. By then, however, its role as a secondary alternate route of the Atlantic Intracoastal Waterway was forever established.

The 1906 report had gone on to consider the various options to the government for the Norfolk - Beaufort inland waterway's two other divisions farther south—from Albemarle to Pamlico Sounds, via Croatan Sound to the east, or inland cuts using the Alligator River. The third division extending from Pamlico Sound to Beaufort Inlet stated the Adams and Core Creek route was preferable. Thus the groundwork was firmly laid for the long-envisaged takeover and operation of a continuous channel, federally maintained and located entirely inside the twin dangers of Capes Hatteras and Lookout.[21]

In due course, pursuant to the River and Harbor Act of June 25, 1910, a contract for the purchase of the Albemarle and Chesapeake Canal was negotiated between the United States government and the Chesapeake and Albemarle Canal Company. This was duly signed in Washington on February 17, 1912, by Secretary of War Henry L. Stimson and company president James M. Edwards. As might be expected, this contract was subject to further ratification and appropriation of funds by Congress, and an immediate point at issue consisted of what should be done with the company's apparently surplus land holdings, items that were over and above the necessary line of right-of-way, along with canal basins, building sites, and maintenance shops.[22]

It should be recalled that the first designator for the canal—as planned by Marshall Parks more than a half century earlier—had been the Great Bridge Lumber and Canal Company, and by the terms of this agreement, forested property in excess of the actual land through which the canal was to run had been acquired by the canal company along with the strips for the right-of-way. Though the canal company at that time never actively engaged in the lumber business, these excess lands were leased for such purposes, and the present owners, the Chesapeake and Albemarle Canal

---

[21] Ibid., p. 5.

[22] U.S. Congress, House, *Chesapeake and Albemarle Canal Company*, 62nd Cong., 2nd sess., House doc. no. 589 (letter, Chief of Engineers Maj. Gen. W. H. Bixby to Secretary of War Jacob M. Dickinson, dated February 15, 1912).

Company, saw no reason to merely hand them over when obviously they were not needed for the government's sole avowed purpose of operating a canal.

Ultimately the question of what land the government would acquire was resolved upon the recommendation of the Norfolk District Engineer, Lt. Col. Mason M. Patrick, and the canal company retained its surplus land to do with as it chose. So it was that even though the company ceased to have any concern with running the canal thereafter, its corporate existence continued on for some more years, and records in the office of the Norfolk County Clerk of Courts indicate land transactions in its name taking place as late as August 7, 1918.[23]

Final documents conveying the Chesapeake and Albemarle Canal to the United States government were signed on March 19, 1913, by William Byrd, assistant secretary of the canal company. They were in agreement with the contract dated the previous year—February 17, 1912—between the company and Secretary of War Stimson representing the United States. The property lying in Virginia was covered by two bills of sale. The first, a comparatively short one, conveyed various buildings occupied by lockkeepers and bridge keepers and by company offices and shops located in and around a twenty-acre tract adjacent to the lock at Great Bridge. Actually the government now owns sixty-nine acres there but only twenty are used at present. Also covered by the first bill of sale was the private ten-mile-long telephone line between the lock and North Landing, together with various items of machinery and floating property—of which, apparently, there was then little left beyond a steam dredge and a couple of lighters.

The second bill of sale, executed on the same date, covered the land of the canal cuts and the right-of-way. This property was then described in careful detail as running from "a concrete monument marked '1' near the southerly shore of the Southern Branch of the Elizabeth River" and extending down the line of the canal to the Virginia boundary line in the North Landing River. As mentioned above, the first bill of sale was for $55,000 and the second for $320,000.[24]

Similar instruments as recorded in Currituck County Courthouse, North Carolina, covered that state's canal property lying between Coinjock Bay and the North River, although in this instance three deeds had to be provided. The first of the Carolina Cut deeds was executed February 13, 1913, and conveyed "all of the canal cut and right-of-way . . . lying between Coinjock Bay and North River" for a consideration of $120,000. A smaller parcel of land farther north comprised 186 acres at Long Point projecting into Coinjock Bay. A mile-long canal cut slicing across the point made an island out of the tip, where a lighthouse was

[23] Clerk's Office of the Circuit Court of the City of Chesapeake, Va., Deed Book 451 (1918), p. 173.

[24] Ibid., Deed Book 389, pp. 244–45.

erected. Cost of this land was $5,000. The final deed, dated March 19, 1913, in the amount of $55,000, included all the canal company's "houses, bridges, telephone lines, machinery, lighters, tools and office furniture." This brought the total cost of the canal's North Carolina property to $180,000—considerably less than the Virginia part.[25]

All aspects of the purchase were fully completed on April 30, 1913, and the very next day, the United States, in the person of Lt. Col. E. Eveleth Winslow, United States Army Corps of Engineers and District Engineer for the Norfolk district, took over the operation and stewardship of the Albemarle and Chesapeake Canal. A new era had dawned.[26]

[25] Clerk's Office, Currituck County Court House, N.C., Deed Book 52, pp. 482, 489, 513.

[26] U.S. Army Corps of Engineers, *Annual Report of the Chief of Engineers* (Norfolk District), 1913, p. 1910.

11

The Canals as
Federal Government
Waterways, 1913–78

Acquisition of the Albemarle and Chesapeake Canal by the United States Government rated front-page coverage in the Norfolk *Virginia-Pilot* of Thursday, May 1, 1913, and a headline proudly proclaimed: "$800,000 is now available for improving Waterway."[1] Final transactions had been carried out the evening before, and a half-million dollars had been turned over to representatives of the three-year-old Chesapeake and Albemarle Canal Company. So was the "conveyance of property formally consumated and deeds filed for record." Lt. Col. E. Eveleth Winslow, USA (fig. 48), the Norfolk resident district engineer, had officially assumed command of the canal works at

this point and promised that improvements to them would begin right away.[2]

In addition to the $500,000 paid out for the purchase, the $800,000 cited in the newspaper headline had been appropriated by Congress for upgrading the facility, and funds were immediately available to the Corps of Engineers to start its work. Colonel Winslow estimated it would take at least four years—and $5,400,000—to complete the entire job of widening the canal cuts and river channels and bringing the depth to a twelve-foot minimum throughout the line

---

[1] Norfolk *Virginian-Pilot*, May 1, 1913, p. 1.

[2] Lt. Col. E. E. Winslow, Corps of Engineers, had succeeded Lt. Col. Mason M. Patrick as Norfolk District Engineer, July 25, 1912.

Fig. 48. *Lt. Col. E. Eveleth Winslow, U.S. Army Corps of Engineers, was Norfolk District Engineer from May 2, 1903, to November 2, 1905, and from July 25, 1912, to October 1, 1914. He accepted the Albemarle and Chesapeake Canal for the United States government. (September 1918 photo, courtesy U.S. Army Corps of Engineers.)*

from Norfolk to Beaufort, as well as replacing worn-out bridges and buildings.

As evidence that there had been many people interested in the government acquiring the canal, the newspaper account quoted North Carolina Representative John H. Small as saying: "This is really a notable event. It marks the realization of the effort of more than a century." The congressman acknowledged the efforts of a "number of men [who] waged an active propaganda" effort for the creation of a free waterway by Congressional action. "Among the most notable," he named the late "Commodore Marshall Parks of Norfolk," but he stated that he himself had personally been working toward government acquisition of the canal ever since he was first elected to Congress in 1898.[3]

As might be expected, the impact of these events on the Dismal Swamp Canal was catastrophic. On the very day that the government acquired the Albemarle and Chesapeake Canal, one of a series of advertisements in a Norfolk newspaper promising "quick transit for traffic" and "prompt towing" was placed jointly by the Lake Drummond Canal and Water Company, the Lake Drummond Transportation Company, and the Lake Drummond Towing Company. But their "inland route, protected from storm," was now no match for the free waterway.[4] Boasting of its superiority was of no avail; the Dismal Swamp toll canal could no longer compete

---

[3] *Virginian-Pilot*, May 1, 1913.
[4] Ibid., April 39, 1913.

on long hauls with the toll-free Albemarle and Chesapeake. Yet somehow, even though under constant threat of financial ruin, the old canal contrived to remain available to ever-declining numbers of shallow-draft local craft, and so provided a lifeline for area inhabitants.

Although at the time it purchased the Albemarle and Chesapeake Canal the government showed no particular concern over what might happen to the more venerable Dismal Swamp Canal, a little more than half-a-dozen years later the possibility of also acquiring the Dismal Swamp Canal was again under investigation. On December 6, 1921, Brig. Gen. H. Taylor, senior member of the Board of Engineers for Rivers and Harbors, recalled to Maj. Gen. Lansing H. Beach, Chief of Engineers, that in 1912 when the Albemarle and Chesapeake Canal was the route selected for government purchase, it was presumed that "the business of the now competing Dismal Swamp Canal will probably be practically ruined." While it had been clearly understood that the Dismal Swamp Canal's owners had "no legal redress" for the damage done to their business, nevertheless it was now thought proper "to invite the attention of Congress to the condition which will then exist" if the Dismal Swamp Canal Company went under.[5]

Now that "it is locally feared [in 1921] that the [Dismal Swamp] Canal Company will be forced out of business and the residents of the contiguous country, whose interests and investments have been largely based upon the existence of the canal, will be deprived of this transportation route upon which they depend," both area inhabitants and government engineers felt that it would be only right that the latter should immediately take over and run the old canal in the same way it was handling the Albemarle and Chesapeake.[6]

For the moment, the amount that should be paid by the government to the Lake Drummond Canal and Water Company was the stumbling block. After having invested about a million-and-a-quarter dollars in the 1896–99 rebuilding effort, the company had initially set a price tag of $1,750,000 on its property, and this considerable amount had effectively swung the balance toward the purchase of the Albemarle and Chesapeake Canal for only $500,000. Eight years later, however, expressing "faith in the integrity and spirit of fairness on the part of the board and likewise on the part of Congress," the Lake Drummond Company indicated it would be willing to accept far less.[7]

In the end, a similar price of $500,000 for the Dismal Swamp Canal was agreed upon; at length, the deal was consumated, and the old canal became a ward of Uncle Sam. Though its purchase was authorized on March 3, 1925, it was not until March 30, 1929, that

---

[5] U.S. Congress, House, *Inland Waterway from Norfolk, Va., to Beaufort Inlet, N.C.,* 67th Cong., 2nd sess., doc. no. 5, February 2, 1922, p. 3 (letter from Chief of Engineers transmitting report on the advisability of acquiring the Lake Drummond [Dismal Swamp] Canal).

---

[6] Ibid.
[7] Ibid.

the Dismal Swamp Canal "and all appurtenances thereto" were acquired.[8]

As far as masters of vessels in transit via the Albemarle and Chesapeake Canal were concerned, that waterway under government control continued to operate pretty much as before. Ships' names and types and their tonnage, draft, hailing ports, and destinations were still recorded while the vessels were locking through at Great Bridge, but no money changed hands. The same civilian personnel operated the facility for the army engineers, and specifically cited in their 1913 *Annual Report* were a lockmaster, a recorder, five lockmen, and a laborer on duty at Great Bridge lock. A bridgetender and a laborer worked at each of the three bridges taken over by the government—Great Bridge, North Landing, and Coinjock.[9] The other three crossings over the canal—the Norfolk and Southern Railroad bridge, the Centerville Turnpike drawbridge, and the Pungo Ferry—retained their own private operators. The condition of the government's three bridges was so poor, however, that replacing them as soon as possible was given top priority by the District engineer.

True to his word, Colonel Winslow immediately got the work under way. He assigned the government dredge *Hampton* to remove an eight-foot shoal spot in the Virginia Cut on which three transiting vessels had recently grounded, in one case delaying traffic for as much as ninety-seven hours. A dredging contract was also signed with P. Sanford Ross, Inc., of Jersey City for enlarging and deepening a 5.5 mile stretch of the North Carolina Cut with the removal of 1,155 cubic yards of material at a cost of 9.48¢ per yard. Two contracts were awarded to the Bowers Southern Dredging Company to work on 6.5 miles of the Currituck Sound channel and on 5.7 miles of the North Landing River, both at 5.9¢ per cubic yard. Within the first six months of federal operation, $16,800 had already been spent on canal improvements. This increased to $63,463.34 by the end of the fiscal year terminating June 30, 1914.[10]

During the first two months free transit was offered, 41,398 tons of freight and 880 passengers were transported through the canal. Some 670 locking operations passed 860 vessels and 43 log rafts through Great Bridge. By June 30, 1914, this had increased to 258,441 tons of freight and 6,582 passengers in 5,342 vessels, requiring 4,120 lockages. Though the projected 12-foot depth was still a future goal, a draft of 8½ feet could now be carried the entire 200-odd miles from Norfolk to Beaufort.

Also contracted for in 1914 was the removal and replacement of the rickety government-acquired bridges. The Penn Bridge Company of Beaver Falls, Pennsylvania, undertook to build steel bascule single drawspans for the three crossings at a cost of $82,890,

---

[8] Brown, *Dismal Swamp Canal*, p. 175.
[9] *Annual Report of the Chief of Engineers*, Norfolk district (1913), p. 1911.

[10] *Annual Report, Engineers* (1914), p. 1944.

FIG. 49. *Steel bascule highway bridge spanning the Albemarle and Chesapeake Canal at Great Bridge (ca. 1930), was built by the Penn Bridge Co. in 1916 for the Corps of Engineers. It was replaced by the present drawbridge in 1943. (Photo courtesy U.S. Army Corps of Engineers.)*

and this work was successfully carried out between June 10, 1914, and March 9, 1916.[11] (See fig. 49.)

Still another project undertaken by the government during its first year of stewardship was the formulation of new sets of rules and regulations for users of the canal. These were put into effect February 10, 1914. One important feature related to the assembly and towing of timber rafts—long an annoyance both to the canal authorities and to other navigators, who were frequently delayed by the rafts' slow progress. (See fig. 50.) The regulations were made necessary by reason of the considerable number of waterlogged timbers which were dropping out of their towing booms, creating hazardous sailing for other craft. This debris had to be grappled for and removed from the channels at considerable trouble and expense.

At the same time, a small house was built on a pile foundation near Beacon no. 9 in the North River for use by the government's newly established inspector of rafts. His job was to make sure that no unseaworthy tows got into the canal. The *Annual Report* of the Chief of Engineers for 1914 observed that the "salutary ef-

---

[11] Memorandum to the author on Albemarle and Chesapeake Canal bridges from J. Thomas Lawless III, U.S. Army Corps of Engineers, Fort Norfolk, June 29, 1972.

S. Q. COLLINS.   J. B. LE KIES.

LE KIES & COLLINS,

MANUFACTURERS OF

North Carolina Pine Lumber.

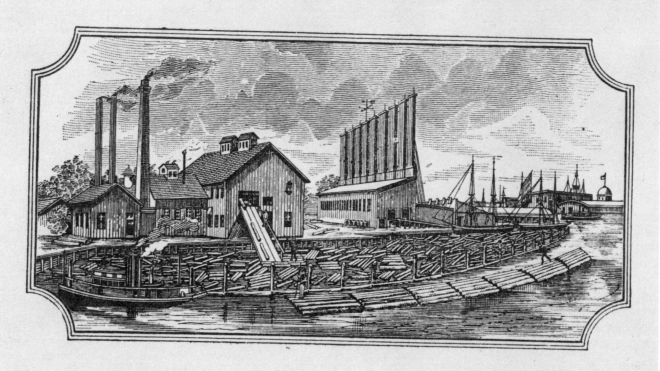

Every board trimmed between two saws, making uniform lengths and perfectly square ends.   Kiln-dried to prevent sap stains.

Capacity per Annum, 18,000,000 feet.

State where you saw this advertisement.

fect of restrictions placed on rafts can already be noted in the more substantial and bouyant character of the rafts using the waterway."[12] Two additional inspectors were added in June 1914.

The good work continued on into 1915, with hydraulic dredging and bank trimming going on uninterruptedly. The three drawbridges were now 65 percent finished, and the new steam dredge *Currituck* was being usefully employed. Contracted for on December 11, 1913, and completed July 23, 1914, the *Currituck* was in effective operation in the Virginia Cut in 1915.

Meanwhile, year after year, ship traffic gradually increased, while the work of improving the facility continued. Routine activities included replacing the private telephone system (1914) and constructing a plant for electric lighting, water supply, and fire protection at Great Bridge (1916–17).[13] Although power is presently supplied by the Virginia Electric and Power Company, this private plant is maintained on a standby basis for use in emergencies.

The *Annual Report* of the Chief of Engineers for 1917 gave a table of expenditures for the "operating and care of the part of the Inland Waterway . . . lying between Norfolk and Albemarle Sound" from takeover in 1913 to the end of that current fiscal year, June 30, 1917:

1913—$ 923.23
1914— 19,774.01
1915— 23,771.66
1916— 15,744.87
1917— 16,557.99

Total—$76,871.76[14]

By this time both land cuts had been considerably widened, requiring some bordering land in Currituck County to be condemned by the government. This became a source of subsequent acrimony on the part of the owners. Although forty years earlier, District Engineer Captain C. E. Phillips had suggested that still another guard lock be installed at the eastern end of the Virginia Cut in order to retain maximum elevation of water in the cut when northerly winds tended to drain the North Landing River,[15] the best twentieth-century professional engineering opinion now advocated eliminating the Great Bridge Lock entirely and having no locks at all. The theory was that the greater width and depth of the enlarged channel of the Virginia Cut would tend to lessen the impact of free-flowing water alternately moving back and forth through the cut as the tides in the Elizabeth River ebbed and floded, so that this current probably would not present any real problem to navigators. It was presumed that an estimated two- to three-miles-an-hour

---

[12] *Annual Report, Engineers* (1914), p. 1947.
[13] Ibid. (1916), p. 527.

[14] Ibid. (1917), p. 2269.
[15] "Phillips Report," pp. 6, 27.

FIG. 50. *Advertisement for the lumber firm of Le Kies & Collins, which appeared in Robert W. Lamb,* Our Twin Cities—Norfolk and Portsmouth *(1881). The woodcut shows lumber storage in the river off the mill and a small tug delivering a timber raft, which undoubtedly had been brought up through the canal.*

FIG. 51. *Iron, side-wheel lighthouse-tender* Holly *tied up to the former north wall of the lock at Great Bridge after removal of the lock in 1920. This photograph of the 1881-built tender was taken about 1932, before a new lock was put in. (Courtesy U.S. Army Corps of Engineers.)*

tidal flow in the canal would prove negligible to vessels having to buck it. Actually, the maximum velocity, as measured shortly afterwards, amounted to no more than 2.2 miles per hour.

This estimation, however, did not square with testimony offered at a public hearing held a decade later by residents who wanted the lock to be restored—as will subsequently be discussed. But for the time being,

in order to put this free-flow assumption to actual test, on April 1, 1917, all lock gates were opened permanently. The continuous use of the guard lock at Great Bridge, carried out from the very beginning of canal navigation, was now over. During 1917, 5,524 vessels and rafts made the transit.[16]

———————————

[16] *Annual Report, Engineers* (1917), p. 541.

Since operations without the guard lock apparently were proving satisfactory, the *Annual Report* for 1918 stated that it "may be [more] advantageous to construct a by-pass around the old lock . . . than to remove the lock."[17] By the following year, however, it was decided to demolish the lock, which was then considered too small anyway, and to retain only the 220-foot stone north wall for use as a wharf as is shown with the light- house tender *Holly* (fig. 51) tied along side. Since a bypass would be necessary while the lock was being removed, the snag-boat *Roanoke* was assigned the task of digging it.

By May 6, 1920, all dredging work in the canal contracted for by the Corps of Engineers had been finished with the removal of 1,523,409 cubic yards of material, "so completing all the dredging contemplated on the waterway north of Albemarle Sound."[18] A project depth of twelve feet and a bottom width of ninety feet was then attained throughout the line.

The government dredge *Currituck* then changed its location to the Beaufort area, and shortly thereafter it was assigned to work on the Alligator-Pungo Canal. This new canal, located about halfway between Norfolk and Beaufort, bisected Hyde County, North Carolina, from east to west. It was to prove a useful improvement to the Intracoastal Waterway system, making it possible for through traffic to cross Albemarle Sound, then proceed up its southern tributary,

Alligator River. The route already navigated by the Fairfield steamers, extends due south—with the river separating Tyrrell and Dare counties. It then bears west around Newport News Point—Virginians may find it hard to believe that they must share this place-name with North Carolina—and then, by way of a 25-mile-long overland cut, it reaches the headwaters of the Pungo River near Belhaven. Now, changing its direction to the south, this well-protected navigation route then crosses the mouth of the Pamlico River, passing down the southern end of Pamlico Sound to the wide mouth of the Neuse River.

For southbound vessels, Roanoke Island was eliminated as a port of call on the line, but the Alligator-Pungo cutoff bypassed the more exposed easterly route from Croatan Sound and the major portion of open Pamlico Sound. The total distance from Norfolk to Beaufort was not materially altered by the new route. Work on the Alligator-Pungo Canal and these river channels was not fully finished until 1929, however, when a railroad swing bridge over the canal was completed on July 21.[19]

World War I came and went without having any noteworthy effect on the Albemarle and Chesapeake Canal other than keeping it busy. Possibly an indication of the increased importance of this area was the appointment of Maj. Gen. Peter C. Hains, USA, as Norfolk District Engineer, the first time that a general officer was placed in this command. But the World

[17] Ibid. (1918), p. 573.
[18] Ibid. (1920), p. 591.

[19] Ibid. (1929), pp. 537–38.

War I upswing in the use of the canal was by no means comparable to the vast amount of vital traffic—subsequently to be cited—carried during World War II. This increased from 823,434 tons in 1937 to 1,037,193 in 1941, then dropped back to only 428,444 in 1946, at the war's end. With Nazi submarines operating with seemingly impunity close to the Atlantic seaboard, the grim name "Torpedo Junction" for the Outer Banks area was well merited. Consequently, as much coastwise shipping as the vessels' draft would permit was diverted to the Intracoastal Waterway as a safety measure for as long as the U-boats were a menace.[20]

During the immediate post–World War I years, the Engineers' snag-boat *Roanoke* continued whittling away at removing the old stone lock at Great Bridge, while traffic went around via the bypass hacked out of the old bed of the Southern Branch. The lock with its masonry walls had been built substantially and did not come apart easily. The 1922 *Annual Report* noted a total of 5,334 cubic yards of mud, sand, clay, and rocks, along with sixty-six piles and forty-three logs, removed from the lock at a cost of $4,752.74. Work on removing the floor and the south wall was finally completed during 1923.[21] Boat traffic now resumed by way of the original canal channel, while the bypass was filled in and the banks were stabilized with sheet piling.

Although, at the outset, operating the canal without a lock seemed satisfactory alike to both Army Engineers and users of the canal—who apparently were little inconvenienced by the current which, according to the state of the tide, ranged through the Virginia Cut—at length objections began to be heard. These came for an unexpected reason and from an unexpected source—the residents of Princess Anne and Currituck counties, particularly the sparsely settled, low, marshy areas of Back Bay and Knotts Island. Once the lock gates at Great Bridge had been abandoned for the current to flow back and forth unimpeded, there began, imperceptibly at first, an influx of salt water from the tidal Elizabeth River into freshwater North Landing River and Currituck Sound. Sewage treatment being then virtually unknown, Norfolk's contaminated water—with attendant trash picked up in the harbor and working its way through the canal—at length began to exert a deleterious effect on the duck-feeding aquatic plants of Back Bay and Currituck. Consequently, sportsmen and residents of the area, fearing a decline in property values accompanying the potential loss of their major industry—market and sports duck hunting—now began to make their objections vocal. Facilities for duck shooting, including some fairly commodious clubhouses and shooting lodges, were estimated to represent an investment of as much as $5,000,000, and the livelihood of many residents depended on this seasonal business.

---

[20] Ibid. (1947), p. 528. This presents a table covering a comparative statement of traffic from 1937 through 1945 by both vessels and rafts. The latter have declined for this period from 26,320 tons to 8,374. This decline has continued, so that all logs today are barge-loaded and no lumber tows pass through the canal.

[21] Ibid. (1922), p. 624.

FIG. 52. *Steamer* Harby *of the Elizabeth City Boat Line: 260 tons, 113 feet long; built at Elizabeth City, N.C., in 1919. (Courtesy of the Steamship Historical Society of America Collection: University of Baltimore Library.)*

Finally, on May 21, 1926, a public hearing on the matter was called by Lt. Col. F. A. Pope, the district engineer, and a considerable amount of information was made public. This was condensed into a pamphlet published the next year, entitled *Do the Facts Require the Restoration of a Guard Lock on the Albemarle and Chesapeake Canal?* The consensus of area residents and users of the canal was a resounding yes.

It was brought out too that canal navigators, as well as sportsmen, were in fact often discommoded by the unchecked current surging back, and forth in the Virginia Cut, which eroded the banks and, under certain conditions of wind and tide, amounted to far more than the estimated two to three miles an hour contemplated when the lock was eliminated in 1917. W. P. Ashburn, operator of the Norfolk to Elizabeth City boat line, whose vessels made some 250 trips through the Albemarle and Chesapeake Canal annually and, unlike tugboats, were required to run on a tight schedule, complained that his vessels had several "narrow escapes from knocking down the bridges." And he stated that, on more than one occasion, his 113-foot screw steamer *Harby* (fig. 52) had to tie up "because she could not stem the tide going through the bridge and we lost nine hours." Other steamboat operators complained because they could no longer take on fresh water in the canal and had to buy it piped in before leaving Norfolk.

Signatures of various notables, including Governors Angus W. McLean of North Carolina and Harry F. Byrd of Virginia, were attached to the document, and it was obvious that they disagreed with the somewhat cavalier view of Army Chief of Engineers Maj. Gen. H. Taylor, dated July 22, 1922, which stated that "the evidence in hand did not indicate a lock was required" when the government set about to eliminate the existing one. When the boat operators and tidewater lowcountry dwellers "earnestly urged the War Department to grant the relief asked for," the Corps finally took a long, hard second look into the matter.[22]

It seems surprising in the present ecology-minded era, when environmental impact studies are required for even the slightest activity affecting wetlands areas, that all this had not been thoroughly investigated before the guard lock was completely done away with. Actually, however, despite continued protests, contamination of the freshwater sounds from this source was allowed to continue from 1917 until—finally succumbing to the pressures of area residents, sportsmen, and watermen—a new guard lock which solved the problem was installed on the canal in 1932, fifteen years later!

In 1913, the operators of the handful of surviving passenger steamers which plied the Albemarle and Chesapeake Canal on their various rounds naturally welcomed the elimination of tolls. Probably the most imposing vessel then regularly navigating the waterway was the old stern-wheeler *Comet*, which has been mentioned on several occasions in this account. Built in 1887 to ply the Roanoke River, the *Comet*, (See fig. 6) was later acquired by the Bennetts' North Carolina line and was plying Currituck Sound in connection with the railroad line to Munden Point when the government acquired the canal. At 120 feet in length, the *Comet* was described as being the "largest local canal

---

[22] *Do the Facts Require the Restoration of a Guard Lock in the Albemarle and Chesapeake Canal between Norfolk, Va., and Beaufort, N.C.?*, pp. 44–45.

FIG. 53. *Stern-wheel steamboat* Currituck *moored at Norfolk. This 105-foot, wood-hull vessel was operated by the Bennett North Carolina Line. Built at Norfolk in 1916, she was laid up in 1931. (Photo William B. Taylor Collection, Mariners Museum.)*

packet."[23] A smaller stern-wheeler was the 1914-built *Waterlily.*

The *Comet's* sands were running out, though, and in 1915, after only two years of free passage, the thirty-year-old steamer was withdrawn and then scrapped. The engine was retained, however, and was promptly installed in a new stern-wheeler, the *Currituck* (fig. 53), a steamboat of similar size built in Norfolk the next year. The *Currituck* had the distinction of being the last of Bennett's seven-ship fleet and the last Currituck passenger boat regularly using the canal. At length, in 1931, she too succumbed to "progress." Her last skipper, still-spry Capt. Ernest L. Ballance, reported when interviewed at the age of eighty-four in 1969: "The paved roads killed us."[24] The Great Depression beginning in 1929 played a considerable part in the demise of its traffic too.

At the time of making her final runs, the *Currituck* left the foot of Brooke Avenue in downtown Norfolk at eight o'clock in the evening, three days a week. Passing on by Great Bridge—with no lock now to slow her down—the steamer negotiated the Virginia Cut and the North Landing River during the night and reached Knotts Island at five A.M., arriving at the end of her run at Poplar Branch, North Carolina, at eight or nine o'clock in the morning, depending on weather and traffic.

[23] Stanton, *Steam Navigation*, p. 14.
[24] Arthur P. Henderson, " 'The Paved Roads Killed Us,' Says *Currituck's* Last Master."

The *Currituck* had eight staterooms, and Captain Ballance recalled that she was a favorite among Yankee sportsmen coming down to Norfolk by train, thence on to Currituck for hunting or fishing. The fare was only $1.55, and the stateroom cost but an additional dollar. Obviously this sportsmen's traffic was not a great revenue producer for the line; the tariff which actually paid the way was gained by hauling freight. Southbound, it was general merchandise for the area inhabitants and storekeepers. Northbound, the principal cargoes consisted of potatoes and freshwater fish for transhipment to markets as far away as New York City. As many as five hundred barrels of potatoes and seventy-five barrels of fish might be carried each trip.

The venerable Captain Ballance admitted that running the *Currituck* down to Coinjock "was not the same as taking a ship around Cape Horn,"[25] but he reported the weather could still present problems, the worst of which were fog on the North Landing River—"it rose out of the marshes like smoke," he said—and the short, nasty, choppy seas which could develop on open Currituck Sound during bad weather.

Through the 1920s, the Bennett Line also operated a fleet of little screw steamers, mostly between Norfolk and Elizabeth City. Some craft served Roanoke Island from the latter port. As has been noted, the federal government ultimately purchased the Dismal Swamp Canal on March 30, 1929, but its subsequent improvement came too late to save these vessels. Long a favorite was the 1890-built *Emma K.*, which was little more than a fifty-nine foot glorified tug with an enclosed upper deck for the convenience of her passengers.

The *Emma K.* had provided a lifeline for Dismal Swamp residents whose farms bordered the canal on the east side, but when, in the early twenties, a bus line was instituted between Norfolk and Elizabeth City along the road which flanked the canal—the original towpath, now Route 17—the *Emma K.* could no longer meet the competition and was switched over to run in the Currituck area. Here she joined such Bennett Line vessels as the 1888-built *Virginia Dare* (100 feet in length), the 1891-built *Severn* (76 feet), the 1892-built *Greensborough* (117 feet), the 1909-built *Clio* (109 feet), and the 1919-built *Harby* (113 feet), the vessel which had trouble stemming the tide.[26]

These little boats in turn made the Norfolk-Elizabeth City run the long way around—via the 85-mile-long combined Albemarle and Chesapeake Canal and lower Pasquotank River route. As late as 1928, the Hampton Roads Maritime Exchange *Ports Annual* advertised "a steamer daily" leaving the Merchants and Miners Pier in Norfolk "at 5 P.M. for Coinjack [*sic.*], Jarvisburg, Old Trapp, Howell's Wharf and Eliz. City, N.C."[27] The next year the depression effectively killed off the service. Only the faithful old paddler *Currituck* survived,

---

25 Ibid.

26 Brown, "Passenger Steamers of Dismal Swamp," p. 209.
27 Hampton Roads Maritime Exchange, *Ports Annual* (Norfolk, 1926), p. 34.

Fig. 54. *Diesel mini-liner* Mount Hope *of the American Canadian Line, northbound in Great Bridge Lock, May 3, 1973, was returning to New England from a winter in Florida waters. (Photo by Alexander C. Brown.)*

the very last of a long and notable line of Carolina Sounds freshwater steam packets.

But commercial passenger craft plying the Albamarle and Chesapeake Canal still continue, however spasmodically. Commencing in 1968, Rhode Islander Luther H. Blount built a trim little diesel-powered 110-foot mini-liner, the *Mount Hope* (fig. 54), for his newly founded American-Canadian Line. In order to employ her profitably the year round (until the boat was sold to the Arkansas River in 1974), he sent her down south every year via the Intracoastal Waterway with a full load of passengers embarked from Narragansett Bay to Florida and the Bahamas. During the winter the *Mount Hope* cruised in the warm waters of Florida and the adjacent islands, then returned northward in the spring—also carrying cruise passengers—

FIG. 55. *Mini-cruise-liner M/V* New Shoreham, *125 feet long, en route to Warren, R.I., entering Great Bridge Lock; view looking east to the drawbridge at Great Bridge, May 10, 1973. (Photo by Alexander C. Brown.)*

for a full season of New England, Erie Canal, and St. Lawrence River operations. The two-week-long north-south trips contrived to put a twice-a-year passenger "liner" through the Albemarle and Chesapeake Canal, so upholding an ancient tradition. In 1971, Blount

added his larger, 125-foot, 60-passenger mini-liner *New Shoreham* (fig. 55), and this little vessel operated as another twice-a-year canal traveler until she, too, was replaced by the 150-foot *New Shoreham II* in 1979.

A rival cruise concern, the American Cruise Lines, Inc., of Haddam, Connecticut, then acquired two new 150-foot mini-liners, the *American Eagle* (1975) and the *Independence* (1976), and they too now make the Albemarle and Chesapeake Canal passage on their annual jaunts up and down the Intracoastal Waterway. Many day-excursion boats, notably the former Wilson Line catamaran cruiser *America* (fig. 56) of Washington, D.C., transfer their base of operations from northern to southern waters during the winter and deadhead down the coast.

I enjoyed a cruise south on board the *New Shoreham* in November 1972, en route from New York to Saint Petersburg, Florida. *Seaboard* editor Samuel Ward Stanton, whose account of his trip south via the Albemarle and Chesapeake Canal in 1892 appears in chapter 9,[28] mentioned that, owing to the early-morning departure of the *Newberne* from Norfolk, he had remained abed and had slept while the steamer was passing through the Great Bridge lock. I braved a memorable early rise, however, and so witnessed the entire canal passage from the *New Shoreham*. A break-of-day view over Great Bridge, as seen from the deck of a passing vessel (fig. 57), has never received suitable

---

[28] Stanton, *Steam Navigation*, p. 10.

Fig. 56. *Johanna Hewlett Brown photographs the diesel cat-amaran excursion-boat* America, *late of the Wilson Line (built 1974, 90 feet long by 40 feet wide), passing through the Pungo Ferry bridge, September 24, 1978, en route south via the Intracoastal Waterway. (Photo by Alexander C. Brown.)*

national acclaim as a visual experience worthy of memorializing. Nevertheless, I felt it was well worth making the effort to view the historic canal, framed by walls of giant cypress trees, doubled by reflection, as dawn's early light bathed it in a golden glow.

At length, in 1930, bowing to the wishes of Princess Anne and Currituck county residents, the federal government carried out an extensive investigation into their complaints of the contaminated salt water in the canal, and the authorities commenced the construction of a replacement lock for Great Bridge. The lock proposed was to be 500 feet long by 75 feet wide with 16 feet over the miter sills. It would cost an estimated $728,000.[29] It will be recalled that, when built, the original Great Bridge lock was the largest in the nation with the exception of the tandem locks of Sault Sainte Marie, Michigan. That Great Bridge lock measured 220 feet long by 40 wide, but at the time it was taken out, it had been outclassed by several other sets of locks, even by the 250-foot, 1899-built locks of the Dismal Swamp Canal.

Some $200,000 of the estimated cost of $728,000 for the new Great Bridge Lock was suggested to be contributed by local interests. But when Congress adopted the project as authorized by the River and Harbor Act of July 3, 1930, that body felt that local cooperation in financing was not either necessary or appropriate and

[29] G. R. Young, "The Great Bridge Lock," p. 552.

FIG. 57. *As she proceeds south via the Intracoastal Water-way, the small cruise ship* New Shoreham *passes through Great Bridge Lock during the early hours of November 16, 1972. (Photo by Alexander C. Brown.)*

$1,000,000, but no more money was allocated for the project.

To build a million-dollar structure and only be allowed to spend half that amount on its construction posed an extraordinary challenge to Maj. G. R. Young (fig. 58), Norfolk District Engineer at that time. But by exercising strictest economy and eliminating all unnecessary frills, the job was done.[30] Certainly there could be no corner cutting in the construction of the enormous double gate assemblies which the lock required, or in the system of conduits with the various complicated valves and cutoffs installed in substantial reinforced concrete monoliths. Instead of masonry walls, however, less costly interlocking steel sheetpiling with suitable tiebacks was recommended. One of the biggest savings in building the lock, however, was realized by dispensing with the traditional solid flooring and merely leveling the bottom and covering it with native sand. It would never be necessary to dewater the lock.

Each of the four sets of double miter gates of the reversible head lock, meeting its opposite at an oblique angle, was securely attached to the monoliths at each corner of the lock chamber. These steel gates measured twenty-six by forty-two feet in size and weighted forty-five tons. Electricity to operate the motors for the gate machinery and to turn the valves came from a central power source. A master control switch located midway along the lock's 600-foot north wall could direct the electrical current to either end of the chamber, but not

that the government should bear the entire expense of construction. It inserted a proviso, however, that under no circumstances should the cost exceed $500,000. Surprisingly, though the money to be made available was considerably reduced, the length of the lock specified was increased from 500 to 600 feet. As might be expected, this would also almost double the construction estimate to just short of

---

[30] Ibid., pp. 552–56.

FIG. 58. *Maj. G. R. Young. U.S. Army Corps of Engineers, was Norfolk District Engineer from August 13, 1930, to June 30, 1934. He was in charge of building the new guard lock. (Photo courtesy U.S. Army Corps of Engineers.)*

closing of one set of gates and then, when all was secure and the water pressure properly equalized, the opening of the other.

The design work on the lock was carefully handled by the Corps of Engineers' Norfolk office, and Major Young was in charge of the entire project. Contracts were let on March 2, 1931, to Merritt, Chapman & Scot of Baltimore for the lock proper; on March 7, to the Berkley Machine Works of Norfolk for the gates; and on May 27, to Foote Brothers Gear and Machine Company of Chicago for the machinery.

Since ship traffic had been using a bypass channel north of the lock for the entire period it was under construction (see figs. 59–61), there had been no interruption in the canal's service. When the new guard lock was completed, its gates were left open while this bypass was closed off, and, at length, on June 16, 1932, the lock was formally declared completed. (See fig. 62.) The ceremonial passage through it of the engineers' handsome 100-foot inspection ship *Falcon* (fig. 63) resplendent in polished brass and gleaming mahogany, marked the occasion. She was a former $150,000 steam yacht built on the Great Lakes in 1925 and acquired six years later by the Corps during the depression at a bargain-basement price of only $19,390.[31]

Major Young was justifiably, proud of his new creation, summing up his accomplishment by stating:

let it go to both ends at once—a safety measure designed to prevent a catastrophic opening of opposite-end gates at the same time. The throw switch would be handled by one of the lockmen as he walked the length of the lock from one end to the other, following the

---

[31] U.S. Army Corps of Engineers, Norfolk District, description of plant data sheet: survey boat *Falcon*. Particulars on this vessel were provided to the author by the executive officer, Fort Norfolk, Va.

F<small>IG</small>. 59. *Great Bridge Lock construction (1930s). Building of the bulkhead on the north side of the canal, showing bulkhead forms and tierods. The water being discharged on the right is pumped by the dredge to form fill. (Photo courtesy U.S. Army Corps of Engineers.)*

F<small>IG</small>. 60. *Dredge pumping fill on the north side of the canal (1930s), view looking east at Great Bridge. (Photo courtesy U.S. Army Corps of Engineers.)*

FIG. 61. *Completing the new Great Bridge guard lock. A 1930s view looking northwest along the Southern Branch of the Elizabeth River as the south side of the lock is being filled in. (Photo courtesy U.S. Army Corps of Engineers.)*

"While this job was not very large, it was one of the most interesting that I have ever handled—and incidentally, at times, one of the most annoying." Having provided the government with the equivalent of a million-dollar facility at half the cost—actually $492,980—he had every reason to be pleased.[32]

Proof that the lock had been well designed and built was amply afforded by the fact that it gave forty years satisfactory service before any major repair work was required on it. At length, though, necessary rehabili-

tation of the lock costing $604,196,40 was carried out by general contractor Thomas J. Crooks of Virginia Beach between June 1972 and April 1974 (fig. 64). This expense was more than $100,000 over the cost of building the entire facility to begin with in 1932. Crooks's work was also performed without any interruption of service, and, interestingly enough, a large part of it had to be done underwater by divers feeling their way about in the murk.

The initial economy of dispensing with a solid floor and using a sand covering instead had finally resulted in parts of the bottom of the lock being scoured out by

---

[32] Young, "Great Bridge Lock," p. 557.

FIG. 62. *The Great Bridge guard lock with gates in place. This view, looking northwest, shows the barge* Winnie T. Robinson *being locked through about 1932. (Photo courtesy U.S. Corps of Engineers.)*

propeller turning action of powerful diesel tugs. (See fig. 65.) These craft would be tied up to the north wall during the locking process and when the gates were opened and they suddenly started up and gave their engines full ahead, the propeller wash would churn up the bottom as they got under way again. Divers now leveled the floor and then three-quarters of its area (along the north lock wall and across the aprons inside each lock gate) was covered over, piece by piece, by placing heavy slabs of precast concrete on the bottom. The one-foot-thick slabs measured ten feet square and weighed 15,000 pounds apiece. Each had to be carefully positioned on the bottom by feel alone, for dewatering a lock which had remained continuously full for forty years was considered too great a hazard to

subject the ancient walls to as they might collapse into the lock chamber under the suddenly released equalizing pressure.

Since operation of the lock had customarily been carried out from the north side, where the controls were located, and vessels in transit were moored to the north wall, this part of the lock chamber was obviously subject to the greatest use—and also abuse, as when unruly barges occasionally smacked into it too vigorously. Switching the operation to temporary facilities on the south side, the contractor in effect, provided an entirely new north wall by driving new steel "H" piles outside the old ones, then placing precast concrete panels between the flanges of the piles. The space between the panels and the old steel sheet-pile wall was

FIG. 63. *The Corps of Engineers official inspection-yacht* Falcon *passed through the new lock at Great Bridge on opening day, June 16, 1932, with the ceremonial party embarked. This 1925-built steam yacht was acquired by the Corps in 1931 and was in use until disposed of in 1955. (Photo courtesy U.S. Army Corps of Engineers.)*

FIG. 64. *Major repairs to Great Bridge Lock were carried out in 1972–74, and a new north wall was installed by contractor Thomas J. Crooks. Here, piling is being put in on October 31, 1973. (Photo courtesy Virginia State Library, Richmond.)*

then poured full of concrete, effectively tying the new structure to the old. This narrowed the 75-foot width of the lock, but only by the comparatively insignificant amount of three feet.[33]

Other major improvements to the canal carried out by the government during the comparatively recent past consisted of removing the single-lane bascule drawbridges at Great Bridge, North Landing, and Coinjock (which had been installed in 1916) and replacing them with the present double-swing spans. The Coinjock bridge was renewed June 12, 1940, at a cost of $175,000. Work began on an identical structure at Great Bridge in August 1941, but was suspended owing to war-material shortages and was not completed until August 15, 1943, at a final cost of $250,000. The third bridge, at North Landing (fig. 66), was finished on August 15, 1951. Its cost was $350,000, a positive indication of drastic price increases in the intervening period.

This was hardly comparable to the $420,000 price tag attached to the subsequent rehabilitation and modernizing of the 1943 Great Bridge span by Tidewater Construction Corporation, begun on June 30, 1969, and completed September 1, 1970. With more than 800 openings per month of a bridge then required to carry up to 18,000 vehicles daily, the draw at Great Bridge received greater demands on its operation than either of the other crossings.

---

[33] Information provided by J. Thomas Lawless III, Corps of Engineers, Fort Norfolk, Va., January 12, 1978.

FIG. 65. *The 61-foot diesel tug* Willie K *shown locking through at Great Bridge on October 31, 1973, is pushing a barge loaded with pulpwood logs destined for the Chesapeake Corporation's mill at West Point, Va. Repairs to the north wall of the lock are clearly visible. (Photo by Alexander C. Brown.)*

While these repairs were being carried out, the drawspans at Great Bridge had to be closed entirely to land travel for more than five weeks. This provided the U.S. Army Corps of Engineers with an interesting extended field exercise for the troops of the 902nd Engineer Company. Starting on July 6, 1970, these men set up and then operated two 180-foot floating bridges across the canal carrying one-way vehicular traffic in each direction (fig. 67). The 98-foot center sections of the bridges were floated out of the way daily at 4 P.M. until 10 A.M. the following morning for waterborne traffic of the canal to pass through. They were then closed from 10 A.M. until 4 P.M. for the benefit of land traffic.

With the pontoons assembled and temporary approach roads laid down by the city of Chesapeake, the floating bridges were successfully maintained from July 15 to August 23 and gave good service, although, as might be expected, not without a certain amount of grumbling by patrons until the regular bridge was back in operation again.[34]

Because of a significant increase in vehicular traffic subsequent to the reopening of the bridge in the autumn of 1970, the bridge, which had been designed to handle a daily average of 6,000 automobiles, was actually transporting 21,000 vehicles according to a traffic count recorded in May 1977. As might be expected, this required that unfortunately the draw be

[34] Hubbert M. Johnson and Lt. James Thibault, "M4T6 Bridges on Intracoastal Waterway."

FIG. 66. *A new swing bridge over the North Landing River was completed on August 15, 1951, at North Landing, Va. (Photo courtesy U.S. Army Corps of Engineers.)*

made more restrictive to navigation. As of September 1976, a schedule of openings was tentatively put in effect by the Corps of Engineers to provide for opening the draw once per hour between 6:00 A.M. and 7:00 P.M., then opening on demand of vessels for the eleven overnight hours. As this seemed to work reasonably well, these hours were made permanent in January 1978. Except in emergencies then, in daylight hours the sailors presently have to wait, since land traffic now has clear priority.[35]

To make these shipboard delays more palatable, however, as of January 1980 the Corps provided mooring facilities on both sides of the bridge where vessels can conveniently wait their turns. On the west side of the bridge in the short stretch of canal between the bridge and Great Bridge Lock, the banks had already been bulkheaded and provided with sufficient dolphins for tugs with tows to tie up to. On the east side, for the benefit of north-bound traffic, a small basin was dredged along the north side of the channel and six dolphins were installed.

Two years after the Great Bridge draw had been rehabilitated, a brief, unexpected forced closure on the canal followed an accident to the North Landing

[35] U.S. Coast Guard, Public Notice 5–400, Portsmouth, Va.: Fifty Coast Guard Headquarters. "Drawbridge Operation Regulations," September 15, 1978.

Fig. 67. *The southbound lane of one of two 180-foot pontoon bridges across the canal operated by the Corps of Engineers from July 6, 1970, to August 23, 1970, while repairs were being carried out on the Great Bridge drawspan. A center section of pontoons was opened daily from 4 P.M. to 10 A.M. for water traffic. (Photo courtesy of U.S. Army Corps of Engineers.)*

bridge. On April 16, 1974 an empty oil barge being pushed by the diesel tug *Ilene L.* was rammed into the draw. It was in the process of being opened for the tow when the clutch of the reverse gear on the tug slipped, and the boat surged forward, ramming the draw with the barge and knocking the twin spans almost a foot off their rollers. At first, it was expected that the accident might close the draw to vehicular traffic for as long as two or three months and to ships for at least a week. Owing to quick action on the part of the engineers,

however, a special set of jacks was brought in to lift the two 250-ton sections and replace them in the open position, and it worked out that vessels were denied passage only for a twenty-four-hour period and that the damage could be remedied to make the spans operational for land vehicles soon afterwards. Repairs were in excess of $100,000, however.[36]

[36] Newport News, Va., *The Times-Herald*, April 17 and 19, 1974. Associated Press dispatches originating from Virginia Beach and Chesapeake, Va.

A far more serious bridge accident than the one sustained by the North Landing draw occurred on August 21, 1978, when the 247-ton tugboat *Roleta* of the Willis Barge Company, pushing two barges up the North Landing River, unfortunately slammed the lead barge into the Pungo Ferry swing bridge's southwest fender system. This made it impossible to close the bridge, and vehicular traffic, estimated at being approximately 1,000 cars daily, ground to a halt while lengthy repairs got under way. (See fig. 68.) These were completed sufficiently by September 29, 1978, to let cars across. The bridge had remained inoperative for almost six weeks.

As the swing span was not affected and remained in the open position, there was no interruption to water traffic using the Albemarle and Chesapeake Canal. The bridge accident, however, immediately produced a state of emergency in the vital transportation of harvested grain throughout this agricultural area of Virginia Beach. Like the little flat-barge cable ferry which preceded it until 1954, Pungo Ferry Bridge serves State Route 726, connecting the boroughs of Blackwater and Pungo. In 1954, a steel swing bridge at Churchland, which had originally carried U.S. Highway 17 across the Western Branch of the Elizabeth River but had been replaced by a fixed bridge in 1951, was barged down the Intracoastal Waterway and adapted to its new location at Pungo Ferry. As already observed, this made the cable ferry obsolete, but the little settlement of Pungo Ferry retained its time-honored name.

In the wake of the August 21, 1978, accident, however, it was imperative that some sort of ferry be instituted as soon as possible. Accordingly, the city of Virginia Beach made arrangements with the firm of Keystone-Richmond, Inc., which specialized in providing ferry service when needed all over the eastern part of the country following bridge accidents. The firm had just concluded operating a ferry across the James River at Hopewell in connection with the inoperative Benjamin Harrison Bridge, damaged by the tanker *Marine Floridian.*

Keystone-Richmond immediately dispatched its equipment to Pungo Ferry. A flat pontoon barge was assembled out of several individual components secured to each other, so creating a craft of about 100 feet in length and sufficiently wide to carry two cars abreast. Its total capacity was 12 automobiles, or three fully-loaded grain trucks. (See figs. 69, 70.)

In the meantime, on both sides of the 400-foot wide river immediately to the north of the bridge, highway department personnel installed temporary roadways with blacktop ramps running out over the beach into the river. Flaps on either ends of the flat barge could be let down onto the ramps when docking, so providing vehicles a smooth and easy access aboard. Power and steering for the new free-swimming ferry were pro-

FIG. 68. *Aerial view of Pungo Ferry drawbridge taken by a Virginia Beach police helicopter, August 23, 1978, two days after a southwest fender was damaged when a barge slammed into it. The draw was put out of commission until September 27, 1978. Note loops and cutoffs in the twisting North Landing River (top), beyond the bridge. (Photo courtesy of the City of Virginia Beach, Va.)*

FIG. 69. *An overall view looking upstream from the damaged Pungo Ferry bridge, September 24, 1978, showing the little diesel tug* Seneca *providing power for a flat-barge ferry across the North Landing River. (Photo by Johanna H. Brown.)*

vided by the little thirty-four foot long diesel tug *Seneca* with its two-man crew. An ingenious swivel attachment secured the bow of the tug to a steel bracket fastened midway along the side of the barge (fig. 71). When the ferry started out on one of its more than two dozen daily river crossings—it operated twenty-four hours a day—the tug's bow would be headed to the shore. Accordingly, the tug had to back out into the river until the barge cleared the ramp. Then the stern line holding the tug parallel to the barge was cast off, and it automatically swung around on the bow swivel to point in the opposite direction. Five minutes later, now going full speed ahead, it ran the barge up the ramp on the other bank.

Meanwhile, pile drivers and floating cranes (fig. 72)

worked around the clock renewing and strengthening the broken fender assembly on the west bank. By September 29, Pungo Ferry Bridge was in operation once more, and the ferry facility was retired. Reputedly, its operation cost $1,250 per day, payable by the errant tugboat's owners.[37]

Owing to fairly universal complaints concerning the operation of the crowded Great Bridge drawbridge—where frustrating delays annoyed both ship and vehicular traffic—discussions on the feasibility of building a high bridge across the canal to carry some of the increasingly heavy traffic of Route 168 had been going on for some time. Chesapeake residents were reluctant

---

[37] Alexander C. Brown, "Errant Barge Revives Pungo Ferry."

to lose their existing ground-level drawbridge, however, since a high bridge would have to commence gaining its required elevation (a minimum of sixty-five feet above mean low water, as established by the Corps of Engineers) at a considerable distance from both banks of the canal. Since the town of Great Bridge lies close to the canal's south bank, a bridge of the required sixty-five feet in height would necessarilly "fly over" the greater part of the business area—so missing it entirely, to the considerable distress of local merchants.

Although the present time-honored low-level drawbridge has been retained at Great Bridge, an alternative fixed-level high bridge was designed to convey motorists across the canal just east of the Atlantic Yacht Basin, about a mile along the canal from the existing draw in the center of town. Bypass roads leading to the bridge branch off Battlefield Boulevard at Oak Grove, 1.6 miles from the canal, rejoining the highway 2.5 miles farther down the line. With Battlefield Boulevard and the present drawspan of Highway 168 maintained at Great Bridge, the southbound motorist with no particular need to stop in the town can take the bypass, speed over the canal sixty-five feet below without delay, meanwhile enjoying an excellent view of both the waterway and the swamp forest surrounding it.[38]

In 1978 the U.S. Coast Guard, one of several gov-

FIG. 70. *Cars loading on the temporary ferry across the North Landing River from the west bank, power and steering being supplied by the tug* Seneca. *(Photo by Johanna H. Brown.)*

ernment agencies concerned, granted its construction permit to the Virginia Department of Highways and Transportation for the high bridge which the Ciambro Corporation of Pittsfield, Maine, commenced building that summer. However, yachtsmen whose sailing craft have lofty masts were not pleased by the now-irrevocable sixty-five foot vertical-clearance restriction, which effectively eliminated the unlimited height

---

[38] City of Chesapeake, Va., Public Works Department, location map for proposed high-level bridge over canal and marsh, December 13, 1977.

FIG. 71. *The swivel attached to the bow of the tug* Seneca *and to the side of the ferry barge permitted the tug to reverse its direction without unfastening itself at the end of each crossing. (Photo by Johanna H. Brown.)*

viously afforded canal navigators. Bowing to the inevitable, some owners who regularly use the Intracoastal Waterway announced that they would cut down their masts to 64 feet so they could still use the canal. Others became resigned to the necessity of sailing "outside," paying more insurance and taking their chances with potentially stormy Cape Hatteras weather in order to go south for the winter. However, with fixed bridges now at both ends of the stretch of waterway between Norfolk and Beaufort Inlet, North Carolina, and with one fixed bridge in between as well, the Carolina Sounds are effectively sealed off to the passage of tall vessels anyway. First built along this stretch was the Morehead City bridge, which opened in January 1965. The Wilkerson Creek Bridge in Hyde County, North Carolina, located at the sound end of the Alligator–Pungo Canal on Route 264, was opened November 21, 1979, and the Great Bridge bypass, all of 65 feet, will open in 1981.

As has been previously mentioned, there are three other low-level drawbridge crossings of the Albemarle and Chesapeake Canal which are not the responsibility of the federal government since they were added after the canal was already a going concern. The Corps of Engineers would like to dispose of the obligations it acquired on the original three bridges, which it necessarily assumed upon the purchase of the canal, but the Virginia cities of Chesapeake and Virginia Beach are apparently satisfied with the status quo of federal government operation. North Carolina, however, has agreed to a plan for replacing the Coinjock Bridge in

FIG. 72. *Floating crane and pile driver working on the damaged fender of the Pungo Ferry swing-span drawbridge, September 24, 1978. (Photo by Johanna H. Brown.)*

Currituck County, plus four other drawspans crossing the Intracoastal Waterway in that state, with the now-standard sixty-five foot clearance fixed bridges, and to pay 25 percent of the project costs.

One of the three independent crossings is the Norfolk Southern Railway bridge over the Virginia Cut, where the present single-track, single-bascule, rolling-lift structure, which opened October 9, 1928, is the third on the site. It adequately handles the two surviving freight trains which cross every day between Berkley Terminal and Elizabeth City.

The present two-lane Centerville Turnpike swing bridge on Route 604 replaced a single-lane span and was built by the Virginia Department of Highways and opened in September 1955. Construction of the present Pungo Ferry swing bridge (See figs. 24, 25), replacing the flatboat cable ferry (see fig. 26) was begun in August 1952 and was completed two years later, in March 1954.[39]

Still another public-canal-crossing facility came into being in the autumn of 1962. On September 4, the seventy-one foot twin-diesel ferryboat *Knotts Island* (which the Norfolk *Virginian-Pilot* said "almost looks like a cute toy"[40] came down from her Wilmington, Delaware, builders to begin service for the North Carolina Department of Highways (figs. 73, 74). Crossing a wide

[39] Memorandum on Albemarle and Chesapeake Canal bridges received by the author from J. Thomas Lawless III, Corps of Engineers, Fort Norfolk, June 29, 1972.
[40] Norfolk *Virginian-Pilot*, September 1, 1962.

FIG. 73. *The diesel ferryboat* Knotts Island, *built in 1962 for transporting school children from the island across Currituck Sound, is shown returning to her slip on Knotts Island, August 19, 1972. (Photo by Alexander C. Brown.)*

part of Currituck Sound, her route was from the southwest end of Knotts Island over to Currituck Courthouse. Although the new ferry was licensed to carry seventy passengers and, as a schedule leaflet proclaimed, had a capacity of "Approx. 6 cars," this leisurely free service was actually instituted principally for the benefit of the North Carolina–resident school children of Knotts Island—which, by reason of the canal, is a completely detached part of Currituck County. A long causeway over the marsh at its northwesterly end connects Knotts Island to the Vir-

ginia mainland, though the island itself is almost entirely in North Carolina. Since the settlements on the island are not large enough to support a fully equipped high school there, it had been necessary to bus the children on what amounted to a daily hundred-mile round trip in order for them to attend school in their own state. The buses left the island by way of the causeway entering lower Princess Anne County, Virginia, and from there they crossed the North Landing River at Pungo Ferry, then proceeded down the west shore of Currituck Sound, across the state line near Moyock,

FIG. 74. *The state-owned ferry* Knotts Island *shown leaving Currituck on her forty-five minute trip across Currituck Sound, bisecting the line of the Intracoastal Waterway, August 13, 1972. (Photo by Alexander C. Brown.)*

and on to the village of Currituck, where the school was located.

The ferry was designed to handle three regular-size school buses on a seven-mile, forty-five minute trip—a considerable saving both in time and in distance from the original bus route. The general public also gets to patronize the *Knotts Island* without charge, and at about nine miles an hour, she makes five round-trip crossings in winter during the school term from September 1 to June 15. This is increased to seven trips in summer, with tourists and campers now taking their turns on board—so providing an enjoyable cruise for all hands except possibly the eighty-odd school children, who might well by now have become bored with it. Halfway across, the ferry crosses the line of the Intracoastal Waterway, with Coinjock the next point along the line, eight miles to the south.[41]

In 1946, the Albemarle and Chesapeake Canal was

[41] Alexander C. Brown, "School Children, Campers, Tourists Ride Free Knotts Island Ferry."

[201   ]

FIG. 75. *Col. Douglas L. Haller, U.S. Army Corps of Engineers, was appointed Norfolk District Engineer on June 28, 1978. (Photo courtesy U.S. Army Corps of Engineers.)*

tion and care of the lower end of the canal, including the North Carolina Cut and the North River, while the Norfolk district continues to maintain the Virginia part of the canal, including Great Bridge lock, the Virginia Cut, and the North Landing River.

Col. Douglas L. Haller (fig. 75), is currently Norfolk District Engineer, with headquarters located at venerable Fort Norfolk overlooking the harbor. Aided by his civilian executive assistant, Gerald W. Barnes, Haller is in overall charge of all Corps of Engineers projects and activities within the Norfolk district. J. Thomas Lawless III is chief of the operations and maintenance branch and is also one of the district's most knowledgable unofficial historians.

Actually, the operation of both the Albemarle and Chesapeake Canal and the Dismal Swamp Canal is carried out at Great Bridge. Here a substantial complex of administrative offices, storage facilities, boat basins, and shops capable of effecting all routine maintenance and repairs, including replacing lock gates and other tasks, is located within a twenty-acre compound on the south side of the lock, as shown in fig. 76. Alva O. Benson is in charge of a caretaker unit comprising a dozen skilled workers, including foremen, mechanics, electricians, workboat operators, carpenters, and other technicians. In the operations unit, also headed by Benson, there are six lock and bridge operators and three park technicians assigned to the Dismal Swamp Canal at Deep Creek and twenty-one lock and bridge tenders assigned to the Albemarle and Chesapeake, for an authorized strength of forty-four civilian per-

divided in half for administrative purposes, following the district boundary lines set up by the Chief of Engineers. Today, the Norfolk district's authority extends southward to the Virginia–North Carolina state line, at which point the Wilmington district commences. The latter, therefore, is now charged with the opera-

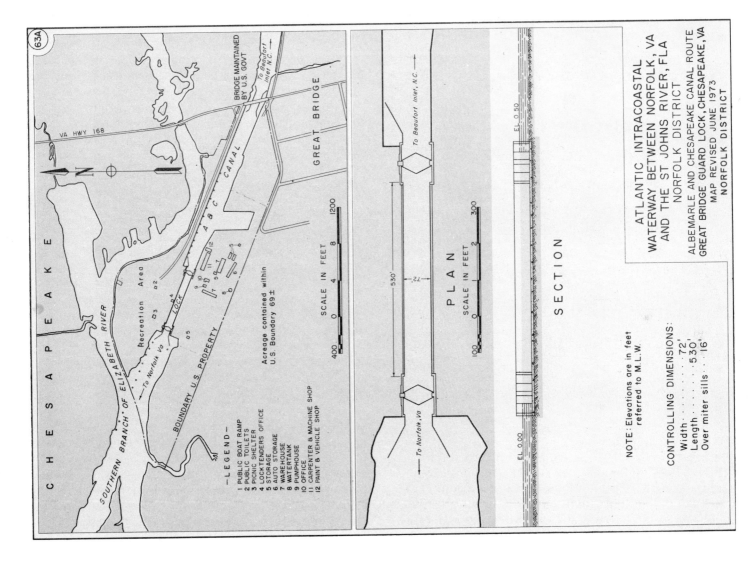

Fig. 76. *A 1973 detail map of the Great Bridge lock area of Chesapeake, Va., with a plan and section of the guard lock. (Courtesy U.S. Army Corps of Engineers.)*

FIG. 77. *Army Corps of Engineers' tender* Johnson, *built in 1965, is shown May 22, 1974, entering Great Bridge Lock westbound. This view is looking southwest across the lock entrance. (Photo by Alexander C. Brown.)*

sonnel. These men keep the canals running smoothly around the clock with a minimum of confusion.

Formerly, the corps maintained a sizable fleet of workboats in the Norfolk district. But routine dredging is now carried out through contract by private op-

erators. The only vessel left at Great Bridge, other than small outboard cruisers used for inspection, is a little all-purpose workboat named the *Johnson* (fig. 77), a thirty-five footer expressly built for the corps at Fall River, Massachusetts, in 1965. The handsome former-

FIG. 78. *Army Corps of Engineers' derrick boat* Roanoke, *built in 1937, is shown working on a bulkhead at the district office, Fort Norfolk, July 26, 1948. (Photo courtesy U.S. Army Corps of Engineers.)*

yacht *Falcon* was disposed of in the mid-1950s, but she is held in affectionate memory by many of those who have enjoyed cruises aboard in local waters. Other former Corps of Engineer craft include the U.S. derrick boat *Roanoke* (fig. 78), constructed for the Corps in 1937 by Spedden Shipbuilding Company of Baltimore. She was converted into a crane barge, *ND-3*, in August 1961 and sold in the spring of 1970. The *Roanoke* was replaced by crane barge *ND-6*, built for the Corps by Tidewater Equipment Company of Chesapeake in December 1969. Another former vessel of the fleet was the tender boat *Staunton*, a forty-foot steel vessel resembling a little tug. She was sold in 1961 and sank in Tangier Sound in Chesapeake Bay a few years later.

Over the years there have been several gradual changes not only in the size and function of the various types of vessels using the Albemarle and Chesapeake Canal but also in the kind and variety of the principal cargoes transported on it. The canal had hardly gotten started at the outbreak of the Civil War when almost immediately the waterway was used for the passage of Confederate naval vessels and transports and also for the shipment of military supplies, stores, and equipment. After the war, small passenger and cargo steamers joined the little steam tugs which daily hauled trains of loaded sailing craft or floating log rafts through the sounds and canals. Wood products, vegetables, and fish for northern markets made up the lion's share of commodities brought through northbound, while manufactured goods and general stores were carried down on the return trips.

Gradually the little schooners which hooked rides through the waterways at the end of towlines were replaced by self-propelled freighters. At the turn of the century, sailing vessels had been almost entirely replaced by power craft, and there was also a gradual attrition in the fleets of steamboats which formerly had so successfully tied the Carolina Sounds communities together. Proliferating railroads usurped more and more of the boats' passengers and perishable food products, since the railways could now provide quicker transport. Improved roads and the advent of motor trucks speeded the process, leaving merely the heavier bulk freights to be handled as waterborne commerce.

The advent of the internal-combustion marine engine saw more and more power yachts using the canal, and with the improvements to the Intracoastal Waterway farther south, up to and following World War I, more and more seasonal traffic ensued—with adventurous pleasure craft changing bases of operation from northern to southern waters in spring and fall. One of the earliest accounts of a full run via the Waterway appeared in the *Nautical Gazette* of November 8, 1911.[42] It was based upon the 1905 report of a Lieutenant Grady, USN, who made the trip in a ninety-foot, twin-screw water barge which drew 5½ feet of water. Today's uniform system of channel marking was then unknown, and Grady recommended taking on local pilots. He stated that his article was prepared at the request of New York underwriters who had recommended that "light draft vessels may save a lot of danger by using the canals and channels inside the reefs and islands."

With the construction of substantial steel barges (for a long time it had been customary to use the eviscerated hulls of former steamers), the practice of towing log rafts through the canal to the various waterfront

---

[42] "Inside Route to Florida," *Nautical Gazette* (New York), November 8, 1911, pp. 9–13, 19–20.

sawmills of the bays and sounds declined. The perennial annoyance to other craft caused by unruly log rafts has been cited by numerous observers, and pulpwood logs are now barged the entire way.

The development of powerful diesel tugs—actually blunt-nosed push boats—has driven steam vessels to the point of extinction. These noisy monsters, thumping along without stopping, represent the greater part of the commercial craft one sees on the waterway today, as they shove big barges ahead of them loaded with pulpwood or fertilizer.

Unknown during the last century, a large number of shallow-draft steel tankers which service the inland waterfront communities are today included in the canal fleets. The transportation of petroleum products reached an astonishing height during World War II. The considerable upsurge of traffic diverted to the Intracoastal Waterway owing to the Nazi submarine menace off the Atlantic coast during the anxious years of 1941 to 1943 has already been noted. Nowhere has that endeavor been more forcefully summarized than in a letter describing the war period written by former Norfolk Corps of Engineers executive assistant John H. Pruhs in response to an inquiry from *Time* magazine.

Stating that the Intracoastal Waterway ranging from New Jersey to Florida "proved to be a vital navigation facility," Mr. Pruhs first cited the enormous shipments of coal from Hampton Roads northward which, by reason of the enlargment and modernization of the Chesapeake and Delaware Canal, were then enabled to remain inside the protected waters of Chesapeake and Delaware bays for the greater part of their journeys. But perhaps the most remarkable movement of vital war cargo took place in the fully enclosed waterway south of Norfolk. Mr. Pruhs mentioned that, by means of a priority crash building program, the federal government was able to construct literally hundreds of both wooden barges and steel tankers for this Intracoastal Waterway service. He stated:

From June 1942 through December 1944, government steel tankers carried 75,000 tons of molasses from Port Everglades, Florida, to Philadelphia for use in manufacture of ammunition. Government wooden barges carried 40,000 tons of steel plating to a southern shipyard for use in building fire-fighting tugs for military use. These wooden barges were also used to deliver supplies via the inside route to military establishments up and down the Atlantic coast.

While certain commodity tonnage appeared constant for war and non-war years, actually these commodities during the war were converted to government use. For instance, 300,000 tons of petroleum products moving south from June 1942 through December 1944 were actually high-octane gas for airplane maneuvers on the South Atlantic coast, and 375,000 tons of pulpboard moving north under government contract reached its destination in Army camps all over the world as waterproof containers, especially milk containers.

As a result of curtailed delivery of petroleum products to Atlantic Coast areas by submarine ac-

FIG. 79. *Prefabricated deckhouse of the United States Trust supertanker* U.S.T. Atlantic, *being barged up the Intracoastal Waterway from Morehead City, N.C., to the Newport News Shipbuilding and Dry Dock Co. Shown May 7, 1978, as it passed through Highway 168 draw at Great Bridge. Viewed is the after side of the 920-ton structure. (Photo by Alexander C. Brown.)*

FIG. 80. *Port-side view of the ULCC (Ultra Large Crude Carrier) deckhouse, being barged to Newport News via the Intracoastal Waterway, is shown in Great Bridge Lock on May 7, 1978. The pair of bridge wings, not yet attached, are loaded on the bow of the barge. (Photo by Alexander C. Brown.)*

tivity off the coast, a pipe line was constructed from Louisiana to Jacksonville, Florida. From July 1943 to July 1945, this line carried 1,650,000 short tons of gasoline which was then barged from Jacksonville to internal points on the Atlantic section of the waterway. The satisfactory condition of the waterway, as maintained by the Corps of Engineers, con-

tributed materially to facilitating the war effort on the Atlantic Seaboard.[43]

---

[43] Letter from John H. Pruhs, executive assistant, Norfolk District U.S. Army Corps of Engineers, dated November 3, 1955, to Mrs. Martha Buckness, Time, Inc., Washington, D.C. Copy filed at Fort Norfolk, Va., headquarters.

FIG. 81. *The diesel tugs* Evelyn Doris *and* Tim Kelly, *shown heading west from Great Bridge Lock into the Elizabeth River, are pushing the barge carrying the 920-ton deckhouse of the supertanker* U.S.T. Atlantic. *(Photo by Alexander C. Brown.)*

Table 10—Ship traffic via Great Bridge route, 1979

Month	Direction bound	Towboats	Barges & scows	Motors & tankers	Yachts & pleasure	Government vessels	Total vessels	Tonnage	Number of lockings
January	North	82	76	4	18	7	187	50,600	100
	South	89	79	4	65	4	241	92,171	134
February	North	70	77	5	9	12	173	47,810	84
	South	71	89	5	13	4	182	52,515	86
March	North	106	155	6	120	12	399	46,136	186
	South	94	89	8	74	22	287	61,799	159
1st quarter Total		512	565	32	299	61	1,469	351,031	749
April	North	103	108	15	554	10	790	58,910	344
	South	104	128	9	146	13	400	63,954	209
May	North	71	89	36	1,113	54	1,363	34,120	450
	South	84	108	25	228	51	496	76,748	236
June	North	88	107	15	764	8	982	63,406	399
	South	94	99	28	325	7	553	54,508	291
2nd quarter Total		544	639	128	3,130	143	4,584	351,646	1,929
July	North	102	145	10	499	19	775	55,960	334
	South	98	96	11	413	22	640	69,890	307
August	North	110	107	8	335	11	571	65,350	276
	South	110	108	6	358	16	598	56,315	312
September	North	103	109	22	271	11	516	76,983	244
	South	95	96	21	626	17	855	96,715	343
3rd quarter Total		618	661	78	2,502	96	3,955	421,213	1,816
October	North	120	129	9	130	9	397	88,983	182
	South	115	109	13	1,317	22	1,576	58,305	427
November	North	97	91	11	54	19	272	61,512	151
	South	94	83	18	717	8	920	62,209	374
December	North	83	91	4	25	9	212	62,919	110
	South	85	134	6	˙211	9	445	57,790	223
4th quarter Total		594	637	61	2,454	76	3,822	391,718	1,467
1979 Total		2,268	2,502	299	8,385	376	13,830	1,515,608	5,961

This was certainly a brave record, and the Atlantic Intercoastal Waterway did its part to insure the final victory.

Over the years, there has on occasion, been a wide variety of interesting vessels and extraordinary cargoes transported via the Intracoastal Waterway, including a showboat that regularly played the Virginia and North Carolina bay and river towns in the 1920s and 1930s. Perhaps the most spectacular of recent transits consisted of the movements by barges of a series of enormous, fully completed ships' deckhouses. (See figs. 79, 80, 81.) The first of these was built for a trio of 939-foot liquefied-natural-gas tankers then being constructed at the Newport News Shipbuilding and Dry Dock Company. They were followed by two even larger bridge houses for 1,187-foot Ultra Large Crude Carriers (ULCC), all subcontracted to Hopeman Brothers, Inc., Carteret Manufacturing Corporation of Morehead City, North Carolina. Weighing 920 tons and measuring 90 feet wide and more than five stories high, these superstructures comprised the ships' navigation bridges, chart houses, radio shacks, captains' and officers' quarters, wardrooms, and other spaces. Loaded sideways on board Loveland Company flat barges, the deckhouses were transported to Newport News from the Beaufort area in a fully completed state—even with carpeting on the floors and curtains at the windows.

The first of these deckhouses, intended for the LNG [Liquefied Natural Gas] *El Paso Southern* arrived at Newport News on August 17, 1976, after the more than 200-mile voyage up from Pamlico Sound. Two more, also completely furnished, were for her sister ships, the *El Paso Arzew* and the *El Paso Howard Boyd*, and they followed along later in the year. The first of the then-unnamed ULCC bridge houses transited the Albemarle and Chesapeake Canal on May 7, 1978, and its passage is recorded in the series of photographs reproduced here. The name subsequently given the ship was the *U. S. T. Atlantic*. To bring these monsters up through the waterway's constricted channels without damaging anything entailed extremely skillful piloting. They made impressive sights towering over the buildings of Great Bridge as they squeezed into the lock on the final leg of their journeys.

Actually, though, it is in the routine movements of thousands of less spectacular vessels—barges, scows, dredges, towboats, motor tankers, and pleasure craft of infinite variety—that the Albemarle and Chesapeake Canal has so effectively demonstrated its worth. In proof of this, careful records are maintained by the Corps of Engineers at all times, and the Corps is to be commended for its quiet and efficient stewardship. Table 10 provides a sample record of such ship movements for the year 1979, broken down by month and by class of vessel. Obviously the A & C Canal will long continue effectively to serve the nation in war and peace as a national asset of incalculable value—commercially, recreationally, and esthetically—in which all Americans may well take pride.

12

A Trip on
the Canal Today

A Personal Chronicle

ow that the growth and development of the Albemarle and Chesapeake Canal have been traced from its inception two centuries ago to the present time, it might be interesting to offer personal reminiscences of a trip through the historic waterway. My first full transit was made on board the sturdy, twenty-seven foot Tartan sloop *Whim*, then owned by Mr. and Mrs. Charles B. Cross, Jr., of Chesapeake, during a late-spring cruise in 1972. It is hoped that this contemporary description of the sights, sounds, and smells encountered on a pleasant 150-mile round trip—down by the Albemarle and Chesapeake Canal and back by the Dismal Swamp Canal—will represent an appropriate conclusion to the foregoing formal history of these famed American canals.[1]

Early on a bright May morning, the *Whim*—with the Crosses, my thirteen-year-old daughter Johanna, and me embarked—set sail from the Cross's pier in Indian River, a small tributary of the Eastern Branch of the Elizabeth River in Chesapeake, and headed west for a junction with the river's main Southern Branch at Norfolk's Town Point. This spot is situated only a few hundred yards south of the flashing red channel buoy

---

[1] This little voyage is recorded in Alexander C. Brown, "A Spring Cruise to the Albemarle."

N-36 opposite the Portsmouth Naval Hospital, where the zero mark of the Atlantic Intracoastal Waterway is located and where it officially commences.[2]

Turning hard left on entering the main, southbound channel, the little sloop, chugging along under power, crossed over the Norfolk-Portsmouth Tunnel buried deep in the mud under the river, leaving Berkley to port and the sprawling Norfolk Naval Shipyard complex to starboard. Barely discernable amidst the various docks, piers, and lofts of what had been originally designated the Gosport Navy Yard lay the old stone Dry Dock Number One—the nation's first such facility, officially opened with the ceremonial docking of the U.S. ship-of-the-line *Delaware*, a three-deck man-of-war, on June 17, 1833. The dock is still in use and was recently designated a national historic landmark.

As usual, the river provided an animated scene, with ships of infinite variety plying the channel and purposeful activity going on both in the shipyard on the west bank and in its St. Helena Annex on the east. Scenes of action also marked the row on row of mothballed naval vessels on either shore.

Now came the first of hundreds of drawbridges that lie athwart the waterway on its long journey south—no less than eight of them in the ten-mile course of the Elizabeth River alone. First passed was the infrequently used railway bridge of the Norfolk-Portsmouth Belt Line, followed by the lift bridge of Highway 337 between Portsmouth and South Norfolk.

Beyond the naval shipyard, river traffic diminished, and commercial establishments and giant warehouses and elevators gradually replaced the Navy's lay-up docks on either hand as the sloop was approaching Gilmerton. Here, where the river made the first part of a long **S** turn, lay the site of the former Roper sawmill and the 1899-abandoned entrance to the Dismal Swamp Canal. The lock chamber made of carefully fashioned blocks of cut stone for the tidewater lift lock are still intact—at a spot which canal buffs would like to see turned into a waterfront minipark.[3]

Tall fertilizer factories made their presence known by both sight and smell as we rounded Money Point with the U.S. Navy's St. Julien Creek Annex—for ammunition storage—to starboard. At the distant end of the **S** curve, the trip was enlivened by the existence of a pair of parallel drawbridges—those of busy Military Highway, Route 13, together with the main line of the Norfolk and Western Railroad coming into Norfolk. Though yachtsmen may presume—as many do—that their watercraft automatically have the right-of-way over mere land conveyances, in practice it works out

---

[2] Routes of both the Albemarle and Chesapeake Canal and the Dismal Swamp Canal are given on opposite sides of a progressively updated navigational strip chart produced by the U.S. Department of Commerce. It is Nautical Chart 829–SC, *Norfolk to Albemarle Sound via North Landing River or Dismal Swamp Canal, Virginia–North Carolina*, available to users of the Intracoastal Waterway at all nautical instrument shops.

---

[3] Alexander C. Brown, "Chesapeake's Stone Lock Would Make a Fine Park."

that the trains go on across without delay, while the sailors wait, anxiously jockeying around to keep their vessels from being swept by the tide onto mud flats near the bridge entrances. Meanwhile, taking their time about it, a hundred or more freight cars may lumber ponderously on across the draw.

Sighing with relief when this navigational bottleneck was safely passed, the *Whim's* navigators then headed her due south again, soon to pass between the lofty towers of the 1970-built high-level highway bridge across the Elizabeth River of Interstate 64. In addition to providing a fine view of the steam generating plant of the Virginia Electric and Power Company, the bridge affords normal vertical clearance of some sixty-five feet. Actually there is a narrow drawspan in the center of the bridge, which, by prior arrangement between a ship's agents and the Virginia state highway personnel, may be opened in the rare event that an even taller masted vessel must go through.

Deep Creek enters the Southern Branch of the Elizabeth River just south of the bridge. Here, as a pair of arrowed signs mounted on piles on the west side of the channel proclaim (See fig. 1), the navigator must decide whether to make a sharp right-hand turn to the west to enter Deep Creek, which leads to the Dismal Swamp Canal's present entrance five miles away, or to continue on southward in the Elizabeth River to the portals of the Albemarle and Chesapeake Canal. We had planned to take the latter route for our cruise down to the sound, and we would be returning via the Dismal Swamp Canal, so we kept on course.

Just beyond yet another railway swing bridge at Mill-ville on the west bank, the Southern Branch makes an easy ninety-degree turn to the east, and as soon as it has passed under the twin-span bascule bridge of Highway 166—appropriately named Southern Branch Boulevard—the channel aims directly for the Great Bridge lock entrance, three miles distant.

This upper reach of the Elizabeth River originally made several meandering curves as it approached its headwaters. Prior to the channel being straightened by the Army Corps of Engineers, one of these loops led past the lumber-stacked wharves of Camden Mills, the sometime venerable facility of the Richmond Cedar Works lying at the doorstep of the great Dismal Swamp. The lumbering concern was organized in 1870, and when incorporated twenty years later, its holdings included more than 300,000 acres of rich timberland, a large part of which lay in the swamp. The head office remained in Richmond, however, where they produced all varieties of wooden ware and furniture. Cedarwood ice-cream freezer tubs were a specialty.

The site of the former sawmill we were about to pass at Camden Mills was established about the turn of the century, and in its heyday a maze of plank roads and narrow-gage railroad lines penetrating deeply into the swamp were designed to bring fresh-cut cypress, cedar, and juniper to the whirring saws of the mill. Ultimately, the logs were trucked in and the tracks were taken up, so eliminating the ever-present hazard of fires set by the wood-burning locomotives.

A major additional source of lumber was obtained in Tyrrell County, North Carolina, south of Albemarle Sound. The company then acquired a fleet of barges

FIG. 82. *Wood-hull pulpwood barge* Richmond Cedar Works No. 2, *built in 1901, is shown along with a square-ended flat barge handling lumber at an Albemarle and Chesapeake Canal wharf near Camden Mills, Va., circa 1905. (Photo by H. C. Mann; courtesy of the Mariners Museum.)*

and tugs (figs. 82, 83) to bring the logs up from loading docks at Gum Neck on the Alligator River. On arrival, they turned off the main waterway channel to unload their cargoes behind the half-moon shaped island in the Elizabeth River caused by the cutoff.[4]

Unfortunately, the large planing mill at Camden Mills burned in the late 1940s, and by 1960 its vessels were sold and the company gradually phased itself out of business. The property along the river is presently owned by Lone Star Industries, Inc., who acquired the site in 1962 and now uses it for the manufacture of a variety of products including gravel and precast concrete.

[4] One of the Richmond Cedar Works' lumber barges was the former U.S. gunboat *Nashville*, built in 1895. The *Nashville* was the first naval vessel constructed by the fledgling Newport News Shipbuilding and Dry Dock Company and had the distinction of firing the first shot of the Spanish-American War three years later. As a unit of the U.S. Atlantic Fleet, the *Nashville* served thereafter on active duty in many areas of the globe until, following World War I, she was decommissioned and sold out of service in 1921.

With machinery removed and all interior partitions ripped out, the old gunboat became converted to a log-carrier barge of 435 tons, then being renamed *Richmond Cedar Works No. 4*. Towed by the 1893-built former steam tug *Elsie* (converted to diesel in 1942), the company's various barges were hauled back and forth from Gum Neck to Camden Mills on week-long trips made by the tug.

The *Richmond Cedar Works No. 4* gave more than thirty years of faithful, if unspectacular, service toting lumber before finally being scrapped in 1957. Particulars about her owners are given in Hanlon, *The Bull-Hunchers*, pp. 295–98. The long career of the gunboat *Nashville* is recounted in Alexander C. Brown, *The Good Ships of Newport News*, chap. 2, pp. 11–16.

FIG. 83. *Richmond Cedar Works diesel tug* Elsie, *1893-built as a steam tug, is shown at Camden Mills on the Southern Branch of the Elizabeth River, January 19, 1948. She was regularly employed from 1947 to 1960 towing log barges to the mill via the Albemarle and Chesapeake Canal. (Photo by Alexander C. Brown.)*

Trees in increasing profusion now appeared along the Elizabeth River banks by the water's edge, giving promise of the forest through which the Virginia Cut of the canal would soon penetrate. Near the eastern entrance to the lock, a materially diminished river meandered off to the northeastward, finally petering out in the extensive swamp-forest leading overland to the headwaters of the similarly meandering North Landing River.

At the village of Great Bridge in colonial days, long before the canal was even planned, two causeways crossing the wide expanse of marshy terrain met at a sixty-foot wooden bridge. This was the original "great bridge" on the vitally important overland trade route leading from Edenton to Norfolk. It was here, as revolution swept the dissatisfied colonies, that patriots routed the superior Redcoat forces of cocky Lord Dunmore, the self-deposed colonial governor. The epic Battle of Great Bridge, December 9, 1775, was dubbed the "Bunker Hill of the South."

The tide lock at Great Bridge is the only lock that a southbound waterway traveler will encounter in the entire thousand-mile journey—unless he starts off on the Dismal Swamp Canal route, with its two lift locks. There is, however, an extensive lockage system in the 'cross-Florida Okeechobee Waterway.

As soon as the green signal light appeared on a semaphore at the Great Bridge lock entrance, the *Whim* chugged into the big chamber, temporarily tying up on the north wall in front of the locktender's shack. (See fig. 84.) In former days of the private canal company,

FIG. 84. *Charles Cross's 27-foot sloop* Whim *tied to the north wall of Great Bridge Lock, April 28, 1972, on her round trip of the Virginia and North Carolina canals. (Photo by Alexander C. Brown.)*

tolls would have been collected at this point. Now, however, all that was wanted was the boat's name, dimensions, hailing port, and planned destination. While this information was being obtained, I stepped ashore, crossing over to the south side of the lock by the west gates catwalk, for meanwhile the gates had closed behind us (fig. 85). My intent was to take some pictures of the *Whim,* which at twenty-seven feet in length—looked mighty small in the 600-foot-long dock.

Having secured the gates at the west end of the chamber, the lock tender (see fig. 86) meandered down to the other end of the lock, throwing, at the halfway point, a master switch, which controls the electric power operating the east gates. In a matter of only a few minutes, the water levels in the lock chamber and the canal cut ahead had been equalized—though we could detect no difference, for the change in elevation measured only a few inches—and the gates ahead swung open. The

FIG. 85. *Reversible-head lock gates at the eastern end of Great Bridge Lock are shown in an unusual situation, when both pairs of gates were closed, May 10, 1973. This can occur only at the change of tides. (Photo by Alexander C. Brown.)*

Whim's lines were then cast off, and now, at last, her trip through the Albemarle and Chesapeake Canal proper began. Passing out of the lock as other yachts approached (fig. 87), we left a tree-shaded park and picnic area on the port hand and the neat, well-tended white buildings of the Corps of Engineers to starboard. From a flagstaff yardarm flew the American flag together with the Corps' standard—the familiar battlemented castle with the twin stone towers.

Stacked on the south bank at the east end of the lock were several spare lock gates lying on their sides. These forty-five ton monsters would be immediately available as replacements should anything happen to damage the existing ones. Visible in the lower inboard corner of each prostrate gate as it faced the canal was a recess (see fig. 88) into which, when the gate was hung in position, a twelve-inch semisphere placed on the floor would enter. These metal half-globes serve as bearings, supporting the entire weight of the gates which turn smoothly on them.

A stretch of only about five hundred yards of canal cut separated the east end of the lock from the present busy twin-span swing bridge of Battlefield Boulevard (Highway 168), the main road bisecting the town of Great Bridge, and today's actual "great bridge"—even though it crosses the canal and not the meandering upper Elizabeth River—now confined to hardly more than a culvert as it passes under the highway.

In response to the customary three toots on the *Whim*'s foghorn, the drawspans swung open ahead of us with a great clanging of bells and flashing of lights. Immediately vehicular traffic began to pile up at both ends as the *Whim* chugged placidly on through, oblivious to the motorists' delay and probable annoyance.

A short distance beyond the bridge on the starboard hand lay the vast boat-storage complex of the commercially operated Atlantic Yacht Basin. Although gas docks and bulkheaded tieup areas paralleled the canal for some distance, and an Atkinson Company dredge makes this her home port (see fig. 89), actual entrance to the yacht storage area was by a narrow channel at the far end, cutting through the canal bank and making the approach to the boat slips from behind. Millions of dollars worth of pleasure craft make this a

FIG. 86. *Former Great Bridge lockmaster Curtis Evans working the controls at the east end of the lock, May 3, 1973. (Photo by Alexander C. Brown.)*

popular winter storage area where—in enormous roofed-over wet docks—they can ride in complete tranquility in the juniper water of the canal with no fear of damage either from the wash of passing vessels in the canal proper or from marine growth or toredo worms as in a saltwater lay-up.

A short distance east of the yacht basin is the site of the new Great Bridge bypass high-level fixed bridge, and a mile beyond the canal was crossed by the bascule single-track bridge of the Norfolk Southern Railway's Elizabeth City line, dating back to 1881 and now only used twice a day. The bridge is generally left in the up position, being lowered only when a train is expected. A fisherman on the trestle provided the only sign of activity.

In this part of the Virginia Cut enormous trees grow right down to the water's edge, making it impossible for the eye to penetrate more than a few feet beyond the banks. The sky above was mirrored as a blue ribbon in the dark water ahead—which the *Whim*, chugging merrily along, resolutely knifed into, churning it into sun-flaked amber bubbles in her wake.

The little sloop now passed a right angle cut into the canal's northern bank, expressly made to provide entrance to a snug mooring basin for a quantity of large pipeline dredges and accompanying workboats and barges owned by the Norfolk Dredging Company. This private fleet is thus provided a safe haven centrally located on the Intracoastal Waterway, and its units may be readily withdrawn to proceed in either direction as work requires.

Then, some five hundred yards ahead, still another drawbridge crossed the canal, this one the swing bridge of Centerville Turnpike (Route 604). The next four miles of the Virginia Cut proceeded uninterruptedly through a leafy defile of seemingly virgin forest with incredibly tall and beautiful cypress trees

FIG. 87. *Charles Cross observes northbound yachts entering Great Bridge Lock, May 3, 1973. An "ice tongues" rig suspended from the davit (foreground) is used to fish floating timbers out of the canal so they will not damage the gates. (Photo by Alexander C. Brown.)*

interspersed with pines and hardwoods hemming us in a straight and narrow channel behind a colonnaded wall of lofty trunks. This was where the artist Edward Bruce had contrasted the giant woods to columns in ancient Thebes or Luxor.

It being the spring of the year, the *Whim* was fre-quently met and passed by northbound yachts return-ing from southern wintering. Occasionally a fully loaded log barge showed up ahead, and momentarily one wondered if there was going to be enough room to get by safely. The *Whim* hugged the right bank while the barge quickly approached, apparently at an aban-doned collision course. As might be expected, it veered slightly to starboard at the last minute, leaving an ad-equate amount of space between the vessels for passing (fig. 90). Because of the suction action in the wake of the powerful tug thumping astern of the barge, our smaller craft was given an uncomfortable twisting mo-tion for a few seconds before the waves subsided and full helm control was regained.

At the end of this straight stretch of canal, appar-ently devoid of all human habitation, the cut bent slightly southward as we approached the hamlet of North Landing, the site of Highway 165's swing bridge. Here the road leads westward from Princess Anne Courthouse. Formerly, lumber was barged to North Landing for the nearby sawmill of the Baird-Roper Lumber Works. Today the community exudes an air of utter somnolence.

The *Whim* now commenced her descent of the North Landing River, with its gentle curves opening new vistas of natural beauty at every turn—a relief from the monotonous, straight-as-an-arrow course of the Virginia Cut. One imagined that the canal builders must have been happy to reach this point, where they could let nature help take over in providing the chan-nel. Occasional tributary streams fed into the main

FIG. 88. *Photographer John W. Lewis examines the bronze semispherical turning recess located at the lower inside corner of a spare 45-ton lock gate stored on the south bank of the canal at Great Bridge, October 31, 1973. (Photo by Alexander C. Brown.)*

river, gradually increasing its width. As at Camden Mills back in the Elizabeth River, the many tight curves of the North Landing River had been cut across to straighten the channel, and in every case the then-abandoned oxbows harbored a variety of gray-weathered derelict craft. They were mostly former wooden barges which had been hauled there out of the way and left to die—but not before the local residents had stripped them of anything of value. In many instances, we noted bushes growing luxuriantly out out of the abandoned hulks, adding to the spectral appearance of these dead fleets.

A couple of winding miles beyond North Landing Bridge, we approached the little settlement of West Landing on the east bank of the river, gloomily recorded on an 1878 map of the Albemarle and Chesapeake Canal as Starvation Farm. The village's proximity was announced by the first of numerous signs one sees along the Intracoastal Waterway warning navigators: "Slow—No Wake." The annoyance, and also potential damage caused by hot-rodding powerboats raising an enormous swell behind them as they proceed recklessly at full tilt, is deemed actionable in many canal-front communities, where sheriffs mete out stiff penalties to those who exceed the posted speed limits. When boxed in by cooperative drawbridge tenders who refuse to open their bridges, miscreants may be readily apprehended by the authorities. The *Whim*, with her maximum five-mile-an-hour speed, would hardly qualify for censure, however.

FIG. 89. *Atkinson Dredging Co. (Chesapeake, Va.) dredge moored to the south bulkhead of the Atlantic Yacht Basin on the Virginia Cut, August 9, 1977. (Photo by Alexander C. Brown.)*

FIG. 90. *Diesel tug* Birgit-Ann *of Charles City, Va., pushing a steel barge, proceeding westward down the Virginia Cut, April 28, 1972. (Photo by Alexander C. Brown.)*

FIG. 91. *The little settlement of West Landing, Va.—protected by its seawall made of old automobile tires stacked up on stakes driven into the river bank—is situated on a bend of the North Landing River. (1972 photo by Alexander C. Brown.)*

West Landing, (fig. 91), a small community composed apparently of equal parts of small frame buildings and house trailers, has the distinction of preserving its curving waterfront by a unique seawall composed of old automobile tires closely stacked up on piles driven into the river bank. This ingenious variety of bulkheading provides protection against the bank being unduly washed by waves caused by passing vessels but certainly does little esthetically to enhance the beauty of the view.

Just below West Landing, the *Whim* passed a mark on the chart indicating that she had come twenty miles from the waterway's commencement off Norfolk. Two larger tributaries now joined the main stream: West Neck Creek to port and Pokety Creek to starboard. The high stands of trees which formerly hemmed in the banks had now withdrawn, and open marshland widened the vistas on either hand.

Five miles from West Landing brought us to Pungo Ferry, now blossomed into a Virginia Beach resort community on the river's east bank. Here, it will be recalled, Edward Bruce on board the *Calypso* had considerable trouble persuading, the rickety drawbridge to open. Today there are a few more than the two or

FIG. 92. *Munden Point, Va., overlooking the northern end of Currituck Sound, shows the abandoned piling of the former railway terminal from a pleasing riverside campground site, August 19, 1972. (Photo by Alexander C. Brown.)*

three houses observed by Army Engineer Charles B. Phillips's party in 1879, and a small settlement has grown up around a marina with boat slips cut into the east bank and docks and a pavillion paralleling the river front. The twin-span swing bridge of Highway 726 obligingly opened before us without delay. Hidden away among the cattails growing by a little slough near the west end of the bridge and abandoned to the tooth of time was the old flatboat which had for many years served as a ferry until replaced by the bridge in 1954.

We passed more half-moon shaped islands formed when the river's curves were eliminated, and they too sheltered more fleets of derelicts showing up as stubble across the marsh. Then, a mile beyond Pungo Ferry, the North Landing River is joined by Blackwater Creek as the main stream makes a final bend to the eastward, then widens as it approaches Currituck Sound. Now, at length, we were afforded an uninterrupted view of the full, north-south sweep of the northern part of the sound into which the river discharges. Channel beacons set in a straight row at half-

FIG. 93. *Northbound diesel tug* Evelyn Doris, *pushing a fully loaded lumber barge out of Coinjock Bay, Currituck Sound, passes a smaller tug, the* Cornwallis, *also designed for pushing barges, southbound on August 13, 1972. (Photo by Alexander C. Brown.)*

mile intervals marched ahead as far as the eye could see, for although open water may lure the navigator to sail wherever he fancies in the sound, actually the water is deceptively shallow, and boatmen without local knowledge must certainly follow the straight and narrow dredged channel or risk running aground.

The town of Munden, Virginia, is the last settlement visible on the east bank of the widened river. At Munden Point in 1896 was located the railhead of the Norfolk, Virginia Beach, and Southern Railroad, which became the Currituck Branch of the Norfolk Southern in 1900. Here, in former days, perishable cargo bound for Hampton Roads ports, including considerable quantities of barreled wild duck shot by the market gunners of the area, was transshipped from canal to rail. Summer cottages were now in evidence, and remains of Munden's once-busy piers, plus a few decaying barges in the vicinity, were all that we could see of past commercial glories. (See fig. 92.) The rails were taken up and the right-of-way abandoned in 1943.

The North Landing River had become more than a mile in width when we crossed the state boundary

FIG. 94. *The U.S. Coast Guard station at Coinjock, N.C., is located on the west bank of the North Carolina Cut of the Albemarle and Chesapeake Canal, as shown in this official Fifth Coast Guard District photograph. (Courtesy U.S. Coast Guard, Portsmouth, Va.)*

line between Virginia and North Carolina, and it now continued to widen rapidly as we proceeded southward. Troublesome Point—then behaving benignly despite the fact that once we left the hemmed-in river we felt the full force of a fresh southwesterly breeze—lay to starboard. We skirted Faraby Island—now well marked by lighted beacons—opposite the marshy outlet of Northwest River. This stream extends in that same direction into the easterly part of Dismal Swamp itself.

Some four miles below the state line, the dredged channel through the sound made a slight bend to the eastward, and we came abreast of the venerable village of Currituck with its handsome, weathered, red-brick courthouse, built in 1876. Currituck derives its name from *coratank*, the Indian for wild geese, and the famous whistling swan winters in this area famed for its profusion of waterfowl.

Opposite Currituck on our port hand, we could see low-lying Knotts Island in the distance. Earlier it was known as Mackie's Island. Here a tenuous connection between the two divided parts of Currituck County was instituted only as late as 1962, by the establishment of the seven-mile-long free ferry line, and we could pick out the diesel ferryboat *Knotts Island* leaving its slip at Currituck bound for the opposite shore.

It was choppy in this part of the sound, and short, steep seas reduced our progress. The *Whim's* crew was not unhappy, then, after passing Bell Island at the northern end of Coinjock Bay, to come into the lee of marshy land lying to port. Literally hundreds of duck blinds standing on stilts were in evidence, and in the far distance to the eastward, we could see majestic high sand dunes bordering the ocean, simmering in the afternoon sunlight. These are characteristic of the entire Carolina Outer Banks country. Farther south were the famed ridges at Kitty Hawk and Nag's Head. It is well known, of course, that early in this century these windswept dunes lured the Wright Brothers—bicycle builders from Dayton, Ohio—to come to Kill Devil Hills to try out their newfangled flying machine.

The channel now cut through a tip of what was formerly Long Point, presently an island inhabited, as far as we could determine, by a few cattle and flocks of goats. Passing a pair of powerful tugs (fig. 93), the *Whim* skirted along close to man-made islands to port composed of spoil dredged from the channel, and then entered the tree-lined banks of the North Carolina Cut. Halfway through lay the village of Coinjock, noteworthy not only for the export of Currituck County watermelons in season but also for its several

rival fuel-oil docks lining both sides of the canal and vividly promoted by billboards placed at vantage points near the entrances of the cut. We selected a mooring on the east bank and spent the first night of our canal cruise securely tied up to a long wharf paralleling the canal. According to the chart, the *Whim* had then sailed forty-three miles from the point where the waterway officially began off Norfolk's Town Point.

Opposite, in a neat compound on the canal's west bank, lay a U.S. Coast Guard station (fig. 94), with its three small cutters and eleven-man staff. From here they maintained Currituck and Albemarle sounds' approximately 115 lighted aids to navigation and 100 day beacons, in addition to carrying out the unit's primary mission of search and rescue throughout the sounds area. Coinjock provides the customary amenities required by both boatmen and duck hunters in the way of fuel and supplies, but not much more is offered by the place in the way of diversion. Nor are many people looking for it, for boatmen who tie up there generally do so merely to refuel and rest before proceeding on their way. Not all vessels stop, however, and at intervals all night long we could hear the asthmatic coughing of passing diesel tugs as the *Whim* nudged the padded pilings of the dock whenever one went by, making our moored sloop rock gently in its wake.

The first order of business on starting out under power the next morning was negotiating the drawbridge that is one of the more important features of Coinjock (see fig. 95). Route 158 crossing the bridge is a busy one, providing as it does sole access to the

FIG. 95. *The swing-span drawbridge at Coinjock, N.C., is shown April 29, 1972, looking south toward the head of the North River, N.C. The bridge connects upper and lower Currituck County. (Photo by Alexander C. Brown.)*

southern part of the county made into an island by the canal. This main road runs in a southeasterly direction down the full length of the Currituck peninsula. At Point Harbor, located at the tip, is the Wright Brothers Memorial Bridge, an almost five-mile-long causeway with a drawspan in the center that was built in 1965 and extends over the lower part of Currituck Sound across to the Outer Banks islands. These have many attractions for tourists and year-round residents alike—the Wright Brothers memorial and museum at Kill Devil Hills, Nag's Head, Roanoke Island with Fort Raleigh, the summer Lost Colony Theater, and the Elizabethan Gardens, and so on down the line of beautiful beaches to Oregon Inlet, the wildfowl refuges, and finally Cape Hatteras with its spectacular

peppermint-stick–striped lighthouse. Other Currituck County roads starting out from Coinjock lead northeastward to Waterlily, with its plush hunting lodges, and southward to Aydlett and Poplar Branch.

After we had gone a mile and a half below Coinjock Bridge, the canal cut entered North River at a place curiously named Bumplanting Creek. It was this region during the Civil War that witnessed some skirmishing and the intentional blocking of the canal by both Confederate and Yankee forces. Here too, the wily Pasquotank Guerillas captured the Union steamboats *Emily* and *Arrow*, considerably embarrassing the federals, who had mistakenly assumed that they had full control of the area.

We were blessed by a glorious day, and there was a

FIG. 96. *Intracoastal Waterway marker 173, on the site of a former lighthouse where the North River enters Albemarle Sound, is the southern terminus of the Albemarle and Chesapeake Canal—as viewed from the sloop* Whim *on April 29, 1972. (Photo by Alexander C. Brown.)*

splendid southwesterly breeze. As soon as possible after leaving the North Carolina Cut, we resolved to turn off the motor and proceed under sail once we could get the wind to draw properly. Though for the most part the *Whim* now sailed southward, close-hauled on a fairly direct course, there was one long and easy **S** curve in the river where we rounded scrub-covered Buck Island at the fifty-mile marker. Approaching yachts around the distant bends in the river gave the curious impression that they were sailing over-land on wheels. Buck Island was once an assembly point for sailing vessels needing a tow up through the canal. Reputedly, the little nineteenth-century steam tugs, such as the *Chowan* or *Croatan*, would take as many as ten or a dozen sailing craft through at one time. South of Buck Island, the river broadened, and navigation markers indicating the channel resumed their necessary function. We noted that, as far as nocturnal navigators were concerned, one of them was failing its mission. An enormous osprey nest was built completely over the beacon light.

Only about ten miles of the North River remained before the end of the line of navigation of the canal as it merged its identity into Albemarle Sound. But even though this river was now from two to three miles wide, sailors must still stick closely to the well-marked dredged channel, which proceeded southward on a series of dogleg courses so that the *Whim's* crew was kept busy trimming sails—sometimes close-hauled, then sailing with easy sheets. The settlement of Jarvisburg, once served by jaunty little steamboats from Elizabeth

City, lay off to the east directly opposite wooded Camden Point, the southernmost tip of Camden County. Below the point, the channel cut through shallow bars extending out from either shore at the true mouth of the North River. Here, we officially entered Albemarle Sound (fig. 96). The point was marked by an automatic flashing beacon set on piles—the original site of a small tended lighthouse. Prevailing depths all around now exceeded the waterway's project depth of twelve feet, and vessels of lesser draft could navigate with impunity in any direction in the sound.

The *Whim* had successfully traversed the entire course of the Albemarle and Chesapeake Canal and had reached the so-called common point of the nineteenth-century surveyors, where the lines of the Albemarle and Chesapeake Canal and the Dismal Swamp Canal—separated back in the Elizabeth River—now came together again. Through travelers proceeding on down the Intracoastal Waterway have the crossing of Albemarle Sound before them, which—prior to digging the Alligator River–Pungo River Canal in 1928—reached Pamlico Sound by the exposed open route lying to the eastward. This served Roanoke Island, proceeding thence through Croatan Sound to the open waters of Pamlico, the steamboat route of yesteryear.

We planned only the Albemarle and Chesapeake Canal voyage, however. So, with a splendid southwest wind now brought on the quarter, the *Whim* bore off into the broad mouth of the Pasquotank en route to Elizabeth City, twenty-five miles distant. The next day, we would be sailing still farther up the Pasquotank to the south end of the Dismal Swamp Canal and so through the canal and on home to complete a memorable round trip of the waterways. I had enjoyed the cruise mightily, as well as the company of my shipmates.

BIBLIOGRAPHY

Albemarle and Chesapeake Canal Company. *Annual Report*. Norfolk, Va.: A & C Canal Company, 1856–81, 1885. (Incomplete sets of bound volumes were found in the Sargeant Room, Norfolk Public Library, and in the U.S. Army Corps of Engineers' Archives, Norfolk District, Fort Norfolk. Holdings of both were copied on microfilm and collated, and duplicate sets were deposited in the archives of the Norfolk County Historical Society of Chesapeake, Va., and in the Library of the Mariners' Museum, Newport News. Va.)

Barrett, John G. *The Civil War in North Carolina*. Chapel Hill: University of North Carolina Press, 1963.

Baum, Jack. "A History of Market Hunting in the Currituck Sound Area" [Part 1], *Wildlife in North Carolina*, 32, no. 11 (November 1968), p. 14.

Brown, Alexander Crosby. "Albemarle-Chesapeake Canal 125 Years Old." Newport News *Daily Press*, September 7, 1980, sec. C, p. 1.

———. "Chesapeake's Stone Lock Would Make a Fine Park." *New Dominion Magazine* (in Sunday Newport News *Daily Press*), May 30, 1971, pp. 1–2, 14–15.

———. "Colonial Williamsburg's Canal Scheme." *Virginia Magazine of History and Biography* 86, no. 1 (January 1978): 26–32.

———. *The Dismal Swamp Canal*. Rev. ed. Chesapeake, Va.: Norfolk County Historical Society of Chesapeake, 1970.

———. "Errant Barge Revives Pungo Ferry." *Peninsularama* (in Sunday Newport News *Daily Press*), October 1, 1979, sec. E, p. 1. Photos by Johanna Brown.

———. *The Good Ships of Newport News: An Informal Account of Ships, Shipping, and Shipbuilding in the Lower Chesapeake Bay Region*. Cambridge, Md.: Tidewater Publishers, 1976.

———. "The Guard Locks at Great Bridge." *Virginia Cavalcade* 24, no. 2 (autumn 1974): 70–79.

————. "Painter of Robert E. Lee—Edward C. Bruce Recorded Tidewater Scene." *New Dominion Magazine* (in Sunday Newport News *Daily Press*), July 23, 1972, pp. 4–7.

————. "The Passenger Steamers of Dismal Swamp." *Steamboat Bill* 29, no. 124 (winter 1972–73): 203–9.

————. "Reversible Head Locks." *American Canals*, no. 34 (August 1980), p. 3.

————. "The Runaway Steamboat Caper: A Daring Wartime Feat Embarrassed the Yankees and Brightened a Dark Day for the South." *The State* (Raleigh, N.C.) 45, no. 10 (March 1978): 12–14.

————. "School Children, Campers, Tourists Ride Free Knotts Island Ferry." *New Dominion Magazine* (in Sunday Newport News *Daily Press*), September 17, 1972, pp. 14–15.

————. "A Spring Cruise to the Albemarle." *New Dominion Magazine* (in Sunday Newport News *Daily Press*), June 11, 1972, pp. 1, 4–7.

————. "Virginia's Watergate: Canal Locks at Great Bridge Control Tide." *New Dominion Magazine* (in Sunday Newport News *Daily Press*), June 10, 1973, pp. 1, 8–10.

Bruce, Edward C. "Loungings in the Footprints of the Pioneers." *Harper's New Monthly Magazine* 18 (May 1859): 741–63 and 20 (May 1860): 721–36.

Burton, H. W. ("Harry Scratch" of the Norfolk *Virginian*). *History of Norfolk, Virginia, 1736–1877*. Norfolk: Norfolk Virginian Job Print, 1877.

Butts, D. Gregory Claiborne. *From Saddle to City by Buggy, Boat, and Railway*. Richmond, Va.: published by the author [Hilton Village, Va.], 1922.

Byrd, William. *Histories of the Dividing Line Betwixt Virginia and North Carolina*, introduction and notes by William K. Boyd, new introduction by Percy G. Adams. New York: Dover Publications, 1967. (Originally published by the North Carolina Historical Commission, 1929.)

Clark, Walter, ed. *Histories of the Several Regiments and Battalions from North Carolina in the Great War, 1861–65*. 5 vols. Goldsboro, N.C.: published by the state, 1901.

Cross, Charles B., Jr. "The Canal" [Albemarle and Chesapeake]. Episode 1 in *An Historical Review*, pp. 11–19. Chesapeake, Va.: Norfolk County Historical Society of Chesapeake, 1966.

Dean, Earl. "Old Albemarle and Chesapeake Canal to Mark 100th Anniversary This Year." Norfolk *Virginian-Pilot*, January 30, 1953.

[Great Bridge Lock]. *Do the Facts Require the Restoration of a Guard Lock in the Albemarle and Chesapeake Canal between Norfolk, Va., and Beaufort, N.C.?* Norfolk, Va., 1927. 59-page pamphlet.

Dunbar, Gary S. *Historical Geography of the North Carolina Outer Banks*. Louisiana State University Studies: Coastal Studies Series no. 3; Baton Rouge: Louisiana State University Press, 1958.

Emmerson, John C., comp. "The Dismal Swamp Canal." Transcripts of articles extracted from various Norfolk, Va., newspapers, 1796–1848; deposited in the library of the Mariners' Museum, Newport News, Va., 1956.

———. *The Steamboat Comes to Norfolk Harbor and the Log of the First Ten Years, 1815–1825*. Portsmouth, Va.: published by the author, 1949.

———. "Steamboats, 1837–1860; 1866–1878." Transcripts of articles extracted from various Norfolk, Va., newspapers; deposited in the library of the Mariners' Museum, Newport News, Va., 1950.

———. *Steam Navigation in Virginia and Northeastern North Carolina Waters, 1826–1836*. Portsmouth, Va.: published by the author, 1949.

———. Untitled scrapbooks and typewritten transcripts and clippings of various articles pertaining to steam navigation and the local scene; deposited in the Sargeant Room, Norfolk Public Library, Norfolk, Va.

Fisher, Allan C., Jr., and photographs by James L. Amos. *America's Inland Waterway: Exploring the Atlantic Seaboard*. Washington, D.C.: National Geographic Society, 1973.

Fitzpatrick, John C., ed. *The Writings of George Washington*. 39 vols. Washington, D.C.: U.S. Government Printing Office. 1931–44.

———. *George Washington Diaries, 1748–99*. 4 vols. Boston: Houghton, 1925.

Forrest, William S. *Historical and Descriptive Sketches of Norfolk and Vicinity*. Philadelphia: Lindsey and Blakiston, 1853.

Fulton, Robert. *Report on the Practicability of Navigation with Steam Boats on the Southern Waters of the United States from the Chesapeake to the River St. Mary's. . . .* 2d ed. Philadelphia: Thomas Town, 1828. (First published December 1813.)

Great Bridge Lumber and Canal Company. *Report*. [Norfolk, Va.: Great Bridge Lumber and Canal Company, 1855.]

Hanlon, Howard A. *The Bull-Hunchers: A Saga of the Three and a Half Centuries of Harvesting the Forest Crops of the Tidewater Low Country*. Parsons, W. Va.: McClain Printing Company, 1970.

Hawkins, Brevet Brig. Gen. Rush C. "Early Operations in North Carolina." In *Battles and Leaders of the Civil War*, edited by R. U. Johnson and C. C. Buel, vol. 1, pp 632–59, New York: The Century Company, 1887.

Henderson, Arthur P. " 'The Paved Roads Killed Us,' Says *Currituck's* Last Master." Norfolk *Ledger-Star*, March 22, 1969.

Hening, William Waller, ed. *The Statutes at Large: Being a Collection of All the Laws of Virginia from the First Session of the Legislature in the Year 1619*. 13 vols. Richmond, Va.: printed for the editor, 1810–23.

Hinshaw, Clifford R., Jr. "North Carolina Canals before 1860." *North Carolina Historical Review* 25, no. 1 (January 1948): 1–56.

Hoehling, A. A. *Thunder at Hampton Roads*. Englewood Cliffs, N.J.: Prentice-Hall, 1976.

Hotchkiss, Maj. Jedediah. *Virginia: A Geographical and Political Summary . . . Prepared under the Supervision of the Board of Immigration*. Richmond, Va.: Public Printer, 1876.

"Inside Route to Florida." *Nautical Gazette* [New York], November 8, 1911, pp. 9–13, 19–20.

Johnson, Eads, comp. *Johnson's Steam Vessels of the Atlantic Coast.* New York: Eads Johnson Publishing Co., 1916–. (This appeared as *Johnson's Marine Manual*, during 1932–52; consulted at the Mariners' Museum.)

Johnson, F. Roy. *Riverboating in Lower Carolina.* Murfreesboro, N.C.: Johnson Publishing Company, 1977.

Johnson, Hubbert M., and Lt. James Thibault, Corps of Engineers, USA. "M4T6 Bridges in Intracoastal Waterway." *The Military Engineer,* January-February 1971, pp. 22–23.

Johnson, Robert Underwood, and Clarence Clough Buel, eds. *Battles and Leaders of the Civil War.* 4 vols. New York: The Century Company, 1887.

Jones, Cary W. *Guide to Norfolk as a Business Centre.* 2nd ed. Norfolk, Va., 1881.

Kennedy, John Pendleton, ed. *Journals of the House of Burgesses of Virginia, 1773–76.* Vol. 13. Richmond: Virginia State Library, 1905. (Earlier volumes have H. R. McIlwayne as editor.)

King, Edward. *The Great South; A Record of a Journey. . . .* Hartford, Conn.: American Publishing Co., 1875.

Kirk, Paul W., Jr., ed. *The Great Dismal Swamp.* Charlottesville: University Press of Virginia, 1979.

Knox, Thomas W. *The Life of Robert Fulton and a History of Steam Navigation.* New York: G. P. Putnam's Sons, 1887.

Lamb, Robert W., ed. *Our Twin Cities of the Nineteenth Century—Norfolk and Portsmouth.* Norfolk, Va.: Barcroft, 1887–88.

Lochhead, John L. "Steamships and Steamboats of the Old Dominion Line." *Steamboat Bill,* no. 31 (September 1949), pp. 52–53.

Lytle, William M., comp., and C. Bradford Mitchell, ed. *Merchant Steam Vessels of the United States, 1790–1868: "The Lytle-Holdcamper List."* 2d ed. Staten Island, N.Y.: Steamship Historical Society of America pub. no. 6. Distributed by the University of Baltimore Press, 1975. (Initially compiled and published by William M. Lytle and Forrest R. Holdcamper, 1952).

M., A. *Pictures of Maritime Dixie—Norfolk, Port and City, Va.* Norfolk: Englehardt, 1893. ("The Chamber of Commerce Book by A. M.")

McKelvey, William J., Jr. *Champlain to Chesapeake: A Canal Era Pictorial Cruise.* Bloomfield, N.J.: published by the author, 1978.

Moore, Frank, ed. *The Rebellion Record: A Diary of American Events with Documents, Narratives, Illustrative Incidents, Poetry, etc.* 8 vols. New York: G. P. Putnam, 1864.

Moore, John W. *History of North Carolina from the Earliest Discoveries to the Present Time.* 2 vols. Raleigh, N.C.: Alfred Williams & Co., 1880.

North Carolina General Assembly. *Report of the Select Committee on the Re-opening of Nag's Head Inlet in North Carolina.* Senate doc. no. 50. Raleigh: Thomas J. Lemay, Printer to the State, 1950. (Consulted in the Library of the Mariners Museum under the title: "Collection of Documents with Reference to Inland Navigation in North Carolina, 1850–1875.")

———. *A Bill to Incorporate the Albemarle and Currituck Canal Company, December 27, 1850.* House doc. no. 94. Raleigh, N.C.: Thomas J. Lemay Printer to the State, 1850.

———. *A Bill to Construct a Ship Canal to Connect the Waters of Albemarle, Currituck and Pamlico Sounds with Chesapeake Bay and for Other Purposes.* Senate doc. no. 8. pp. 67–74. Raleigh, N.C.: William W. Holden, Printer to the State, 1854.

———. *Governor's Message and Busbee's Report on the Albemarle and Chesapeake Canal Company.* 1860–61 session. Doc. no. 22. Raleigh: State Printer, 1861. (Referred to as *Busbee's Report.* Busbee was the reading clerk of the state senate as appointed by Governor Ellis).

———. *Communication from the Governor* (to the General Assembly of the State of North Carolina: report in relation to the Albemarle and Chesapeake Canal Company, made by Augustus M. Moore, Raleigh, February 24, 1875) 1874–75 session. Doc. 25. [Raleigh, N.C.:], Josiah Turner, Public Printer, 1875.

———. *Laws of North Carolina.* Chap. 46. Raleigh, N.C.: State Printer, 1857.

North Carolina State Board of Agriculture. *North Carolina and Its Resources.* Winston, N.C.: State Board of Agriculture, 1896.

Nowitzky, Geo. I. *Norfolk: The Marine Metropolis of Virginia and the Sounds and River Cities of North Carolina—a Narrative.* Norfolk, Va., and Raleigh, N.C.: Geo. I. Nowitzky, 1888.

Platt, Joseph C. *Examination into Proposal of Improving and Enlarging the Dismal Swamp Canal now Owned by the Lake Drummond Canal and Water Company.* New York: published by the author [35 Wall St., New York, N.Y., April 20], 1894.

Prince, Richard E. *Norfolk Southern Railroad, Old Dominion Line and Connections.* Millard, Neb.: published by the author, Omaha, Neb., 1972.

Pollock, Edward. *Sketch Book of Portsmouth.* Portsmouth, Va.: G. W. Purdie & Co., 1886.

Purdy, T. C., special agent. "Report on the Canals of the United States." In U.S. Congress, House mis. doc. 42, vol. 13, pt. 4. Department of the Interior, Census Office. *Report on the Agencies of Transportation in the United States.* Washington: Government Printing Office, 1883, pp. 725–64.

Ruffin, Edmund. *Agricultural, Geological and Descriptive Sketches of Lower North Carolina.* Raleigh, N.C.: n.p., 1861.

Simms, L. Moody, Jr. "Edward Caledon Bruce: Virginia Artist and Writer." *Virginia Cavalcade* 23, no. 3 (winter 1974): 30–37.

Sloan, Thomas H. "Inland Steam Navigation in North Carolina, 1818–1900." M.A. thesis, East Carolina University, 1971.

Stanton, Samuel Ward. *Steam Navigation on the Carolina Sounds and the Chesapeake in 1892*. Edited by Alexander C. Brown. Salem, Mass.: Steamship Historical Society of America, reprint series no. 4, 1947. (Reprint of *Seaboard Magazine* [New York], vol. 4: April 7, 14, 18, May 19, and June 16, 1892.)

Stewart, Col. William H., ed. and comp. *History of Norfolk County, Va., and Representative Citizens, 1632–1900*. Chicago: Biographical Publishing Co., 1902.

Stick, David. *Graveyard of the Atlantic*. Chapel Hill, N.C.: University of North Carolina Press, 1952.

Thomas, Bill. *The Swamp*. New York: W. W. Norton & Co., 1976.

Tredwell, Adam. "North Carolina Navy." In *Histories of the Several Regiments and Battalions from North Carolina in the Great War 1861–65*, edited by Walter Clark. Vol. 5. Goldsboro, N.C.: published by the state, 1901. pp. 298–313.

Trout, Dr. William E., III. "The Kempsville Canal." Three-page unpublished monograph; no. 19 in Trout's series on Virginia canals and inland navigation. 1969.

Turlington, Sarah Woodall. "Steam Navigation in North Carolina Prior to 1860." M.A. thesis, University of North Carolina, 1933.

U.S. Army Corps of Engineers. *Annual Report of the Chief of Engineers, U.S. Army, on Civil Works Activities*. Washington, D.C., 1913–. (Reports of Norfolk District consulted.)

————. *Atlantic Intracoastal Waterway, Dismal Swamp Canal Route*. Norfolk district. January 9, 1970.

————. *The Intracoastal Waterway Atlantic Section*. Washington, D.C; U.S. Government Printing Office, 1961.

————. *Report of the Chief of the Bureau of Topographical Engineers*. Washington, D.C., 1872–.

————, U.S. Army Engineer Division Lower Mississippi Valley. *Waterborne Commerce of the United States, Calendar Year 1976*. Compiled under the supervision of the division engineer. Part 1, Waterways and Harbors Atlantic Coast. Vicksburg, Miss., 1977.

U.S. Commerce Department, U.S. Coast and Geodetic Survey. *Coast Pilot Information: Intracoastal Waterway, Norfolk, Va., to Key West, Fla*. Washington D.C.: U.S. Department of Commerce serial no. 670, May 1945.

————. *Inside Route Pilot, Intracoastal Waterway—Norfolk to Key West*. Washington, D.C., 1936.

————. *Norfolk to Albemarle Sound via North Landing River or Dismal Swamp Canal—Virginia–North Carolina*. Nautical Chart 829–SC. 15th ed. Washington, D.C., February 1977. (This Intracoastal Waterway strip chart is progressively revised and reissued).

U.S. Congress. House. Copy of Major [James] Kearney's report of November 5, 1816. House doc. no. 93. [Washington, D.C.: Government Printing Office,] February 20, 1817.

————. Senate. Report of the Chief of Engineers, February 21, 1876: *Survey of a Line to Connect . . . the Waters of Norfolk Harbor. . . .* 44th Cong. 1st sess. Exec. doc. no. 35.

————. House. *Navigation from Chesapeake Bay to Pamlico Sound*. (Letter from the Secretary of War, Wm. W.

Belknap, transmitting a report of the Chief of Engineers, Brig. Gen. A. A. Humphreys, on the extension of navigation from Chesapeake Bay to Pamlico Sound, January 12, 1876.) 44th Cong, 1st sess. Exec. doc. no. 45.

———. House. Letter from the Secretary of the Treasury, John Sherman, in relation to the interests of the government in the Dismal Swamp Canal, January 15, 1878. (House report no. 802, vol. 4, May 10, 1878.) 45th Cong., 2nd. sess. House exec. doc. no. 19.

———. Senate. *Water Routes from Norfolk to the Atlantic Ocean.* (Letter from the Secretary of War, Alexander Ramsey, transmitting report of Capt. C. B. Phillips, Corps of Engineers. Chief of Engineers Brig. and Bvt. Maj. Gen. H. G. Wright, February 9, 1880.) (This is cited in this volume as "Phillips Report.") 46th Cong., 2nd sess. Exec. doc. no. 73.

———. House. *Report on the Agencies of Transportation in the United States, Including the Statistics of Railroads, Steam Navigation, Canals, Telegraphs, and Telephones: Compiled and Published Pursuant to Acts of Congress Approved March 3, 1879, April 20, 1880, and August 7, 1882.* 47th Cong., 2nd sess. Mis. doc. 42, vol. 13, pt. 4. Washington, D.C.: U.S. Government Printing Office, 1883. (Binder's title: Tenth Census of the United States—Vol. 4: Transportation.) (T. C. Purdy, special agent. "Report on the Canals of the United States," appears on pp. 725–64 of this volume.)

———. House. *Waterway from Norfolk, Va., to Beaufort Inlet, N.C.: Report of Examination and Survey.* (Letter from Acting Secretary of War, February 19, 1904, and letter of Chief of Engineers, February 18, 1904.) 58th Cong., 2nd sess. Doc. no. 563.

———. House. *Norfolk–Beaufort Inlet Waterway, Virginia and North Carolina.* (Letter from Secretary of War, transmitting, with a letter from Chief of Engineers, reports of examination and survey, Washington, D.C., December 3, 1906.) 59th Cong., 2nd sess. Doc. no. 84.

———. House. *Chesapeake and Albemarle Canal Co.* January 5, 1912, and March 4, 1912. (Letter from Chief of Engineers, Maj. Gen. W. H. Bixby, to Secretary of War, Jacob M. Dickinson, dated February 15, 1912.) 62nd Cong., 2nd sess. Doc. no. 391 and doc. no. 589.

———. House. Committee on Rivers and Harbors. *Inland Waterway from Norfolk, Va., to Beaufort Inlet, N.C.* (Letter from Chief of Engineers, Maj. Gen. Lansing H. Beach, United States Army, transmitting report of the Board of Engineers for Rivers and Harbors on the advisability of acquiring the Lake Drummond [Dismal Swamp] Canal, February 25, 1922.) 67th Cong., 2nd sess. Doc. no. 5.

U.S. Navy Department. *Official Records of the Union and Confederate Navies in the War of the Rebellion.* 30 vols. Washington, D.C.: Government Printing Office, 1894–1922; index, 1927.

U.S. Treasury Department. *List of Merchant Vessels of the United States.* Washington, D.C., 1868–. (Published annually by Bureau of Statistics.)

———. *Report of the Secretary of the Treasury on the Subject of Public Roads and Canals.* Washington, D.C.: Government Printing Office, 1808.

U.S. War Department. *Official Records of the Union and Confederate Armies: The War of the Rebellion.* 70 vols. Washington, D.C: Government Printing Office, 1880–1901.

Weaver, Charles Clinton. *Internal Improvements in North Carolina Previous to 1880*. Baltimore: Johns Hopkins University Studies, ser. 21, nos. 3–4, March-April 1903.

Wertenbaker, Thomas Jefferson. *Norfolk: Historic Southern Port*. 2d ed. Edited by Marvin W. Schlegal. Durham, N.C.: Duke University Press, 1962. (First published 1931.)

Wingo, Elizabeth B. *The Battle of Great Bridge*. Chesapeake, Va.: Norfolk County Historical Society of Chesapeake, 1964.

Young, Maj. G. R., Corps of Engineers, USA. "The Great Bridge Lock." *Military Engineer* 24, no. 138 (November-December 1932): 551–57.

CARTOGRAPHY

Some nineteenth century charts and maps, ranging from Chesapeake Bay to the North Carolina Sounds, relating to the Albemarle and Chesapeake Canal and the Dismal Swamp Canal, arranged chronologically

Albemarle and Chesapeake / Canal / Connecting Chesapeake Bay / With Currituck, Albemarle and Pamlico Sounds / and Their Tributary Streams / by / John Lathrop, Civil Engineer / 1859 / Hosford & Co., 57 & 59 William St., N.Y.
(Folding map included in Albemarle and Chesapeake Canal Company *Fourth Annual Report*, 1859.)
(22½″ by 28¾″)

Map / of the Line of / Inland Navigation / From New York to the South / Albemarle & Chesapeake Canal Company / Norfolk, Va. / 1859 / Hosford & Co., 57 & 59 William St., N. Y.
(Folding map included in Albemarle and Chesapeake Canal Company *Fourth Annual Report*, 1859.)
(13″ by 18¾″)

Dismal Swamp / Canal / Connecting Chesapeake Bay / With Currituck, Albemarle and Pamlico Sounds / and Their Tributary Streams / by D. S. Walton, Civil Engineer / 1867 / Hosford & Sons, 57 & 59 William St., N.Y.
(Folding map in U.S. Congress, House, 45th Cong., 2nd sess. 1867, exec. doc. no. 19.)
(16″ by 21″)

Albemarle and Chesapeake / and / Dismal Swamp Canals / with Their Connecting Waters / From surveys made in connection with the / Survey of Water Routes / from the Harbor of Norfolk to the Atlantic Ocean south of Hatteras / Under the direction of Capt. Chas. B. Phillips, Corps of Engrs. U.S.A. / By Fred[k] W. Frost, C.E. / C.P.E. Burgwyn, C.E. Pr. Ass[t]. / 1878–9 / Engineer Dept. U.S. Army / BVT Maj. Gen. H. G. Wright / Brig. Gen. & Chief of Engineers. (46th Cong., 2nd sess., 1880, Senate exec. doc. no. 73.)
(9½″ by 14″)

General Map / illustrating the / Survey of Water Routes / from Norfolk Harbor, Va., to the Atlantic Ocean / south of Hatteras and to the Cape Fear River, N.C. / Surveyed under the direction of / Capt. Chas. B. Phillips, Corps of Engrs. U.S.A. / By / Fred[k] W. Frost, C.E., C. P. E. Burgwyn, R. U. Goode / C. M. Yeates and J. P. Darling / Pr. Ass'ts / 1878–9 / Engineer Dept. U.S. Army / BVT

Maj. Gen. H. G. Wright / Brig. Gen. & Chief of Engineers (46th Cong., 2nd sess., 1880, Senate exec. doc. no. 73.) (15″ by 21¾″)

Dismal Swamp / and / Albemarle and Chesapeake Canals (Illustration in T. C. Purdy, "Report on the Canals of the United States." in U.S. Congress, 47th Cong., 2nd sess. House Mis. doc. no. 42, vol. 13, pt. 4, Department of the Interior, Census Office, *Report on the Agencies of Transportation in the United States, . . . 1880–1882*

[Washington: Government Printing Office, 1883]. (7″ by 9½″)

Map of the / Albemarle and Chesapeake Canal / Connecting Chesapeake Bay / with Currituck, Albemarle and Pamlico Sounds / and Their Tributary Streams / By Marshall Parks, President, 1855 / Fairfield Canal and New Berne & Beaufort Canal / Norfolk & Virginia Beach Rail Road / 16th edition / revised and corrected / 1885. / Compiled & drawn by A. Lindenkohl, Washington, D.C. (10″ by 14¾″)

MISCELLANEOUS BOOKS BY ALEXANDER CROSBY BROWN

Written for the Mariners' Museum, Newport News, Va.

Lake Maury in Virginia. Museum pub. no. 1, 1936.

Twin Ships: Notes on the History of Multiple Hull Vessels. Museum pub. no. 5 (reprint *Marine News*), 1939.

The Old Bay Line, 1840–1940. Richmond, Va.: Dietz Press, for the Mariners' Museum and the Baltimore Steam Packet Company, 1940. (An enlargement of Museum pub. no. 6; extract *William and Mary Quarterly,* 1938.) Facsimile edition. New York: Bonanza Books, 1977.

The Steamboat "Pocahontas," 1893–1939: Typical East Coast Side-Wheeler of the 1890's. Museum pub. no. 10 (reprint the *American Neptune*), 1942.

Paddle Box Decorations of American Sound Steamboats. Museum pub. no. 11 (reprinted the *American Neptune*), 1943.

[With Harold S. Sniffen] *James and John Bard: Painters of Steamboat Portraits.* Museum pub. no. 18 (reprint *Art in America*), 1949.

The Mariners' Museum, 1930–1950: A History and Guide. Museum pub. no. 20, 1950.

The Sheet Iron Steamboat "Codorus": John Elgar and the First Metal Hull Vessel Built in the United States. Museum pub. no. 21 (reprint the *American Neptune*), 1950.

Sea-Lingo: Notes on the Language of Mariners and Some Suggestions for its Proper Use, 1980.

Written for the Norfolk County
Historical Society of Chesapeake, Va.

The Dismal Swamp Canal, 1967.

The Dismal Swamp Canal. New, enlarged edition, 1971.

Chesapeake Landfalls. 1974

Other Historical Publications

Horizon's Rim. New York: Dodd, Mead and Company, 1935

Editor. *Newport News' 325 Years.* Newport News: Newport News Golden Anniversary Corporation, 1946.

Editor. *Mr. Hardy Lee: His Yacht,* by Chinks [Dr. Charles Ellery Stedman]. (Reprinted from the 1857 edition published by Dr. Stedman.) Boston, Mass.: Club of Odd Volumes, 1950.

Women and Children Last: The Loss of the Steamship "Arctic." New York: Putnams, 1961.

Steam Packets on the Chesapeake: A History of the Old Bay Line since 1840. Cambridge, Md.: Cornell Maritime Press, 1961

Editor. *Longboat to Hawaii: An Account of the Voyage of the Clipper Ship "Hornet."* Cambridge, Md.: Cornell Maritime Press, 1974.

The Good Ships of Newport News. Cambridge, Md.: Tidewater Publishers, 1976

Newport News' Historical Markers and Memorials. Newport News, Va.: Newport News Historical Committee, 1980.

INDEX

italic page number = illustration

NORTH CAROLINA ROOM
NEW HANOVER COUNTY PUBLIC LIBRARY

For Reference

Not to be taken from this room

NCR